CONFLICT AND COMPROMISE: POLITICS AND PLANNING IN GUELPH, 2000 TO 2015

Fred Dahms

ISBN

ISBN-13:978-1523717965

ISBN-10:1523717963

Self Published by Fred Dahms

Fred Dahms

Conflict and Compromise

Fred Dahms

CONTENTS

Conflict and Compromise

ACKNOWLEDGEMENTS

This book was conceived on a summer evening at the home of my good friend and colleague, Mike Moss, in Aboyne. After consuming a respectable quantity of red wine we began a slightly inebriated discussion of possible new retirement activities. In his somewhat foggy wisdom Mike exclaimed, "Why not write book about Guelph politics?" At the time this seemed to be a reasonable successor to my *Wellington County,* so I concurred. After five years of scouring newspaper archives, municipal and provincial websites and many documents, this volume emerged. I have Mike to thank for the original inspiration.

Many others contributed ideas and useful suggestions that have greatly improved this book. The following reviewed my detailed outline and proof copies of the book: Oxanna Adams, Betty and her husband Ric Jordan, who was my wonderful copy editor; Liz and Brent McArthur, Dr. Robert Miller and Carl Visser. Many thanks for their valuable assistance.

The City of Guelph provided helpful information that allowed me to include important details that were otherwise unavailable. Mario Petricevic supplied data that explained the long delays in renovating the former Via Station, and Lynne MacIntyre provided lists of former Senior City Staff. Ann Pappert, Guelph's C.A.O., ensured that I received information that a city department was reluctant to provide. I thank them all. Any errors are the author's alone.

Finally, thanks to my wife Ruth for her patience during years of listening to me complain when things progressed too slowly. She is my chief literary and grammatical critic who helped me to make the book readable and hopefully more enjoyable. I thank her for her love and support during a number of very difficult years in her life.

INTRODUCTION

The years between 2000 and 2015 constituted one of the most important and exciting periods in the history of Guelph. During this period, Mayor Joe Young was replaced by Karen Farbridge who in turn was replaced by Kate Quarrie. Quarrie and her supporters instituted a free market, right wing administration in the city. During her mayoralty, City Council dealt with some sensitive issues and indulged in considerable hot debate and numerous recriminations. In 2006, Farbridge mounted a well organized campaign that resulted in a purge of most Quarrie loyalists on council.

After Kate Quarrie was defeated, a more cohesive council that some labelled "left wing" took over. The new administration continued to grapple with many of the problems that had confronted the Quarrie council while attempting to reverse some of the questionable decisions made by their predecessors. Unfortunately, a number of decisions taken by the previous council presented a host of difficult challenges for the incoming politicians. The pages that follow will examine important issues and describe the actions of councils in Guelph from 2000 to January 2015 after the November municipal election, which resulted in major changes on city council.

Between 2000 and 2015, Guelph Councillors were presented with many contentious and often costly issues. How were they to provide more group homes and affordable housing? Would Walmart be allowed to locate in Guelph? How should they manage waste disposal, recycling and landfills? The Guelph Museum had outgrown its Waterloo Avenue building; where should its replacement be situated? Should a new Civic Administration Centre be built? How could the termite problem be solved? Should buses continue to transfer passengers at St. Georges Square? Where would they construct a new central library?

How would the city reconcile environmental stewardship with plans for the new Hanlon industrial park? Could central city "Brownfields" be rehabilitated to accommodate new developments? Was the Lafarge property near Howitt Park appropriate for new big box plazas? Was it appropriate to pass a pesticide By-Law to control lawn and garden spraying? How could traffic be calmed in residential neighbourhoods? Were watering restrictions adequate to preserve the aquifers supplying water to the city? Can residential and commercial uses be integrated successfully in Guelph? What should be done about rowdyism downtown on weekends?

Should a new transportation terminal be built on the site of the Greyhound Bus terminal? What should be done about recycling and organic waste? Is it possible to accommodate the population targets for Guelph mandated by the *Places to Grow* legislation passed by the province? And after all these issues had been confronted, how could councils keep municipal tax increases to a reasonable level? These are but a few of the themes to be discussed below.

Organization

Many of the issues noted above persisted for all the years under discussion, while others disappeared only to be revisited later. Some were resolved very quickly and others continue until the present. To complicate matters, the province introduced a series of amendments to the *Planning Act* and passed the *Greenbelt Act* in 2005, both of which modified Guelph's future growth patterns and density. Downtown Guelph was designated as a growth node and the city is expected to accommodate 54,000 new residents and 31,000 new jobs by 2031. Forty percent of all population growth must occur through intensification rather than in suburban "greenfield" areas. The *Greenbelt Act* and related provincial policies had a major impact on Guelph's planning and politics and will continue to do so.

This book will outline the important political and planning issues that persisted between 2000 and 2015. It will also address a number of major problems that were resolved more expeditiously. The conclusion will evaluate the major accomplishments and failures of respective City Councils. First we will describe the major political debates informing the decisions made by each council.

The Political Landscape 2000 – 2003

When Mayor Joe Young retired in November 2000, Karen Farbridge defeated Gary Walton, Phil Cumming, Jim Sinclair, David Kendrick and Michael Klotz for the position of mayor. Young then ran for alderman and was elected in Ward 1, while former mayor and alderman Norm Jary retired after 37 years on city council. After several tempestuous years under Joe Young, Mayor Farbridge promised to initiate a new era of cooperation and harmony in Guelph.

Much of Young's term had been devoted to budget matters and answering the harsh criticism of Councillor Dan Schnurr who pronounced the 1997-2000 council "very, very weak in financial matters." He chaired council's finance committee for several months after the 1997 election but was demoted by council after the 1998 city budget process which was riddled with dissent and recriminations. Council often became embroiled in hot debates led by Schnurr who seemed to delight in criticizing any ideas that were not his own. On many occasions he levelled personal attacks on other councillors who disagreed with his views or suggested something contrary to his desires." It was one of my worst nights on council," said Councillor Cathy Downer who, with Councillor Bill McAdams, was the target of a personal harangue by Councillor Dan Schnurr for her position on the lawn watering issue. In 1999, Prof. Hugh Whitely took

Schnurr to court, alleging that he should have declared a conflict of interest when he voted on allowing Big Box development on University land. The court ruled that although Schnurr was an employee of the University, he had no conflict, and in 2000 Whitley was ordered to pay Schnurr's $10,000 legal fees.

During his year-end address, Young rejected Schnurr's allegations that council had been weak and ineffective on budgets. On the other hand, some felt that Schnurr was working hard to protect the interests of taxpayers. A local news report stated: "While [Dan Schnurr] needs to learn much about the graceful, interpersonal art of effective persuasion, his tight-fisted viewpoint is shared by many people in this city. His main specific complaint is about council's ability to make the best financial decisions. Although his style may be offensive, councillors and citizens who intend to run for council should not ignore his message." During the next few years, Schnurr did his best to make sure that his viewpoint was not ignored.

During 2000, Mayor Young became obsessed with the idea that the province wanted to merge Guelph with the Regional Municipality of Waterloo. He felt that this would be accomplished if Guelph continued to remain a member of the Technology Triangle with Kitchener, Waterloo, Cambridge, and the Waterloo Region, all of which had agreed earlier to contribute $120,000 each. Eventually Guelph Council voted to leave the Triangle and cease paying the annual fee. Nevertheless, the Province never did push Guelph to amalgamate with Waterloo Region.

The solid waste issue which later became a major problem was also tackled by Young's Council. The Eastview Landfill site was becoming full and nearby residents wanted it closed. At that time, the city thought that the site could be used for a few more years and considered expanding it to accommodate additional waste. Neighbours formed a ratepayers association and hired an environmental lawyer, David Estrin to advise them on tactics and help them deal with the environmental assessment that would be necessary to expand the dump. Subsequent councils devoted considerable time to this and other waste issues which will be discussed in greater detail later.

Guelph's growth, which became increasingly important was discussed and debated during Young's term. Assistant Planning Director Jim Forbes stated that Guelph "doesn't really have a set of policies for short term growth management." He estimated that it would take two years to finalize a growth management plan. Forbes said that there were strong trends toward low-density housing and warned that Guelph could become "more or less a bedroom community as part of the GTA." He stated that the rapid development of single family subdivisions "will lead to pressures for low income families" because of a shortage of affordable rental units. He added that most municipalities now plan their growth in stages, whereas Guelph's planning staff had only been able to react to growth. Very soon, Provincial *Places to Grow* legislation would echo and reinforce the position taken by Forbes.

Another major event during Young's term was the resignation of Police Chief Lenna Bradburn who had become very unpopular with the force. In December 1999, Guelph Police Association members voted 148 to 10 to support a non-confidence motion against Bradburn's administration. Soon thereafter she resigned and was given a very substantial severance package which was criticized by many. By the end of his term, Joe Young seemed ready to step down and let someone else carry the torch.

2000 - 2003 Farbridge as Mayor

Many issues were debated during Farbridge's term as mayor. It was punctuated by fiery rhetoric and major ideological differences. Councillor Dan Schnurr, a right-wing incumbent, seemed to become the "Official Opposition". His bias was revealed immediately after the election when he complained about "left wing politicians" (Farbridge and Maggie Laidlaw among others) being elected to council. This outburst set the tone for much of the remaining three years during which he opposed most financial motions in an attempt to keep tax increases to zero. Some would suggest that his philosophy was that council should never spend any taxpayers' dollars on anything. His numerous interjections, hostile demeanour and unpleasant comments contributed to a poisonous atmosphere on council between 2000 and 2003. Despite the conflicts, the Farbridge council made significant progress on a number of important issues discussed in detail below.

2003 – 2006 Quarrie as Mayor

By 2003, the political mood in Guelph had become even more toxic than it was under Farbridge. Many groups that were opposed to the "left wing" councillors decided to end their incumbencies by fielding strong right wing candidates. The time seemed ripe for a "purge" at city hall. Their champion was one Kate Quarrie, a financial analyst who had been President of the Rotary Club of Guelph. She was backed and funded by some of Guelph's most influential builders and developers along with a number of conservative politicians and organizers who had tired of the "Green" Farbridge Council. Quarrie's efforts were successful as she and five new councillors replaced Farbridge and half the previous council. In her inaugural address, to council, Quarrie pleased her supporters by making the following statements:

"We will be open for business." "Early in our first term, we will ask council to revisit the controversial, long-running Ontario Municipal Board battle into rezoning for big-box retailers on Woodlawn Road and Stone Road." "The citizens of this city made their wishes known throughout the election." "We want retail choices like our neighbours," she said. Quarrie referred to the current development application approval process as a "source of dissatisfaction" for both the development industry and local neighbourhood residents" and pledged a review of current practices.

Between 2003 and 2006, watching council was entertaining for some and frustrating for others, but it was never dull. Some appropriate decisions were taken, but others were clearly misguided. In March 2004, Quarrie abruptly adjourned council and walked out after being asked why names of some councillors were omitted from the agenda. In May 2004, the Quarrie council, despite the objections of many voters, approved the location of Walmart in Guelph. By any measure, Quarrie's time in office was even more fractious than that of her predecessors. Old and new councillors clearly disliked each other and accusations flew that Quarrie supporters often met secretly before council to determine the outcome of votes. Dan Schnurr continued to oppose most financial decisions and vociferously locked horns with Quarrie on numerous occasions. He was joined by Peter Hamtak, the "mystery man" from the south end who would reveal no personal information and often appeared to be following his own inscrutable agenda. On numerous occasions, David Birtwistle seemed to talk just to hear his own voice, while Dan Moziar, Ray Ferraro and Rocco Furfaro appeared to enjoy opposing almost anything supported by the previous council.

By the end of 2004 things had deteriorated to the point where council hired a consultant, George Cuff for $100,000 without tendering the contract. His mandate was to assess council's procedures and report back on methods to improve its performance. His task was complicated by the fact that Councillor Birtwistle declined to be interviewed for the review. Cuff's forty-seven recommendations in November 2004 were unequivocal; he pronounced the Quarrie council "dysfunctional". Councillor Christine Billings summed up the situation by saying that "the attitudes, the bickering, the lack of leaving personal agendas or personalities at the door," were reasons why council did not function as well as she would have liked. "I would love the grandstanding to stop" she said. Unfortunately, council ignored most of Cuff's recommendations. He suggested that seating around the horseshoe change every month to force councillors to get to know each other. This did not happen. Quarrie ignored his advice to provide equal opportunities to all members of council to serve as acting mayor and to represent her at official functions to "avoid the appearance of favouritism." After attending meetings where citizens addressing council were treated rudely, one reporter commented, "I used to see thoughtful debate and respect for fellow councillors and the public. I saw instead a dysfunctional environment in which only the most thick-skinned citizens would have the stomach to participate."

In the opinion of many, the most foolish act of the Quarrie council was its decision not to buy the former Canada Post Office to be used as the new central library. Wellington County Council then purchased the building in 2005 and assessed the City of Guelph $2.7 million for its share of renovation costs to cover joint services administered from the building. Some estimated that this decision cost the city $2 million more than if they had purchased the Post Office building. It also left Guelph without a location for a new library. This council also added a pipeline to Lake Erie to its long range water supply plan. If possible, these decisions increased the acrimony among councillors even more and inspired Farbridge/left wing supporters to organize for the

2006 election.

The 2006 Campaign

Frustrated by three years of a fractious right-wing council, citizens in Guelph organized the Guelph Civic League to bring some balance back to municipal politics. It was decided that the best approach would be to establish a citizen led organization committed to protecting the city's quality of life by keeping voters informed and encouraging their active participation in local politics. The league was an umbrella group for neighbourhood associations and other local organizations including the University of Guelph's Central Student Association, the Guelph and District Labour Council and the local branch of the Council of Canadians. Its first president, James Gordon noted that it also had over 200 individual members. In addition to providing information on candidates on its website, the League distributed surveys and encouraged citizens to vote. One of the key reasons the Civic League was formed in 2004 was to speak against a majority on council who often ignored public input before voting. During the days leading to the election, many of its members campaigned for Farbridge.

Although several others participated, Quarrie and Farbridge were the primary candidates for mayor. Both promised to focus on managing Guelph's growth, on repairing the wet-dry waste system and on creating more jobs in Guelph. Growth and water supplies were also recurring themes among the council candidates. Farbridge characterized Kate Quarrie's term as one in which staff struggled with political interference and during which developers had free reign, bloating Guelph's tax rate through new subdivisions that the city could not afford to service. Farbridge attacked everything in Quarrie's record and used the slogans "I will put Guelph back on track" and "Now more than ever Guelph needs a leader with integrity and vision," throughout the campaign. In contrast, Quarrie ran a very business-oriented campaign focusing on her accomplishments with the slogan "Kate gets it done."

During several debates, Quarrie claimed that Farbridge had incurred $16 million in unbudgeted expenses before leaving office in 2003, which increased subsequent property taxes. Farbridge accused Quarrie's city hall of raiding reserves and tripling the city's debt in three years, which "sounds more like bankruptcy planning" than good financial management. A major flaw in Quarrie's campaign was her assertion (later withdrawn) that the city had breached a contract with Subbor, a local energy-from-waste test facility while Farbridge was mayor. This allegation turned out to be false and damaged Quarrie's credibility with many voters.

On election night, Guelph voters decisively removed eight councillors, including Mayor Quarrie. Three years ago she had been elected on her promise to bring Walmart to Guelph, which she did, but voters were clearly dissatisfied with the divided, dysfunctional and sometimes nasty council that she led. The severe divide on council that contributed to raucous, bitter meetings was erased by the 2006 election results. Instead of chairing a council with a significant group hostile to her leadership, as was the case from 2000-2003, mayor-elect Farbridge now presided over a council that reflected many of her philosophies and ambitions for the city. She appeared to be firmly in the driver's seat after 2006. With Kate Quarrie, Ray Ferraro, Dan Moziar, David Birtwistle, Dan Schnurr, Peter Hamtak, Rocco Furfaro and Laura Bailey gone, Farbridge was presented with a very sympathetic council composed of Bob Bell, Kathleen Farley, Vicki Beard, Ian Findlay, Maggie Laidlaw, June Hoffland, Gloria Kovach, Leanne Piper, Lise Burcher, Karl Wettstein and Christine Billings. With only three men and nine women including the mayor, the composition of council had changed dramatically.

The 2010 Election

In November 2010 after a relatively quiet campaign, Karen Farbridge defeated David Birtwistle for the mayoralty. Several incumbents were replaced: Vicki Beard by Andy Van Hellemond; Mike Salisbury by Cam Guthrie. New councillors Todd J. Dennis and Jim J. Furfaro were elected. There were some accusations that Birtwistle had made false allegations during his speeches and on his website, and there was controversy about election blogs without names, but in contrast to the 2006 election, 2010 was comparatively tame. These results seemed to indicate widespread support of some of the previous policies, with enough new councillors to encourage introspection and possibly some modification of policies in 2011.

WATER SUPPLY: DROUGHT AND CONTROVERSY

Most of the important decisions taken by Guelph politicians had effects that lasted for many years. Many were altered or reversed by subsequent councils. Some were minor matters of zoning or traffic calming, while others such as population growth, waste disposal, tax rates and water supply will affect everyone in the city for many years. Each of these will be discussed below. Crucial decisions by various councils that changed their approach to problems will be noted, but the main emphasis will be on the issues and their implications for the citizens of Guelph.

Guelph is one of the few communities in Ontario that relies on ground water for its municipal supply. City leaders bought 70 acres (28 ha.) of farmland in Puslinch Township almost 100 years ago to establish the Arkell Spring Grounds, which still supplies most of the city's water. Now 865 acres (277 ha.) outside city limits provide water to the springs, but this still is not enough. During dry periods, the springs are recharged by water drawn from the Eramosa River, but when there are severe droughts, the Grand River Conservation Authority does not allow this to happen. Some wells in other areas of Guelph have had to be abandoned because of pollution from industries or polluted runoff. During the last ten years, the city has attempted to conserve water with bans and restrictions. Recent population growth mandated by the province and encouraged by Guelph politicians has exacerbated the problems of water supply and wastewater disposal.

1999-2000

Watering restrictions in the city have been relatively recent, and if climate change continues may well become more frequent. The city has also offered incentives to homeowners and builders who install water-saving toilets, but even this measure encountered resistance. In 2000, opponents argued that individual homeowners would include people who were planning to buy low-flow toilets anyway, but were just waiting until they could get a rebate, so incentives were also offered to landlords.

Toilet rebates became available to owners of properties with more than 20 units using over 500 litres of water per day if they replaced 13 and 20-litre gravity tank toilets. Rebates of $100 were offered for replacement of high-use commercial toilets and urinals. This two year pilot project could cost the city $100,000 a year and would pay for 500 toilet replacements and 15 washing machine replacements each year. Since multi-residential units comprised a significant portion of the Guelph's housing stock; (3,917 townhouses; 1,375 multi-plex units; 8,839 apartments and 451 mixed commercial/residential units), the programme had the potential to conserve a significant volume of water.

In response to prolonged dry weather in the summer of 1999 city council had decided that lawn watering would be permitted only on alternate-days from 7-10 a.m. and 7-10 p.m. That year, Guelph's emergency water level dropped so low that an outright ban was put in place during the worst periods of dry weather. In 1999 the city issued 130 warnings to those ignoring the restrictions, but no fines were levied.

Early in 2000 when droughts again became severe, waterworks superintendent Peter Busatto recommended reducing the hours to 7-9 but this was initially rejected by council despite staff arguments that a complete watering ban might have to be imposed. However when levels continued to drop, Bosatto's recommendation was adopted and watering was restricted to alternate days at the times that he had suggested.

In 2000, *Places to Grow* had not yet been passed by the

province so water use planning continued to be based on Planning Department's population projections. At that time, building permit and draft plan commitments in Guelph placed the 2016 population at 127,000. Staff suggested that as many as 10 new wells should be operating before 2016 to guarantee enough water for emergencies such as a major fire or an extended drought. Provincial environmental regulations required the city to make long term projections of water supply and demand. Based on these, existing capacity was well below what would be needed. Depending on how the city managed its water use, it could spend from $2.8 million for six new wells to $6 million for ten. Busatto reported that the city had a healthy supply of water when total consumption was considered. During the year, average daily demand was 51,539 cubic metres, well below the capacity of 82,760. Unfortunately, future provincial legislation and climate change soon made a mockery of such predictions.

The Years of the "Fifty Year Drought": 2001 and 2002

2001

After another dry summer, Guelph City Council began to take water conservation seriously. On Wednesday, Aug. 8, residents used an all-time daily high of 74,000 cubic meters of water. Normal daily water use was about 53,000 cubic meters. On that day at 6 p.m. the city prohibited, on pain of a fine of up to $5,000, watering established lawns, gardens, and shrubs by manual or automatic sprinkler system or by hose. It also banned car and driveway washing. Under the ban, residents could use a watering can to water only gardens, flowers, trees or shrubs. To get a watering permit for newly laid sod or treated lawns they must call city waterworks and apply. By the end of September, alternate day lawn watering, car and driveway washing were again permitted. During the eight-week lawn-watering ban, 70 warnings were issued but no one received the minimum $75 fine. The ban, even without enforcement, resulted in a 15 per cent reduction in exterior lawn watering while it lasted. During this period, council received many complaints, particularly from south end residents about brown lawns and parks. For some, aesthetics seemed to be more important than water conservation.

2002

After its experience in 2001, the city held 3 focus groups to discuss water conservation strategies. They were informed that about 60 per cent of exterior water is used to water established lawns, while 20 per cent is applied to new lawns. Treated lawns, recreational water use, car washing, and watering gardens, shrubs and trees each account for about five per cent. Focus groups seemed most concerned that children would be allowed to run through sprinklers, so it was recommended that this not be restricted unless the drought became severe. Regulations stated that those with odd-numbered addresses could water only between 7 and 9 a.m. and 7 and 9 p.m. on odd-numbered days, and conversely even-numbered addresses on even-numbered days at those times. Alternate day and time restrictions were also imposed for watering trees, shrubs, flowers and gardens and residential vehicle washing. Odd numbered addresses could water on odd numbered days and even numbered addresses could water on even numbered days from 7 to 9 a.m. and from 7 to 9 p.m.

The drought in 2002 was the second year of the "one-in-fifty year drought" and resulted in very low levels in the Eramosa River. Flows behind the city's York Rd. Water station were reduced to 200 litres a second; roughly equivalent to a bathtub full moving down the river every second. In these circumstances, the aquifers from which Guelph's wells draw water are not being recharged since the groundwater level is so low. Drilling additional wells cannot compensate for the water deficiency induced by over-use and climate change. The following is an opinion piece by the author that appeared in the Guelph *Mercury* on August 24:

Guelph councillors should read recent headlines in the local press.

A few examples: "'Critically low' water level looms; Five water violation charges laid; Province's call to turn off the taps; Be prepared for more drought; Weather records scorched; Dams used to keep rivers flowing; City busily preparing for worst case scenarios; New reservoir won't end water bans; Private water sources still sprinkling on some lawns; Large water users asked to show how they cut back." Council's recent actions and the following headlines make one wonder whether members of city council have made the connection between rapid growth, climate change and water supply: "Another boom building year in Guelph; Development plan to council; New subdivision approved despite neighbour's worries."

Just as we endure our second "fifty year drought" in two years, council has approved a new subdivision for up to 733 homes to accommodate 2,500 or more people. They will require water for drinking, bathing, showering, watering, washing cars and filling pools.

Residents will drive cars and many will require schools, parks and roads. Others will want access to our already stressed medical and social services. And all this while "SmartGuelph" is supposed to be planning our future. What motivates council to approve all these applications?

Record construction in Guelph has surpassed building in Kitchener, Cambridge and Waterloo. This has been the case for the last five years; wonderful news for the development industry. But what of homeowners in Guelph? Will they continue to enjoy alternate day watering between 7 and 9, with more restrictions to come? How will business such as car washes and golf courses react when the "Black" condition exists and they can no longer draw water? We have too little water for our existing population, but are prepared to accommodate new residents.

Guelph already has an oversupply of zoned residential land. This is the result of draft approvals made when water supply did not seem to be an issue. Before the implications of climate change were recognized completely, council and staff pushed rapid growth as the solution to all our problems. Now some are not so sure!

Our infrastructure planning engineer recently reported that even with projected wastewater treatment expansion, only 19,000 new housing units could be serviced. Unfortunately, almost 25,000 units have already been approved. These could accommodate up to 75,000 new residents, and will attract more businesses, not to mention the water they will require!

And speaking of "more", why did council reduce development impost charges to attract new industry? Why did they decide to cover the "deficit" by a surcharge on residential water bills? Was this fair or even intelligent?

Guelph's impost charges have always been lower than those of competing cities and our growth has been faster, so what was the point of this move? Apparently it has had little effect on our ability to attract new business, which comes because of our excellent quality of life. As a result of council's misguided impost policy, citizens whose water use is now severely restricted are paying more for water to "attract new growth."

Another headline: "City wants more control over growth." But council can slow our growth. If water and sewer services are unavailable, no development can occur. If there is inadequate wastewater treatment capacity, no development can occur. If land is inaccessible, no development can occur. So, why do they continue to support extended services, new roads and expanded wastewater treatment capacity? Unfortunately, council's policies have exacerbated our water problem. Given that taxpayers are already complaining, should there be a moratorium on infrastructure expenditures until the water situation improves? Council must heed the warnings (and recent history) suggesting that "fifty year droughts" will occur much more frequently.

Without water release from dams, the Speed River would be almost empty. Brantford and other downstream communities would be drinking our sewage effluent. If droughts continue, reservoirs may not fill to increase summer flows.

Ground water tables are dangerously low and will take many years to recover. The Eramosa River, which once augmented our aquifers is now so low that only the "equivalent of a bathtub full" of water flows along it every second.

This is too little to recharge anything, and the Ministry of the Environment will not allow it to be pumped into our aquifers. Climate change research suggests that drought and hot weather will become even more frequent in the future.

Despite the fact that Ontario "planning" legislation favours economic growth and development, we can take action to slow development.

Several school boards have had the courage to disobey the government's "no budget deficit legislation". Maybe city council should defy the province's directive that we accommodate "our share" of growth. Why don't they stop extending services to new areas? Our water shortages have made a

mockery of Ontario's growth policy.
What can the average taxpayer do to change
council's direction? The only effective process for
citizens who don't like city policies is to vote for
different councillors.
Maybe this will be the ultimate solution to our growth
and water problems. But someone will have to
articulate better options and then be elected to city
council on a platform of care and conservation. Our
future is in the hands of voters, but they must rise to
the challenge of changing environmental conditions.

"SmartGuelph" referred to above, was a planning process instituted by Mayor Karen Farbridge in 2002. It involved hundreds of citizens in advisory panels and was intended to guide the city's growth and planning for a number of years. Since it was the object of considerable discussion, dissension and debate at City Council and among interest groups, it will be discussed in detail in a separate section of this book. Here we will continue to discuss Guelph's water problems and policies.

In 2002 a system of four colour codes was employed to inform citizens of watering restrictions. Some considered these a bit confusing, but the threat of fines rather than warnings for infractions made compliance more frequent than in 2001 when no fines were levied. The maximum fine for non-compliance with Guelph's watering ban was $5,000, with most fines between $100 and $500 per incident. The combination of very low levels in the Eramosa River and Provincial drought regulations also encouraged citizens to conserve ground water. Low flows in the river reduced the city's water supply by 10 percent. During several weeks in mid-July, Guelph recorded less than two millimetres of rain. The total amount of precipitation in the Grand River watershed was about 400 millimetres less than normal. The drought-like conditions depleted groundwater which supplies municipal wells and provides fresh water for rivers and creeks.

The hot, dry weather and the possibility of fines encouraged users to reduce peak demand below 2001 levels. In mid July, temperatures reached 34 Celsius and the humidex rose to over 40, higher than in tropical communities such as Miami Beach and Acapulco. Residents were frustrated by the lack of rain but generally complied with the ban on lawn watering. Guelph had received only one quarter the amount of rain typical for August, and almost 70 per cent of the water in the Speed River was coming from storage at the Guelph Dam. Guelph imposed greater restrictions than other parts of the Speed River watershed because its streams, the Speed and Eramosa Rivers, and Mill Creek in Puslinch Township, received less rain than fell elsewhere.

Across the Prairies 50 to 70 per cent of all farms were severely affected by drought, some for the third consecutive year. Crops withered (if farmers had bothered to plant them at all) and grazing pastures were barren causing cattle that normally feed on them to sold off at rock-bottom prices. In 133 years of record-keeping, nearly three-quarters of Alberta's agricultural land had never been drier. During July and some of August, Guelph was at the Red level which prohibited lawn watering entirely. With the Red restrictions in place, street cleaning machines were not used in Guelph. At the end of August, the city stopped bulk water sales, but noted that lawn watering is the biggest user (about 60 per cent) while bulk water sales constituted less than four per cent of outdoor water use.

During this year of drought, many people objected to bulk sales of water to commercial enterprises. The topic of Nestlé's use of water for bottling became more and more controversial. For a number of years it had been drawing large amounts of water from its wells in Aberfoyle for its bottling plant. This ultimately led to the formation of groups attempting to stop or control the use of groundwater for commercial purposes. For some reason, the province levies only minimal fees for ground water-taking permits. However, in September, owners of water-taking permits along the Eramosa and Speed Rivers were being asked by the province to aggressively curb their water usage voluntarily to avoid additional restrictions. By mid October Guelph water restrictions were reduced to their lowest level, but not removed. Guelph's average rainfall for August should be around 100 millimetres, but was instead only 20 millimetres in 2002, among the lowest on record.

Almost Back to Normal

2003

By the end of May, water levels in the Speed and Eramosa Rivers were back to normal and local reservoirs were full. However, ground water remained lower than average, requiring some restrictions until it was recharged. Cool temperatures and adequate precipitation helped to avert severe drought. During this summer, council increased the charges for bulk water sales and discussed water use and conservation in the city. Council was pleased with the wetter summer of 2003 and the positive response to restrictions during the severe drought of 2002.

2004

In 2004, rivers flowing at higher levels resulted in not having to release as much water from the reservoirs. Temperatures cooler than normal prevailed over the summer. The Guelph Dam saw 900 millimetres of rain to the end of July in 2004, compared to 863 millimetres for the same time period in 2003, and 796 millimetres for the January to July period in 2002. This led to a year without watering restrictions in

Guelph in 2004.

Continuing Water Woes in Guelph 2005 – 2012

By 2005, precipitation had again decreased and Guelph officials began to study water use and supply in detail. Fifteen years earlier, finding new supplies of water to feed Guelph's growing population was relatively easy. Few people paid attention to the process. Water came out of their faucets. They didn't concern themselves with the crucial questions of its origins or how much was available. Guelph seemed to have an endless pool of clean water in Arkell Springs; 865 (277 ha.) acres outside city limits that had been providing Guelph with its water for 100 years. Glacial till acted as a natural purifier as rainwater seeped through layers of sand and gravel and gathered in underground aquifers.

According to a Planning Department projection, Guelph was expected to grow by more than 40 per cent over the next 20 years. "In just 11 years, Guelph will outgrow its ability to supply its residents and businesses with the water we need," said Peter Busatto, manager of Guelph Waterworks. He felt that with constant water use and conservation, the supply would last until 2016. To address this situation, city staff were working on a *Water Supply Master Plan* for the next 50 years. The other major challenge was the disposal of waste water and sewage. This report generated considerable debate,including suggestions that Guelph should build a pipeline from the Great Lakes.

The province regulates the amounts of effluent that can be released into the Speed River based on its flow rates, water quality and fish habitat. If Guelph is to grow significantly, its sewage treatment plant will have to be upgraded considerably. Two of Guelph's 23 municipal wells went off-line in the early 1990s due to chemical industrial contamination. Because of regulations about surface water imposed by the province after the Walkerton E-coli disaster, a shallow water collection system at Arkell Springs was also terminated in 2000. No new wells have been drilled to supply Guelph since 1997.

Plans for two new wells at Arkell Springs were blocked by Puslinch Township. The site, although owned by the city of Guelph, is within the township's limits. Township officials believed that more pumping would adversely affect river flows and fish habitat in the Eramosa River, and could affect the levels of private wells within the township. Puslinch officials also disputed Guelph's estimates of the amount of water available from Arkell Springs. By the end of 2004, the City was still grappling with the related problems of urban growth and water supply. Unfortunately, in 2006, the Ontario Government's *Places to Grow* legislation complicated matters even more. By August, the city had once more imposed watering restrictions because levels were again low. Fortunately, the drought in 2005 was neither as long nor as severe as those in 2001-2002.

2006

This year was distinguished by several important events. After consultants recommended a pipeline from Lake Erie to alleviate Guelph's water problems, the Quarrie council added this option to Guelph's long range water plan. It was encouraged by the fact that Waterloo Region had expressed interest in such a facility and by consultants' assertions that infrastructure at the Nanticoke wastewater treatment plant would make this option less expensive than originally estimated.

Early in 2006, Provincial *Places to Grow* legislation stated that by 2015 Guelph must locate at least 40 per cent of new homes in built-up-areas. It also mandated at least 150 residents and 150 jobs per hectare in the downtown core. In new subdivisions built on greenfields there must be at least 50 residents and jobs per hectare. Quarrie's Council informed the province that it would create its own growth plans that would not conform to all the directives in this legislation. However, after Karen Farbridge and a primarily like-minded council replaced Kate Quarrie and seven of her supporters in November, the city changed its stance. Guelph's planning and population projections were revised by the new council to align more closely with *Ontario's Places to Grow* legislation that had passed on June 16. The new council also dropped the pipeline that had been recommended by the Quarrie Council.

The Farbridge Council also made more immediate recommendations, such as a conservation plan that would see Guelph reduce daily water use by about 10 per cent. This plan also recommended that Guelph investigate increasing the amount of water drawn from existing wells and exploring with neighbouring municipalities the possibility of drawing additional water from their sources. While worthwhile to consider before recommending a pipeline, tapping into neighbours' water supplies may be difficult. Residents and politicians in Puslinch have been arguing for years about the potential impact on private wells of additional water pumping from the Arkell spring ground and consistently have opposed approval of any new wells.

2007

Ontario's Places to Grow legislation had a profound effect on Guelph's planning for increased population and water use. It mandated much greater population growth than previously anticipated by city officials and had major implications for water use. In 2007, the population of the city was approximately 115,000 and that of Wellington County about 80,000. Ontario's demands resulted in Guelph planning for a projected population of 169,000 in 2031; a 47 percent increase. Guelph and Wellington County together were projected by the province's plans to have between 175,000 and 195,000 residents by 2031. Guelph would have to accommodate an additional 54,000 new citizens and 3,100 new jobs. To satisfy Ontario's plans for higher densities they would have to be located in the downtown, along major traffic corridors and in high density nodes on the periphery. Such growth would undoubtedly increase air pollution, and the demand for urban services, especially water supply and wastewater treatment. It would also attract significant opposition from those in areas where densities were to increase.

Unfortunately, many residents when confronted with nearby residential growth, and all too often, any change from the status quo, have resorted to the "NIMBY" syndrome. This acronym for *NOT IN MY BACK YARD* has led to many long and expensive delays when Council or developers have attempted to increase densities, change local zoning or take any action considered by citizens as decreasing their property values. Objections to perceived changes such as additional noise, more traffic, different land uses, more residents or any alterations to a neighbourhood inevitably encourage NIMBY. For some, NIMBY has become the standard response to any change, regardless of its merits or lack thereof.

To alleviate some of the anticipated opposition, Guelph's planners designed questions on the city's website asking how new people moving to Guelph should be accommodated. They also questioned people about planning policies on transportation and the environment. Using results from the survey, higher density designs would then be constructed to bring commercial, industrial and residential uses closer together in more efficient patterns than before. This approach was based on focusing growth within built-up areas, where roads, bus routes and water pipes had already been established. According to Mayor Farbridge, "We're going into areas where we already have a lot of infrastructure in place, so it's a type of growth that's less costly for the residents." In addition to the possible NIMBY challenges, few developers favoured higher density plans where significant opposition from residents might develop. Here we will continue to focus on the challenges posed for water supply. Additional planning challenges confronting Guelph from 2007 to 2010 will be discussed below.

During the summer of 2007, Guelph residents complied with the minimal watering restrictions imposed in June, but by September low rainfall and levels in the Eramosa River required level 2 "Red" to be imposed. During this year, local opposition to Nestlé Ltd. which had been drawing water for its Aberfoyle bottling plant for many years became more critical. A group called Wellington Water Watchers was formed with James Gordon as its first Chair. Even though Nestlé's wells extracted water from the Mill Creek watershed, Water Watchers felt that additional pumping from this well would have a negative impact on shallow groundwater discharge. All summer, they questioned Nestlé's water taking and opposed Nestlé's request for a five-year renewal of its permit to draw up to 3.6 million litres of water a day in Aberfoyle, where its bottling plant is located. In May, city council decided to ask the province to renew the permit for only two years.

By the end of the year, the province, which wanted more tests on the effects of Nestlé's operations, had not yet made a decision on the permit application. Despite the fact that Nestlé drew from a different watershed, opponents realized that water resources were not unlimited and that aquifers often joined between watersheds. Several years of droughts had inspired a much greater appreciation of the importance of water conservation, especially in a city that relies on groundwater supplies.

2008

By April, the Ministry of the Environment (MOE) had renewed Nestlé's permit to take up to 1.3 billion litres of groundwater a year, but it reduced the term from five years to two. It felt that the current 3.6 million litres taken per day was sustainable but required Nestlé to conduct ongoing studies and monitoring during that period. While pleased with this decision, Wellington Water Watchers emphasized that a public resource continued to be given away practically free and then sold back to consumers for more than the price of gasoline. Furthermore society must continue to dispose of all the plastic waste generated by the sales of bottled water. For some reason, the Provincial Government had not yet put a reasonable price per litre on ground water taken for commercial purposes, but seemed content to levy a token permit fee. Given that other jurisdictions charge dearly for the use of ground water, one wonders why Ontario has chosen not to utilize this potentially major source of revenue.

By April, after a winter of very heavy snowfall, ground water levels in the Guelph area had returned to normal. Water at the Guelph dam was rising and the dam was filled by May. There were no watering restrictions during the summer of 2008. By August, Nestlé stated that it was seeking a backup well but would not look in Puslinch because of concerns about levels in local wells. By the end of the year, both the Upper Grand District School Board and city council began discussions about banning bottled water in their buildings.

2009

In May, the Grand River Conservation Authority noted that water levels were high in local streams and rivers after days of heavy rain. However, by September Grand River Conservation Authority (GRCA) officials warned that Eramosa River levels were low and that it should not be used to recharge wells, but a watering ban was not imposed. Controversy about Nestlé's water taking activities continued, as did discussion of the recycling of their plastic bottles. The company adopted thinner bottles to reduce criticism and held an open house to support its position. Neither the city nor the school boards banned bottled water in 2009.

2010

Wellington Water Watchers made presentations to local schools supporting the reuse of water containers and Nestlé objected to this activity. The Water Watchers avoided getting into a statistical war with Nestlé, but noted that the facts about bottled water and its expensive eco-footprint spoke for themselves. More and more municipalities were banning bottled water, more information was reported on high bacteria levels in bottled water and there was a worldwide problem with plastic waste. Schools realized that the sale of the product sends a wrong message to its students, and television commercials showed people being active and fit while drinking from reusable bottles.

By September because of consecutive wet summers, Nestlé hadn't been able to conduct "dry conditions tests" or "low flow tests" to determine the amount of water available during the driest of conditions. There was some evidence of reverse flow at Mill Creek, but none to indicate the effect on the aquifer. Nevertheless, Nestlé continued to request approval from the Ministry for a back-up well. Despite early worries about low water levels in 2010, no onerous restrictions were placed on watering that summer. As a result of public education and several years of severe restrictions on watering, many Guelph residents replaced their lawns with bushes, flowers and shrubs which required far less water than lawns.

2011
Early in the year, Nestlé applied to the Ministry of Natural Resources for a ten year water-drawing permit. This was vigorously opposed by Wellington Water Watchers which suggested that a two year permit would be more appropriate. In May, the ministry renewed Nestlé's permit for five years with the proviso that amounts be reduced if drought conditions occurred. Fortunately the area received adequate precipitation during the rest of the year and restrictions were not imposed.

2012
After a very dry winter and spring, Guelph once again began to feel the effects of drought. By July the city had imposed Level 1 restrictions, limiting lawn watering to between 7 and 9 am. and 7 and 9 pm. on alternate days. Precipitation was at only 22 per cent of historical averages for this time of year and Guelph Lake had received only five per cent of average rainfall during five weeks in July. Aside from a few brief thunderstorms, there had been no rain.

With decreasing Speed and Eramosa River levels and low groundwater levels, the city raised restrictions to Level 2 early in August. This banned lawn watering entirely without a permit, and limited watering of gardens or shrubs to alternate days and times as in Level 1. By then an extended drought in eastern Canada had greatly decreased flows in rivers, and reservoirs like Guelph Lake were beginning to be drained. Conservation authorities attempted to keep rivers high enough to dilute sewage effluent by drawing down local reservoirs. By mid-month, lawns were brown and local reservoirs were very low. The extended drought not only affected urban dwellers, but farmers were selling cattle because of the shortage of hay and corn crops had been greatly reduced. Some earlier rain had helped soybean crops, but the situation in rural areas had become severe. It began to rain in earnest shortly thereafter, so hopefully the drought had ended by September.

There is no doubt that Guelph will experience droughts for many years and that water shortages will continue to occur in this area. *Places to Grow* legislation mandating much higher populations in Guelph than projected earlier by city planners will make water conservation even more important. Despite assertions by hydrological consultants, there is no guarantee that drilling additional wells in the same aquifer will ensure adequate water supplies for Guelph. Neither is there any guarantee that groundwater levels in Ontario will remain adequate, especially if climate change continues as in the last few years. With a pipeline politically and economically unpalatable, Guelph politicians may well have to curtail population growth despite provincial targets. Such a scenario will pose major challenges for politicians and planners at the provincial and municipal level.

Nestlé continues to take water from its Arkell wells to bottle and sell across North America. Disposal of plastic waste will remain a major problem, and the question of the value of groundwater will continue to be debated. Wellington Water Watchers and similar groups will persist and press governments to explain why ground water is given away at a token permit fee only to be sold for a large profit by commercial enterprises. Why is it not being priced as an essential public resource, generating revenue for the province? Many other jurisdictions require water bottling corporations to pay a lot for their groundwater. What is wrong with the government of Ontario? During the next few years some interesting debates will undoubtedly occur, especially as citizens become increasingly militant and the frequency of droughts continues to increase.

WASTE DISPOSAL: PROBLEMS AND PROGRESS

2000

Between 2000 and 2010, Guelph politicians were confronted by the problems of how to dispose of household waste and with opposition to the Eastview landfill site which had almost reached its capacity. Neighbours of Eastview became increasingly concerned about leaching and methane gas from the site that might adversely affect their health. Some charged that hazardous waste was being dumped there; an accusation vigorously denied by city officials. Nevertheless, pressure to close the facility continued to mount. Guelph had been a pioneer in wet-dry recycling and in 2000 began an experiment with promising new technology. The era of Subbor (Super Blue Box Recycling) was to begin just off Watson Road near the existing wet-dry facility.

Proponents of Subbor planned to use Guelph's waste for a trial period at no cost to the city to demonstrate that its process worked. The $18.9 million project was being funded by Toronto-based Eastern Power Limited and its subsidiary company Super Blue Box Recycling Corp., plus a government loan of just under $5 million. It worked by recycling everything without the cost of sorting, which during their process was done by machines. It also reduced greenhouse gases by producing and collecting methane gas that would normally escape from landfill sites and then using it to generate electricity. Because of the success of the city's Wet-Dry garbage system, Guelph was chosen as the test site for Subbor at a plant still being constructed in the southeast area of the city. Though the Wet-Dry centre would continue to operate, Subbor was brought to Guelph for a trial testing period of two years, processing as much garbage as the city was willing to provide. After that time the city would decide whether or not to invest in the new technology.

Subbor used a process called digestion (an anaerobic reaction without oxygen) rather than composting. Microbes break down non-recyclable material and remove heavy metals in the digested material which becomes peat. For every 100 tonnes of garbage, 15 tonnes of peat are generated. Subbor was the first of its kind in the world and the technology is purely Canadian. The idea has been developing since 1995.The Guelph facility would be able to process 25,000 tonnes of garbage each year and was a fraction of its potential size. Larger Subbor facilities will be able to handle between 100,000 and 500,000 tonnes of garbage each year. Unfortunately, Subbor never completely lived up to expectations and eventually became embroiled in a lawsuit with city council.

In 1995, Guelph had built a $36-million Wet-Dry recycling centre with the help of an $11 million government grant. Since then city residents have divided their waste into two streams; wet and dry. Wet waste is composted and sold to gardeners and landscapers, dry waste is sorted and recyclable materials are recovered and sold. The centre employed 50 people working in two shifts. Sales of recycled materials were just $500,000 in 1996, the first year of operation, but have increased by $500,000 each year since. For 2000, the centre projected $1.8 million in sales, but because markets are volatile the number could change. Each household in Guelph paid 16 cents a week to have garbage collected and processed in that year, successfully diverting garbage from the landfill site. It kept about 58 per cent of residential garbage out of the dump in 1999, compared to about 20 per cent in 1995. While the city wants to reduce garbage in the landfill site, it also requires more garbage to be recycled to increase sales. Thousands of tonnes of compost made from garden waste have been sold and with more recycling this could increase considerably.

2001

During 2001, Subbor began to operate and residents became increasingly concerned about the Eastview landfill which was scheduled to close in 2002. If this were to happen, a transfer station would have to be built near the existing wet-dry facility off Watson Road. Here garbage would be packed into trucks and shipped away for disposal. Opponents claimed that this would create as many odours and as much pollution as the Eastview site, but in a location ill suited for such a facility.

Pressure to close Eastview as soon as possible continued to increase, but the city explained that it would try to get approval under the Environmental Protection Act for both the Eastview closing and the building of the transfer station. This might take some time. Meanwhile, the wet-dry facility was temporarily closed because fumes from hazardous waste caused a sorter to faint and others to become ill. Once again the city urged citizens to bring hazardous waste to the hazardous waste depot rather than putting it into their recycling boxes. Opposition to the transfer station and pressure to close the Eastview site was sustained through public meetings throughout the year. On several occasions, residents in the Stone/Watson Road area complained bitterly about noxious odours coming from the vicinity of the wet-dry and Subbor facilities. Problems with glass in compost and low prices for coloured glass required Guelph to acquire several new machines for its wet-dry facility.

In June, Janet Laird was appointed as Guelph's Head of Public Works with responsibility to manage the waste and landfill problems. She replaced long-time head Ray Funnell who retired at the end of May. Meanwhile, Subbor management suggested that Guelph sweeten their financial deal because they were removing solid waste from the garbage stream and thus prolonging the life of Eastview.

The facility could take both dry and wet waste streams now going to the wet/dry plant, calling into question whether the city would need to run its facility if Subbor were successful. They could start by accepting all the residential waste going to the Eastview Road landfill site, about 10,000 tonnes annually, but within a year the company would like to handle another 10,000 tonnes of city waste. The city was considering a draft agreement proposed by Subbor to replace a contract expiring in November.

2002-2003

After a trial in the north end of Guelph, a three bag recycling system was recommended in September 2002 for the whole city. This system would use one bag for wet garbage, one for recyclables and one for bypass destined for the landfill. According to city officials, the three-bag system would eventually stop 70 per cent of waste from having to be buried in the ground; much better than the 44 per cent diverted from landfill under the two-bag system. The other option after Eastview closed was to have bypass waste trucked to Michigan or St. Thomas, both expensive and environmentally unsustainable options.

When the three bag system was implemented in March 2003, many complaints were heard. First there was a shortage of clear bags for bypass waste. Many residents had difficulty deciding which waste was recyclable and which was bypass. Others complained that clear bags which were to be collected only every two weeks were not picked up. The local press and council received numerous complaints during the implementation of this system. Councillors Dan Moziar and Rocco Furfaro suggested that the city consider scrapping the new wet/dry programme, and use all non-compostable materials (waste and recyclables) to help fill Guelph's landfill, which was due to close by the end of the year. The city had been forced in the past to ship some recyclables directly to Eastview because of capacity issues at the wet/dry facility, but the province tolerated that because Guelph has had a long term plan to maximize recycling, the new three bag system.

In April, several councillors suggested that the city revisit the possibility of incinerating waste, but Mayor Farbridge reminded them that Guelph had initiated the wet-dry recycling programme because of negative citizen reaction to incineration when it was suggested in 1998.

Guelph filed court papers in June seeking a declaration that the agreement with Subbor to process its waste had expired. The City of Guelph was heading to court to fight off a $30 million breach of contract lawsuit launched by the company that had been told to shut down a waste processing test plant on municipal property. The Subbor court documents pointed out that many actions by the city, such as levying an unexpected $50,000 in development charges against the plant and blocking access to waste for testing purposes, were breaches of the 1998 contract. If the issue goes to trial, Guelph lawyers will move to have a 1998 deal with Subbor quashed and a court order for Subbor to "quietly and peacefully" surrender the Stone Road municipal property where the company has been testing its waste management technology. Under the 1998 agreement the plant had been constructed next to Guelph's wet/dry recycling centre, now called the Waste Resource Innovation Centre.

2004

By 2004, neighbours were again complaining about foul odours emanating from the wet/dry plant. However, bad odours were expected to decrease near the city's wet/dry recycling facility when a $200,000 retrofit and upgrade of the operation's air filtration system has been completed.

2006

After several years of operation, the city began to consider whether to shut down its wet/dry facility. Their consultants said that the city should have known about likely wet plant failure more than a decade ago. The city's wet recycling plant, which is part of a three-stream waste collection system that also involves 'dry' recyclables and regular garbage, collects the organic waste thrown out in residents' green bags and converts it into compost, which is then sold.

As indicated in a report from the city's environmental department, the wet plant, located on Dunlop Drive, would require $3.8 million to replace its roof, upgrade its air-management system and install a water scrubber to remove odours from the air. The alternative outlined in the report was to close the decade-old facility indefinitely, ship the waste to Quebec, and reinforce the roof so the plant could re-open if the city decided to use it again in the future. But when council learned that it would cost only a few more dollars a tonne to ship waste out of town than to continue treating it in Guelph, some councillors questioned the rationale for keeping the plant open.

Most of the funding for plant improvements would come from the federal and provincial governments, leaving the city to pay about $900,000. A city staff report said that money was available in the city's capital budget. If the funding came from the Province and council decided to proceed with upgrades, the plant would be closed for at least a year while repairs were made starting in the fall.

Area residents had long complained about unbearable odours coming from the east end plant. A family about two kilometres south of the Dunlop Drive plant, said that there have been days when children would not play outside because of the smell. The Ontario Ministry of the

Environment inspected the plant and found several areas where it wasn't complying with standards. The city responded with short and medium-term repairs, which reduced odours around the facility. On March 6, council voted to proceed with a ministry-funded pilot project to test a scrubber in the wet plant. The test period would be from May to August. But the city waited to see if it would receive $2.5 million from the provincial and federal governments to proceed with long-term plans, including a permanent scrubber and roof repairs. That announcement was expected in June.

The city had planned to replace the roof when it built the facility which was completed in 1995, but not this soon. The steel deteriorated because it's a corrosive environment, and decayed much faster than originally estimated. The city had been paying about $102 to process a tonne of waste, plus another $40 or so for screening the compost at another facility. Shipping it out-of-town for treatment would cost about $150 per tonne. Given these options, councillors proposed competing ideas and indulged in heated debate about the fate of the plant, which continued sporadically for a number of months. By June, more problems with the three bag system were encountered. Other composting facilities disliked the plastic bags used in Guelph because little pieces of plastic were mixed with the compost. If it closed the wet/dry plant, the city could have a hard time finding another compost facility to process its green bags of organic waste.

The debates about recycling continued, but another factor now entered the discussion. Starting Feb. 5, consumers would pay a deposit of 10 to 20 cents when they bought alcohol, and were encouraged to bring the empties to The Beer Store for refunds of their deposits. A lot of glass could be recycled at the Beer Store and therefore might not become part of the city's wet/dry stream, thus decreasing the city's revenue.

When the organic waste plant was closed, Guelph lost its leadership role in waste processing and recycling. Residents who were aware that their wet waste was no longer being turned into compost began to sort very poorly because wet was no longer being composted. It was shipped to Niagara Falls, New York to be incinerated and dry waste was sent to Green Lane landfill site near St. Thomas. Meanwhile, council dithered about a long-term solution to its recycling problems, and worried that citizens would no longer sort carefully if a new facility were built. As a result of all these problems, a number of concerned citizens formed a watchdog group to monitor the city's waste disposal efforts. The wet plant was finally demolished in May. In August, the city was informed that it had won the $30 million lawsuit brought by Subbor and could proceed with closing their facility. This was one piece of good news during an otherwise difficult year for Guelph council.

2008

The Province announced that it was to levy fees on sales of TVs, computers and other electronics to offset the costs of recycling. In Guelph such items could be left at the landfill for a fee, but on Eco Days they were accepted free. The city considered adding Eco Days to accept more electronic waste if the Provincial fees could be used to offset local recycling costs.

The Ontario Ministry of the Environment (MOE) agreed that Guelph could construct a new composting plant without an environmental assessment if it complied with all provincial regulations. Council then called for tenders and began planning its new facility. Out of fourteen preliminary bids,only two met the requirements of the the city and the MOE. A number of critics of the failures of Guelph's original composting plant recommended that the city scrap its plans for a new facility and just ship its waste out of town. Nevertheless, Council decided to build a new composting plant.

2009

By 2009, the value of recycled material had fallen precipitously. It had been decreasing along with other commodity prices in recent months, and some municipalities were now getting just pennies on the dollar for selling their reusable waste. The going rate for plastic tubs and lids was down 98 per cent from the high of about $295 a tonne. They were now worth only $6 a tonne. These price declines made it much more difficult to operate a recycling programme on a cost recovery model, much less on a profitable basis in Guelph. A schedule in the city's waste management plan suggested that testing of the new facility should be done in the summer of 2010, and cited a city goal to keep 55 per cent of Guelph's trash out of landfill through composting and recycling by 2011.

2010

During these debates, Ken Spira, Chair of the Citizens' Coalition formed in 2007 to monitor the city's waste disposal policies, directed some severe criticism at the plans:

The city clamours to be seen in the light of environmental leadership. But the real ill-conceived and failed experiments from SUBBOR (the Super Blue Box Recycling Corp.), the three-bag system and the discarded compost plant, bulldozed ahead with complete disregard for protection of the environment, Guelph's future water supply, the compost plant's neighbouring residents' quality of life and the taxpayers of Guelph."
"Guelph city council was against shipping Guelph's trash out

of town due to the pollution from trucking and extra traffic mandating that municipalities should look after their own garbage. So it appears the cost to Guelph will be somewhere between $280 and $320 per tonne. One would think that Guelph taxpayers would be somewhat sensitive to this huge increase, as well as offended considering they were first told the per-tonne costs would be $114, then $236, and then 70 cents a week. It is still a mystery why Guelph will not disclose how much this will cost."

A number of councillors, columnists and other citizens questioned everything about the new composting plant from its cost, the value of the waste, its potential for foul odours and the possibility of ground water pollution. Despite these criticisms, Council finally voted to build a new "State of the Art" composting facility.

The New Composting Facility

In September when Councillors inspected the new plant, they were very enthusiastic. "I'm really excited we're finally getting it underway," Councillor Ian Findlay said moments after seeing the site, noting that, while campaigning for election four years ago, residents called for a city composting facility to replace an older one.

"We're addressing all concerns," Findlay said, referring to odour-control measures and solid construction for the new facility under the direction of Mississauga-based builder Maple Reinders which won the contract for the facility. Mayor Karen Farbridge commented that the plant incorporates design and construction advances over the previous composting centre that puts Guelph back on "the leading edge; technology improves through new ideas and innovation."

"We took great pride in being pioneers in organic waste

management," said Mayor Karen Farbridge. "It was fundamental to our identity as a green community. This building is much more than a place to handle our organic waste. It's a symbol of Guelph reclaiming its place as an environmental leader in this province. The city has gained "significant expertise in waste management" by planning and building the facility, and such expertise could be promoted globally. The plant will also include an education room for sharing knowledge with visitors. By having its own facility, Guelph maintains autonomy over its own waste management program, and has the capacity to accept waste from other municipalities, the mayor said. The community is "not at the whim of price increases from a processor in another municipality."

According to the Mayor, residents were unequivocal about what they wanted. "They wanted to process our organic waste in our own municipality," Farbridge said. She added that some options for dealing with organic waste: burying, burning or shipping it elsewhere are cheaper than composting it locally. "But Guelph city council rejected all of these options and made a commitment to a new organic waste processing facility," she continued during her address. "And the reason is simple: It's the responsible thing to do."

Some Potential Problems

To accommodate the MOE certificate regulations,City council approved major changes to Guelph's waste collection system, including adoption of a fully automated cart system of waste collection for all three waste streams. The city also planned to reduce collection of recyclable waste at curbside from the current weekly schedule to collection every two weeks. Collection of the landfill-bound "clear" waste stream would continue to be on a biweekly basis, and the city would continue collecting organic waste every week.

Councillor Gloria Kovach questioned whether the proposed 80-litre green carts, which she described as "small," would be large enough to take yard waste in addition to the organic waste generated by households during peak gardening times in spring and fall. "I think we are being over-optimistic," she said, in thinking the city will be able to eliminate the spring and fall yard waste collections, which cost about $85,000 annually.

The requirement that the city stop collecting organic waste in plastic bags was the most significant change required by the MOE's certificates of approval. The other major change required by the certificates was that diapers and sanitary products will not be allowed in the organic stream when the new composting plant begins operations. Instead, they will become part of the clear bag (bypass) stream, which is used for waste that can't be composted or recycled.

2011:

Major Problems With the New Composting Plant

After the new plant opened in November it worked well, but after about seven weeks, neighbours began complaining about foul odours from the facility. The city and the Ministry investigated and determined that indeed, the odours were coming from the plant. Janet Laird, the City's Director of Environmental Services stated: "We did an initial review last week and we weren't able to determine the cause of the odours." "We are not finished yet. Our investigation is still ongoing. We're doing a thorough review of the odour management system, and if we do identify any issues we will resolve them, and then we will resume accepting waste again." She went on to say: "The province is encouraging municipalities to stop the landfilling of our garbage, and we are doing our best in our community to do that. This is just a minor hiccup, I'm hoping, and that we will very shortly see the return of the full, odour-free operation of this facility and the acceptance of organic waste."

Ken Spira, on behalf of the Citizen's Coalition, continued to level harsh criticism at the city for the problems with the new composting facility. "I can't believe they've built the facility with such faults" he said in an interview. Later he commented: "My opinion? It doesn't work. Compost stinks. You cannot eliminate odours from compost." Problems continued throughout 2011 during which the city, Reindeers and the Ministry attempted to discover the cause of the odours and prevent this problem in the future. By the end of the year, the plant had stopped receiving organic waste and was shut down until odours could be eliminated. Meanwhile, the city incurred costs for consultants examining the plant. On December 13, the Guelph *Mercury* printed an editorial entitled:

The city deserves a public inquiry into the wet plant project:
The smells emanating from the new compost plant near Watson Road have oozed into the hallowed halls of city hall.
I'm intrigued by the city's recently released question-and-answer statement about the plant and its present problems. It is revealing in what the Q-and-A doesn't answer as opposed to what it communicates.
The new plant stopped receiving green bag waste Nov. 25, which is now shipped to a St. Thomas landfill. This cost is stated "about $61 a tonne."
There is no estimate by city officials in the Q-and-A as to when the contractor, Maple Reinders, will fix the odour problem and to Ministry of Environment specifications.
The city does say the cost of processing the green bag waste at the new plant is "about $79 a tonne."
This is where things get murky.

Not included in that $79 operational estimate is the price of borrowing the $32 million capital cost, the depreciation of the facility, the maintenance and the insurance, as well as the cost of road repairs in the city caused by trucks delivering Waterloo Region's waste to the Watson Road plant. The interest rate must be included in the cost of operation of the facility. For example, let's assume the city has borrowed the $32 million at an interest rate of four per cent per annum. That is $1.28 million in interest alone, not including repayment of principal.

The lifespan of the plant is estimated to be 20 years. If the $32 million debenture borrowed matures in that time frame, the cost of this misadventure is more than $57.6 million. That does not include millions to be spent switching from plastic to green bins.

This is where it gets interesting. The Q-and-A does not reveal the terms of the agreement with Maple Reinders. This contractor controls an outfit named Aim Environmental Group and its subsidiary Wellington Organix. All three of these entities are getting a piece of the pie. Maple Reinders is the designer and contractor to build the facility. Its subsidiary, Wellington Organix, operates the plant. And Aim Environmental negotiated the $117 price per tonne for the Region of Waterloo to send its wet waste to Guelph.

That arrangement includes guaranteeing Waterloo Region access to two-thirds of the plant capacity. So the taxpayers of Guelph have financed a wet waste composting plant to provide a service to another municipality that does not cover the real operating costs of the plant.

All liability seems to lie with the taxpayers of Guelph. If the city is paying $61 a tonne to send green bag waste to a St. Thomas landfill with no maintenance, depreciation or cost of capital affecting the price, one

*can only conclude the $79 operating cost of the new
plant is vastly understated. Hey! These aren't my
figures, but are found on the city website.
This project has been riddled with secrecy, a
selective offering of facts for the public, and
questionable management. The only solution to clear
the air is a judicial inquiry to investigate what
happened and expose the expenses of this project.
That giant sucking sound is our tax dollars going
down the toilet.*

This editorial reflected increasing scepticism by many taxpayers, some Councillors and the Citizen's Coalition about the value and effectiveness of Guelph's approach to recycling its wet and dry waste. Because the city was working diligently with the builder and consultants to remedy the problems at the composting plant, the Ministry did not lay charges because of the odours.

2012 Success?

Early in January, the Ministry indicated that the city could again accept organic waste to keep up the bacterial activity inside its biofilter. After a few more problems that seemed to be addressed, the city was given permission to resume operations on February 14. After reviewing the air containment and odour management systems with input from a citizens' advisory committee, a plan was devised to eliminate future odours. A number of changes to equipment and procedures, supervised by the Ministry, to solve odour problems were instituted. Hopefully they will be successful and Guelph will once again resume its leadership position in waste treatment and recycling.

2013

By July of 2013, Guelph's new composting plant had been

operating successfully for a number of months. Ken Spira, a neighbour who founded the Guelph Waste Management Coalition citizens' group to fight odours from the original organics processing facility agreed that it seemed to be operating successfully without producing offensive odours. Susan Antler, executive director of the Compost Council of Canada, commented that Guelph deserved to "blow its own organics horn." She said that they are very proud of the Guelph facility and noted that when Guelph first entered the organics processing business in the mid-1990s it turned a lot of heads. Until then, not one community the size of Guelph had such a facility. When Guelph, with a population of about 100,000 began its programme, the notion that communities of this size could not successfully operate a waste recycling plant was challenged. Guelph demonstrated that smaller communities could operate successful facilities. But being first came with challenges, and Antler said that other municipalities considering organics recycling also learned from Guelph's high-profile mistakes. "Bravo to Guelph for going through what it had to and coming out the other side," she said. At this point it seems that Guelph has been successful, but the cost of organics recycling continues to pose a challenge.

Waste Bins: More Local Controversy

During the Fall of 2012, the City of Guelph began to publicize its planned introduction of waste carts to Guelph. These would enable the city to use automated trucks to pick up and empty the new waste containers rather than handling bags or garbage cans manually. The new carts came in three colours, green for organic waste, blue for recyclable material and grey for bypass to be landfilled. The blue and grey carts were available in four sizes, with the smallest holding 80 litres (21 gallons, equivalent to approximately one standard bag) to the largest holding 360 litres (95 gallons, equivalent to approximately six standard bags). Residents were given a choice depending on their waste history and were advised by the city to choose carts larger than they thought that they would need. For an initial period, exchanges were to be permitted without cost. Green carts were to be emptied every week while the blue and grey carts would be emptied on alternate weeks. The city supplied calendars to each area illustrating the weeks when blue and grey carts were to be emptied.

Purchasing the carts cost the city over $5 million, new trucks were almost $4.5 million and promotion/publicity/education cost almost $300,000. The grand total of $10,148,262 was offset by government grants of $1,335,519, leaving the City with an expenditure of $8,812,743. The annual operational savings of approximately $460,000 would equal the initial cost in about 19 years. In addition, when this programme has been adopted completely, the amount of waste sent to be landfilled will be reduced significantly.

As usual with any innovation in Guelph, the automated cart programme was criticized severely by numerous opponents before it was implemented. Letters to the editors of the *Mercury* and *Tribune* included the following questions and complaints: Where will we store these unwieldy carts? How will we roll them to the curb in the winter? Where will we place them when there are snowbanks? They will be too heavy to be rolled to the curb. The green carts will be very difficult to clean and soon will be infested by maggots and flies. The green carts will soon smell. The cost is far too high. The green carts are much too small to take garden waste as well as organic waste. There is no room at our apartment for carts. Our condominium has no storage place for the carts. This is a heritage neighbourhood and the carts are unsightly! Etc. Etc. Etc.

The author has found that the carts are much more convenient than the former three bag system. It is simple to hose the green carts and a piece of newspaper effectively prevents messy organic waste from adhering to the sides and bottom of the green cart. No liners are needed. We always have room for some garden waste in our green cart. Given their excellent design, even the largest carts are easy to roll. Their sturdy construction and secure latches have completely defeated the hungry local dogs and raccoons.

It seems that most of the very vociferous complainers had never used carts and had little imagination about how they might perform. Unfortunately, such a negative reaction is typical of a group of citizens who seem determined to oppose any change in their neighbourhoods or in municipal procedures. Far fewer complaints have appeared after they were introduced than when the carts were proposed. However, a few important and legitimate shortcomings will have to be addressed during the three-year phase-in for the programme.

Initially some homeowners placed the carts too close together preventing the automated arms from grasping them securely. A number of people placed their carts at the curb on the wrong week. Others forgot to leave the latch on the green cart open for collection. Some used plastic bags which are not permitted inside their carts. Others overfilled carts, resulting in spills during collection. With publicity and time, most of these problems have been eliminated.

One unforeseen problem was the appetites of the voracious raccoons and squirrels in wooded parts of the city. Unfortunately, they have taken to gnawing not only on wet waste receptacles, but on those for bypass and recycling. In some cases they have made holes large enough to enter and to allow matter to escape from the containers. Despite the supposedly sturdy materials constituting the bins, no satisfactory solution has been discovered to protect them from these marauding rodents!

In May 2013, Guelph Council voted against a $35 fee for exchanging waste carts. However, staff proposed the idea again as one revenue generating option. A phone survey that sampled the opinions of the first residents using the bin system found that 70 per cent of them support covering the costs of cart exchanges through a user fee instead of an increase in property tax. The city allows residents to choose from a variety of bin sizes for blue recycling carts and grey garbage carts. Staff proposed a three-month "grace period" after people received bins, during which they could change to a different size of blue or grey bin without a fee. Residents wanting to exchange their carts after the grace period might be given the option of a lower $15 per cart exchange fee if they were willing to clean their original cart, return it to the city and pick up their new cart. Initially, all households received a green 80 litre organics cart and a food scrap container for kitchen use. Unless a resident makes a different choice, the city will also deliver "extra-large" blue and grey carts; a 360-litre recyclables cart and a 240-litre garbage cart.

One major, legitimate problem does remain and that is the plight of residents of certain apartments and condominiums. Most condominium owners can't use the city's three-stream waste removal system and must pay for a private company to remove their waste. The city's trucks are too large for narrow condominium streets, and there is too little space for condominium owners to place bins along the curb. Condominium owners, who are also municipal taxpayers, argue that because they cannot use this city service, they should be reimbursed a portion of their municipal tax. They point out that Waterloo Region provides a $31 a year rebate to condo units which do not receive municipal solid waste services.

Representatives of Condominium owners suggested that the city establish a condominium advisory committee that could be consulted on issues related to condo living. There are about 6,000 condo owners in the city with and more condominiums are under construction. This committee could offer input on condo property design in the planning stage so that city garbage trucks could be accommodated in these communities. City council agreed to explore such a possibility, but no committee was formed. The issue of waste disposal for condominium owners continues to be discussed in the press and at City Council.

There is also a major problem with introducing the three cart system to businesses in the centre of the city. There is often inadequate space in which to store them. It is sometimes difficult to find a location where trucks can easily empty the carts. Permanent carts along the curbs make it difficult to exit cars. Some worry about the whole street being lined by carts on garbage day, while others are concerned about the smell. City officials and downtown businessmen are working to find acceptable solutions to these problems.

Organic Waste Controversy

In August 2013, Guelph's contract with the Waterloo Region to process its organic waste became the topic of considerable debate. Waterloo Regional Council signed a $23 million contract beginning in October to have their organic waste processed at Guelph's new $32 million composting facility. The 10 year contract requires Regional Council to pay Guelph to process 20,000 tonnes of food waste a year. However, the region currently collects only 9,100 tonnes from its unpopular green bins. The shortfall means that Regional taxpayers will be paying Guelph up to $1.3 million a year for garbage not processed. Guelph also hopes to sell the Region's missing tonnage allotment to other municipalities even though it will charge Regional taxpayers for the amounts contracted to be processed. A Guelph councillor argued that Guelph taxpayers deserve any extra cash to help pay for the plant that they built and paid for. Since Guelph sized its plant for regional waste, it will not renegotiate the processing contract and will not allow the Waterloo Regional Government to sell its missing tonnage for its own benefit.

This debate highlights the high cost of green bins, an

expensive program made more expensive after Regional Council overestimated participation and processing needs. Only 15 to 35 per cent of Regional houses put green bins at the curb. If Regional residents don't increase their use of green bins, program costs will increase to $654 per tonne in October. This makes curbside composting five times more expensive than dumping waste in the Waterloo landfill. Later this year Regional Council may consider encouraging more residents to use green bins, by making them mandatory or by reducing bagged garbage collection. By choosing Guelph, Regional Council rejected a pay-as-you-go processing bid from Hamilton that would have been cheaper by almost $1.2 million a year given current tonnages. A number of Waterloo Regional Councillors are very unhappy about the Guelph contract, but it is too late to renegotiate.

Possible Energy From Waste

Ten to fifteen per cent of all waste cannot be reused or recycled and it is now possible to divert much of this from landfills by incinerating it and using the heat to produce electricity. Recently there appears to have been a softening of public opposition to incineration. In an energy-from-waste facility, a significant amount of the capital investment is in pollution-control systems. Nevertheless there's a lot of fear-mongering from people who simply don't want the technology. In Guelph, some city officials are now seriously considering the idea of burning rather than landfilling waste that cannot be recycled or composted. At the moment, Guelph's landfill haulage contract commits the city to shipping 20,000 tonnes of waste annually. Last year the city sent 54,000 tonnes to landfill, so there is plenty of excess capacity if council wants to explore other options. Some councillors believe that the time to consider those options is now.

Energy from waste options were considered during the city's waste management master plan process five years ago, and likely will be reconsidered during the master plan update now underway. Given the large investment required to construct an efficient, low pollution incineration facility, a joint endeavour between Guelph and the Region of Waterloo might be the appropriate procedure. There are currently four plants extracting energy from waste in Canada, with seven more being developed. Since such facilities are very expensive to build, and require enormous amounts of residual waste to keep operating, they are therefore not realistic options for individual municipalities. Guelph could explore options for sending residual waste to an existing facility. Guelph Council has not yet decided on whether it should proceed with such a plan.

Waste Management

In January 2014, The City of Guelph's received the Ron Lance Memorial Award from Waste Diversion Ontario for being the leading diverter of residential waste in the province. Its new composting plant and a new cart-based residential waste collection system resulted in in Guelph diverting 67.72 per cent of its residential waste from landfill in 2012. This waste diversion rate was the best in Ontario in that year. The latest waste diversion figures showed that Guelph is years ahead of its waste diversion targets.

Given the costs and controversy surrounding the new composting plant and the implementation of the cart system, this may become a major issue in the civic election in November 2014. A number of incumbents and prospective councillors were very critical of the process and costs that led to such an excellent rate of waste diversion. The city gave considerable credit to its citizens, many of whom had supported the diversion initiatives and the new cart system. Many others were not very happy about the cost and inconvenience of the changes and may well vote for councillors who also opposed the programme. They point out that city communications about this award did not specify the municipal investment to achieve these numbers, or the comparative cost per tonne of waste management here and elsewhere.

Recyclables Deal

In May 2014, Council signed an agreement to process some of Detroit's recyclable waste and to send some garbage from Guelph to be burned in Detroit's energy from waste facility. This deal is expected to generate an annual profit for the city of about $300,000 and will result in an additional four large trucks entering the Guelph facility every day. It will add a second shift of 36 new employees who will work from 3:30 p.m. to 11:30 p.m.

Up to 22,500 tonnes a year of Guelph's garbage is to be burned to generate thermal energy for an underground steam loop serving downtown and midtown Detroit. Much of Guelph's garbage was going to a landfill near Sarnia, which isn't much closer than Detroit. The recyclables collected in the Detroit area and trucked to Guelph will be single stream. Single-stream recycling is also the system used in Guelph, where all sorts of recyclables are collected in one blue bin or bag. The city signed a separate contract with Recyclable Material Marketing for the Guelph garbage to be shipped to Detroit in some of the returning trucks.

PESTICIDES: FINESSED BY THE PROVINCE

2001

Guelph City Council decided to initiate a public process to consider banning cosmetic use of pesticides on private property. The mere mention of pesticide control by Council attracted numerous opponents, including owners of lawn care companies, golf course superintendents and suppliers of pesticides. Several opponents accused "activists" of promoting regulation of an industry that was already employing sustainable environmental practices. Many proponents and opponents addressed Council which eventually voted that its Planning, Works and Environment Committee "be directed to initiate a public process to review pesticide use in the city of Guelph and to develop recommendations." This was but the beginning of a long, difficult and often contentious process.

2002

Given the intense debate about pesticide control, Council decided to form a committee to review the problem and make recommendations for it to consider. At first it was difficult to find enough potential members for such a committee and then it became difficult to establish procedures and determine the scope of its mandate. A considerable amount of time and effort and many presentations to Council occurred before a committee was formed and began its work.

In December, after a four-month public consultation process by a citizen's panel on pesticides comprising six randomly chosen residents, the panel made its recommendations to the City's Planning, Environment and Transportation Committee. The panel recommended that all pesticide use in Guelph be banned unless a permit is issued by a city inspector, likely only in cases of severe infestation. It also recommended an aggressive education programme to promote alternatives to pesticide use. These recommendations were considered to be the most stringent in the country for reducing pesticide use on private, commercial and city property.

The permit process, which would require homeowners to prove serious infestations to a city inspector, seemed to be the most contentious issue. Amendments to the recommendations introduced at a City Planning, Environment and Transportation Committee meeting included permit exemptions for golf courses and for pesticide research at the University of Guelph. More than 100 people crammed the Guelph Music Centre for a meeting to hear 13 delegations argue the pros and cons of banning pesticide use. A gallery of academics, environmental activists and representatives from both the lawn care and pesticide manufacturing industries attempted to influence the city committee. During this discussion, the citizen's panel was criticized for lack of expertise and for its recommendations. However, Councillors pointed out that the panel had an expert adviser to consult before making its final recommendations. After this long and contentious public meeting, the city's Planning, Environment and Transportation Committee voted 4-1 to send its report to city staff for more study. This report was not expected until February 2003.

2003

Early in the year, some councillors and citizens recommended a referendum on the pesticide issue while others thought that this would be too expensive. In March, Council heard arguments for and against a referendum and eventually voted not to proceed. Opponents argued that a referendum would have to be held before the citizens' pesticide committee appeared before council and before the Planning, Environment and Transportation Committee made a recommendation to council on how to proceed.

A staff report on the pesticide plan suggested that most of the Citizens' Panel's report be implemented, but that it be phased in gradually. It recommended that staff return to Council with by-laws in June, but that only the education portion of the programme and training of enforcement officers begin in 2004. Regulatory provisions of the proposed By-Law would come into force in June 2005, but no fees for permits would be charged that summer "in an attempt to encourage greater compliance and assist in the transition."It recommended that the By-Law be fully implemented in June 2006, at which time fees for permits would begin. Enforcement would be administered by the city's By-Law enforcement officers, "similar to the enforcement of the water restriction By-Law," if time and workload allowed. The permit fee might be $20 per inspection.

By April, opposition to the proposed pesticide by-law necessitated several public meetings. The first, held at the River Run Centre was long and contentious, resulting in a series of recommendations by Mayor Karen Farbridge. "My goal is to decrease pesticide use," she said. A permit system would "galvanize the overall opposition," she said, something that had already started to happen, as some of the 50 people attending the meeting sported no pesticide ban stickers. A permit system could still be required, said Farbridge, but she didn't think that Guelph was ready for permits. A total of 37 speakers made presentations to the committee over two nights. Part two of the highly divisive pesticide debate ended with a fast, unanimous decision by the city's Planning, Environment and Transportation Committee to scrap the controversial pesticide permit system. After the vote, anti-pesticide groups were pleased while the Chair of the Citizens' Panel, several councillors and other proponents were very unhappy that the permit system had been scrapped.

By May the pesticide issue had almost been resolved. Guelph's plan to reduce cosmetic use of pesticide on private land had the support of many within the lawn care industry as well as anti-pesticide activists. Health reasons for decreasing pesticide use were challenged by some, but there was also first-hand evidence offered that many people are adversely affected when neighbours sprayed pesticides. Despite all the evidence presented about the adverse effects of pesticides, a number of speakers strongly opposed any pesticide regulations. One said the the whole process "stinks of bias." A defeated former councillor commented that the discussion had been "hijacked by the Mayor." One particularly vehement opponent said that she and her family would flagrantly and repeatedly break the By-Law and that she would willingly fight this to the Supreme Court of Canada by becoming the first test subject in Ontario."If my neighbour wants to tell me what I can or cannot do on my property, he better buy it," she said.

At the end of a five-hour meeting at the Italian Canadian Club, after an emotional debate, City Council voted ten to three in favour of the Mayor's proposal with minor modifications. The controversial permit system was scrapped, but there would be spot spraying by members of the lawn care industry who had shown their commitment to reducing pesticides by becoming accredited in Integrated Pest Management (IPM). There would also be buffer zones where no pesticide would be sprayed. A stakeholder committee, including the lawn care industry, University of Guelph, citizen and health care representatives, would assist staff in developing the plan. An education program on how to grow grass without chemicals would also be instituted.

2004

A new committee of nine people representing the public, the lawn-care industry, city officials, the health unit and the University of Guelph was constituted to refine the pesticide by-law. It was to advise city council on educating the community about pesticides and a formal program to encourage best practices for using weed and pest killers for cosmetic purposes. It would recommend including buffer zones for schools, health-care facilities and parks. It discussed whether to ask council to put some teeth into measures such as buffer zones by incorporating rules into a By-Law.

The new committee reviewed a draft "healthy landscape program," which proposed some restrictions on pesticide use, but only on a voluntary basis, including:

written notification to neighbouring properties at least 24 hours before applying pesticides;
that pesticides be applied only under certain wind, temperature, weather and smog conditions;
that pesticide use not be permitted next to groundwater wells;
that by January 2006, all lawn-care companies be accredited in integrated pest management, which emphasizes the last-resort use of pesticides;
that integrated pest management be "strictly adhered to" in a buffer zone with a 50-metre, or 164-foot radius for any school, day care, park, church, seniors' residence, hospital or university.
that on city property, a 60-metre, or 200-foot buffer zone be imposed around playground equipment where pesticides would not be sprayed.

2005

Led by Mayor Kate Quarrie, Council continued to discuss the banning of pesticides and actually drafted a By-Law. It banned pesticide use on hot, windy or rainy days but stopped short of creating buffer zones around schools, licensed day cares, seniors homes, parks and hospitals. It then approved a proposed Bylaw to prohibit pesticide application in certain weather situations, but never passed the By-Law.

2006

No progress was made on the pesticide issue until after the November 2006 election when Karen Farbridge and her supporters swept Quarrie and most of her right-wing supporters out of office.

2007

In May 2007, the City Council, led by Mayor Karen Farbridge finally passed a pesticide By-Law. This issue had been under consideration since 2000 with Council's decision finally outlining a plan to ban the use of pesticides in all but exceptional circumstances. The ban was to be phased in over the next two years. A public education campaign was mounted in 2007 to advise the public of the changes and to suggest alternative treatments. The by-law would come into effect in 2008 with enforcement limited to commercial applicators. In 2009 year, full enforcement was to begin.

Councillors all agreed with the efficacy of reducing pesticide use, but were also concerned that some flexibility be built into the by-law to deal with possible infestations and the need of businesses such as golf courses to maintain healthy turf. The motion directed city staff to work with those affected and to review the need for exemptions in certain circumstances.

2008

By 2008, many Ontario communities had enacted pesticide bans of one sort or another and the Province was seriously considering provincial pesticide legislation. A number of provincial announcements were made, including one in which Premier Dalton McGuinty said that municipal pesticide By-Laws could remain in effect when the provincial legislation had passed. He subsequently admitted that he "screwed up" when he said that municipalities could enact stronger anti-pesticide bylaws and was determined to bring in a "single, solid, safe and effective" provincial pesticide standard that would supersede all municipal pesticide By-Laws. This news was disappointing to some who had worked for many years to enact tough pesticide regulations for Guelph. Meanwhile, the City of Guelph initiated its "Healthy Landscapes" programme which was designed to assist homeowners with designing sustainable and ecologically friendly yard and gardens.

2009

On April 22, Earth Day, the Provincial pesticide ban took effect. It included a number of provisions that Guelph committees and Councillors had adopted, but was not as strict as the Guelph proposals. In a way, the Provincial Act was anti-climactic for many citizens of Guelph. The Provincial Act contained the following provisions:

> *Residents in Ontario are no longer permitted to buy and use pesticides for cosmetic purposes.*
> *The Ontario Cosmetic Pesticide Ban will regulate the sale of products containing certain ingredients with controlled sales or banned sales.*
> *Under the new ban one will still be able to buy certain*

types of pesticides for use in and around the home to protect the health or safety of your family.
With the Ontario Cosmetic Pesticide Ban affecting all property owners in 2009, residents are encouraged to explore natural alternatives to pesticides and practise proactive landscape maintenance to help maintain their properties and mitigate the effects of common landscape pests. The City's Healthy Landscapes program provides assistance and support to all members of the community to ensure compliance with all aspects of the Cosmetic Pesticide Ban. The Act contains exemptions for Golf Courses that meet certain criteria and for scientific research.

Enforcement

The ministry manages its approach to compliance and enforcement through education and outreach, inspections, response to incidents, voluntary abatement, orders, tickets and prosecutions. In the case of the pesticides ban, the ministry will focus its initial efforts on education when responding to reports of suspected non-compliance. After many years of effort, the City of Guelph finally had an effective ban on most dangerous pesticides, courtesy the Provincial Government.

PLANNING IN GUELPH

All planning in Guelph is guided by the city's *Official Plan* (OP) which was revised in 2012 but has not yet been approved because some of its contents are being appealed. Nevertheless, the existing OP guides all development, subject to changes required by appeals to the OMB. These often occur because developers do not like decisions made by council, or because neighbours do not like projects near their homes planned by developers. Unfortunately, such appeals are at times lengthy and expensive for all parties involved. The Walmart appeal was a classic example of how multiple appellants and complicated issues can cause lengthy OMB hearings.

Guelph's OP has the following objectives:

a) Establishes a vision, guiding principles, strategic goals, objectives and
policies to manage future land use patterns that have a positive effect on
the social, economic, cultural and natural environment of the City.
b) Promotes long-term community sustainability and embodies policies and
actions that aim to simultaneously achieve social well-being, economic
vitality, cultural conservation and enhancement, environmental integrity
and energy sustainability.
c) Promotes the public interest in the future development of the City and
provides a comprehensive land use policy basis which will be
implemented through the Zoning By-law and other land use controls.
d) Guides decision making and community building to the

year 2031.

The OP is divided into thirteen sections that outline comprehensive policies intended to guide the development of the city. Compared to earlier OPs, this version is extremely detailed in that it ensures conformity with *Places to Grow* and all other recent provincial planning policies, and spells out how the city will achieve these goals. The 297 page document includes Secondary Plans and Schedules containing maps showing precisely where each planning policy applies. Major topics included in the OP are as follows:

Vision, Mission, Guiding Principles, Strategic Goals, Urban Structure, Growth Management Strategy, Planning a Complete and Healthy Community, Natural Heritage Protection, Cultural Heritage Conservation,Water Resource Protection, Energy Conservation, Integrated Transportation Systems, Municipal Services, Community Infrastructure,Urban Design, Land Use, Implementation.

In 2012 the City amended the *Official Plan* (OPA 48) to conform with Provincial policies. There was considerable discussion when it was learned that the River Systems Advisory Committee had not commented on wording changes that they felt weakened protection for the Speed and Eramosa Rivers. In particular they objected to using "Natural Heritage Systems" in place of "River Systems" in the amendment. Planning staff asserted that adequate protection was afforded by OPA 42 which covered the river systems in Guelph and had received input from interested citizens. Despite objections, Council adopted the OPA 48 amendments at its meeting on 6 June, 2012. Because a number of sections of the new *Official Plan* remain under appeal, it has not yet come completely into force and will not until the results of the appeals are released. This may happen in 2016 or later, but until then, only the approved sections of the OP will be in effect.

Each section of the OP elaborates on planning topics and provides policies and practices to implement the polices therein. The latest version of the *Official Plan is* available on the city's website, but the issue of appealed amendments has not yet been resolved and not all sections in this draft have been implemented. The Draft OP indicates the sections that are under appeal, those that are new and those that came from the previous versions of the OP.

The OP website is:

http://guelph.ca/uploads/PBS_Dept/planning/OP/Jan%2030%20release/Attachment%204%20-%20Draft%20OP.pdf

Smart Guelph Initiative

In February 2003, City Council adopted eight SmartGuelph Principles to provide guidelines for growth management for the next 25 years. Nearly 1200 people had participated in developing the *SmartGuelph* Principles. Citizen input was solicited through 23 focus groups, workshops, community forums, a mobile input centre, a Web site, the Mayor's Tours, a session with city staff, two community forums, a speaker's panel and a call for briefs. Literature was translated from English into several other languages. Guelph Mayor Karen Farbridge, who initiated the process, led a bus tour and a bike tour to encourage participation. Participants were asked what they valued about their community and about the benefits and opportunities provided by growth. They were also asked to enumerate the challenges and issues confronting the city. The author was a member of a focus group.

All this consultation resulted in the following principles that were sent to City Council for approval. They suggested a city that is:

Inviting & Identifiable
A distinctively appealing city, scaled for people, with a strong sense of place and a pervasive community spirit which respects and welcomes diversity.

Compact & Connected
A well-designed city with a vital downtown core and a commitment to mixed-use and higher
density development; a safe community conveniently connected for walkers, cyclists, users of
public transit, and motorists.

Distinctive & Diverse
A culturally diverse city with a rich mix of housing, unique neighbourhoods,
preserved heritage architecture, attractive common spaces, and educational and research
institutions integrated into city life; with an abundance of recreational choices and art, ethnic, and
cultural events.

Clean & Conscious
A city with a healthy and sustainable environment, vigilantly demonstrating environmental
leadership; a citizenry that values environmental and social advocacy, participation, and
volunteerism.

Prosperous & Progressive
A city with a strong and diverse economy, a wealth of employment opportunities, robust
manufacturing, a thriving retail sector, and the good sense to invest a meaningful portion of its
prosperity in research and development and the advancement of education, training, wellness,
art, and culture.

Pastoral & Protective
A horticulturally rich city where gardens abound; a

community that preserves and enhances its significant natural features, rivers, parks, and open spaces, and makes the planting and preservation of trees a priority; a city committed to the preservation of nearby agricultural land.

Well-Built & Well-Maintained

A city willing and able to invest in high-quality infrastructure and public buildings, ensuring they are beautifully designed and maintained, engineered to last, and civilizing in their effect on the community.

Collaborative & Cooperative

A city with an effective and collaborative leadership that consults with citizens and other municipalities, manages growth based on the 'triple bottom line' (environmental, economic, social), and makes decisions about development, city services, and resource allocation consistently in keeping with these core principles.

These principles were to guide the city council in decision making in the future. Council would have to evaluate its actions against the principles. The following strategies were to be adopted to conform with *Smart Guelph*:

> *Creation of a Smart Guelph secretariat to ensure compliance with Smart Guelph by City Hall and the community.*

> *Adequate funding to allow the secretariat to achieve its goals*

> *A corporate training programme on Smart Guelph principles as core values for municipal staff and council.*

> *Education and communications to lobby senior government and educate staff, council and all sectors of the community.*

An annual report card tracking how well municipal and community initiatives are doing.

A decision-making filter to ensure the Smart Guelph principles are incorporated into all council and staff decisions.

A report to identify current city initiatives consistent with the Smart Guelph principles.

Audit of existing programmes, services and policies for consistency with the Smart Guelph principles.

Benchmarking to measure future progress of Smart Guelph initiatives.

Calculation of the city's 'ecological Footprint' or impact on the environment.

Audit of city budgets for Smart Guelph priorities.

Long-term fiscal strategy to set aside financial resources for specific Smart Guelph priorities such as implementing the city's existing transportation strategy, affordable housing plan and parks and recreation strategy, as well as stepping up tree planting and creation of trail, sidewalk and cycling systems, acquiring river land, improving downtown and renewing city infrastructure.

Financial incentives for development that is consistent with Smart Guelph principles (such as brownfields and city core redevelopment and affordable housing).

Establishment of 'cornerstones' for economic development activity such as attracting environmentally responsible businesses, enhancing partnerships with the University of Guelph and Conestoga College and enhancing downtown as a major destination.

Priority for approvals and servicing for developments that are consistent with the Smart Guelph principles.

Review of municipal infrastructure, development standards and regulations (such as street parking policy) for consistency with the Smart Guelph principles

Update of Official Plan policies, zoning regulations and development standards to promote mixed use development, compact development, tree protection, community 'connectedness,' protection of significant natural areas and open space, enhancement of river corridors, redevelopment in established neighbourhoods and innovative development.

Consultation with development industry in Guelph and elsewhere for 'best practices' on how to implement Smart Guelph and improve approval processes.

Community identity and sense of place as a core element of development decisions and municipal practices.

The cost of the process, funded primarily by development charges was $200,000. *Smart Guelph* provided a comprehensive and long-term strategy to guide and control Guelph's future development. Despite the solicitation of input from many diverse interest groups, a number of developers and councillors were uncomfortable with the concept and spoke out against it.

A *Smart Guelph* secretariat would be funded by the city and outside sources to be a watchdog, complete with an executive director who would have an arm's length relationship with City Hall, to make ensure that *Smart Guelph* initiatives were implemented. Development approvals would be prioritized based on *Smart Guelph* thinking, and criteria to be developed would go into effect in

2004. These criteria would be developed in collaboration with the development community. However the Guelph Development Association and the Guelph and District Home Builders' Association called for the *Smart Guelph* process to be slowed so it could be debated during the municipal elections in November 2003.

City Council debated the *Smart Guelph* plan until May 20, 2003 when the following councillors voted to defer the implementation of *Smart Guelph* until the funding for infrastructure sustainability had been decided: Joe Young, Rocco Furfaro, Dan Schnurr, David Birtwistle, Dan Moziar and Gloria Kovach. *Smart Guelph* failed on a tie vote, because Councillor Sean Farrelly inexplicably left the meeting early and did not vote on the issue. Councillors Downer, Laidlaw, McAdams, Shapka, Wettstein and Mayor Farbridge voted against the motion. Councillors voting to defer were supported by the Guelph Development Association and the Guelph and District Homebuilders Association both of which viewed *Smart Guelph* with suspicion. Rather than perceiving it as a visionary plan to enhance the city's prosperity, they saw a new level of city bureaucracy.

On June 16, 2003 a motion by Councillor Downer seconded by Councillor Shapka that the *Smart Guelph* Implementation Initiatives report dated May 12, 2003 be reintroduced to Council for approval resulted in a recorded vote as follows: In favour: Councillors Birtwistle, Downer, Farrelly, Kovach, Laidlaw, McAdams, Moziar, Shapka, Wettstein and Mayor Farbridge(10). Voting against: Councillors Furfaro, Schnurr and Young (3). Council had finally voted to adopt the *Smart Guelph* initiative as a framework for future planning decisions. As recently as 2012, critics continue to debate whether Smart Guelph has had any influence on the city's commercial and transportation planning policies. Others have wondered whether it influenced decisions on high rise apartment buildings proposed for the CBD.

The York Road Innovation District

In 2005 the Ontario Realty Corporation decided to dispose of a large parcel of land that the province owned in Guelph. The tract, bisected by the Eramosa River, lay south of York Road and east of Victoria Road. It contained three parcels: the Guelph Correctional Centre lands on the east side of the river, the Wellington Detention Centre lands at the northeast corner of Victoria and Stone roads, and the Ontario Ministry of Agriculture Food and Rural Affairs Guelph Research Station extending from Victoria Road to the west side of the river. The 1,052 acre (425 ha.) area also included the Turfgrass Institute and the city's wet/dry plant. Planning staff developed seven options for its use and recommended one that proposed employment, commercial and mixed uses on the west side of the Eramosa River. Employment, institutional and commercial uses were suggested for the east side of the river. Existing residential lands there would be recognized. The whole area had been designated as Institutional in the *Official Plan.*

The Ontario Realty Corporation indicated that it wanted to sell the land and buildings thereon. It conducted a heritage study of the century-old buildings and filed divestment related documents with other government bodies, including the City of Guelph. The ultimate use of these lands and buildings would have a major impact on the future of residential and industrial land uses in Guelph. Considerable debate accompanied decisions about the ultimate fate of the area. The disposition of the Guelph Turfgrass Institute portion of the land became a major issue between the city and the province.

The Turfgrass Institute was founded in 1987 to conduct research and provide information on grass production and management. People in the grass industry, community members and politicians became very concerned when they discovered that the province might sell the facility's 150 acres (60 ha.). Moving the institute would ruin important research and delay progress for years. As a result, the city instituted a participation process to discuss the future of the whole area, and to provide input into the secondary plan being developed.

In 2007, Liz Sandals, Guelph's MPP, convened a meeting of the Turfgrass Institute, the Ministry of Agriculture, the University of Guelph and the Agricultural Research Institute of Ontario. As a result of that meeting, the Ontario Realty Corporation and the ministry cooperated with the Turfgrass Institute, the university and the research institute to complete an independent assessment of the issues related to potential relocation of the Turfgrass Institute. They focused on research and education, and on the cost of moving the facility. This was the first time that the Realty Corporation had agreed to consider the research implications of a move instead of only the financial implications. The entire tract became the subject of a secondary plan study by the City of Guelph. It would assess future land use proposals from the Ontario Realty Corporation which managed real estate on behalf of the province.

Ontario's minister of culture was interested in designating the administration building of the former Guelph Correctional Centre, which is visible from York Road, as a heritage building. However, the Wellington Detention Centre wasn't a heritage structure, so that building north of Stone Road and just south of the Turfgrass Institute was demolished to allow cleanup of the site to begin. Heritage Guelph, the city's heritage advisory committee, decided to add the Guelph Turfgrass Institute to the city's heritage inventory for possible future designation. Meanwhile, consultation and public meetings occurred to solicit citizen input into the development of plans for the area. The City of Guelph preferred that the Turfgrass Institute not be moved and that the former Guelph Correctional Centre remain intact. It favoured more businesses than homes in the the York District.

AuthentiCity Consultants were hired by the city to propose plans and a vision for the York lands. They hoped to link the proposals to a capital investment plan, including the local economy, municipal policy, environmental sensitivity and the University of Guelph in their recommendations. The province and the city were both committed to preserving the river corridor and some of the natural areas on the property.

Interested citizens proposed many uses for the land. Some felt that it should all become a park while others thought that the former reformatory should become a museum. The president of Conestoga College suggested that it might become a full campus for the institution which was running out of space at its Speedvale location. By November, a planning report suggested that the land be divided into four areas with open land along the ponds and the approach to the jail complex to provide a view corridor of the heritage jail buildings. It proposed that the southwest precinct be turned into a biological products commercialization park, which would be a business park with a combination of light industrial and office buildings. The focus would be on research applications and commercialization to create products developed from the research. One component could be a biological products design centre that would develop and accelerate the commercialization of biological products such as plastics, fibres and fillers to help the automotive industry create lighter vehicles and meet fuel reduction standards. Guelph Innovation District was suggested as an appropriate name for the area.

By 2008, additional opinions had been heard. The Guelph Wellington Men's Club made a submission to the AuthentiCity Consultants recommending that the city create a focus for environmental education and the design and production of sustainable products and services. The contract with the consultants instructed them to consider strengthening the city's tax base and identifying economic sectors that need space. They were to consider live-work units and agricultural innovation, industry, heritage and natural systems. The final plans were intended to help the city to achieve its *Places to Grow* targets for residential and employment development in the future.

By the middle of 2009, the Federal Government announced $85,000 in funding to assist the Guelph Partnership for Innovation consortium to create a detailed proposal for the Guelph Innovation District. It would support research into agricultural, biological and environmental technologies and enable Guelph to become a leader in Green technologies. Indications were that it would include agri-technology and bio-science, alternative energy and advanced manufacturing businesses along with some institutional uses such as university, college and health care facilities. Pedestrian-oriented medium to high-density residential developments were incorporated into early plans.

In 2010, Ontario and the City of Guelph signed a Memorandum of Understanding (MOU) that would help to enhance the local economy and create future jobs in the Guelph Innovation District. The city hoped to turn this area into a sustainable development including the creation of homes for 3,000 to 5,000 people and 8,000 to 10,000 jobs, primarily in the fields of research, green energy and innovation. By mid 2011, the province and the city were actively seeking a developer for the area. A provincial document identified 70 acres (28 ha.) of land between York Road and the jail as a heritage area. Several buildings were also marked as heritage buildings. The 49 acres (19 ha.) behind the jail were deemed the development zone. The majority of developmental land was provincial property which the province prized for much more than its monetary value. Conestoga college continued to consider the land for a new campus or partnership with the University of Guelph.

By mid 2012, after many meetings with citizens and stakeholders, the city had developed firm policies and a Secondary Plan to guide future uses of the York Lands/Guelph Innovation District. They are all available on the city's website and contain excellent maps, drawings and concepts describing the proposed ultimate functions of this land. As recently as February 2012, the director of the Turfgrass Institute stated that the Innovation District development might require the facility to leave Guelph. At the time of writing, the Institute continued to operate as usual. Given the time that it will take for the Innovation District to become active, the Institute could remain in the city for many years. Given the current economic climate, it might also be many years before all the recommendations of the new Secondary Plan are implemented.

2014: New Ideas for the York Lands

A group with an interest in the environment has been working to transform part of the York Innovation District lands into a demonstration hub for education and research. The "Yorklands Green Hub" concept suggests that 36 acres (14 ha.) of land, the gatehouse and the superintendent's house at the former Guelph Correctional Centre (GCC) could become an innovation and research centre. It would support sustainable local food production, wise water use, water protection, energy conservation and renewable energy technologies. The organizer, Norah Chaloner, a well-known local activist, has met with Guelph MPP Liz Sandals, who told her that with enough community support, such a green hub could be developed. The hub group has been lobbying like-minded organizations such as the landscape architecture program at the University of Guelph, Wellington Water Watchers, FarmStart and Guelph Environmental Leadership for support.

The buildings and field being proposed for the Green Hub extend from the entrance driveway on York Road to the former Legion Hall. All have heritage designations and cannot developed. However, the administration building could become an environmental exhibition site. The farm could illustrate best practices and be a prime location to use and illustrate solar power, geothermal heating, ways to reuse grey water and greenhouses. Teachers in the Upper Grand School Board's CELP environmental leadership program are interested in holding classes at such a centre which would be a perfect destination for class trips. It would provide an opportunity to teach about energy, water and food all in one place.

According to Chaloner, the province would support the proposal because it is paying $1 million a year for security and maintenance of buildings at GCC and it wants to decrease these costs. The Green Hub concept would also work well with other ideas that have been suggested for the site. The Hub group requires people with expertise to assist with the project and is applying for grants from several foundations to initiate the plan. They hope that the hub will be sustainable in five to seven years. The city's corporate manager of community energy also supports the Yorklands Green Hub as a community plan, but has suggested that it may take many years to implement.

Approval: May 12, 2014

Guelph Council voted unanimously to support the Yorklands Green Hub group's vision for about 36 acres (14.5 Ha. of land as it approved a Secondary Plan for the 1,077 acre (436 Ha.) Guelph Innovation District. The Plan envisions a new community that is expected to be home to almost 7,000 people and 9,000 jobs. The mix of land uses it describes includes a new "urban village," a mixed-use main street, a research park and two new recreational parks. It calls for adaptive re-use of the area around the historic reformatory complex, which was a jail for about 90 years before closing.

The Plan promotes the conservation and adaptive reuse of existing cultural heritage resources, such as the decommissioned Guelph Correctional Centre. It includes the protection and enhancement of the site's extensive natural heritage system, including the Eramosa River valley and Clythe Creek. Pedestrians, cyclists and transit users will have priority over motor vehicles in the area. Buildings will typically be two to six stories, with some up to ten stories allowed in some areas. Given the long wait times for Provincial approvals, no timetable for development was adopted. However Council did vote unanimously to support the Green Hub's vision for development of the land.

The Downtown Secondary Plan

This plan was approved in 2012 and sets out many goals for the central area of the city. One of the most contentious issues is the proposal to replace the retail uses along the Speed River beside Wellington Street between Wyndham and Gordon streets with a riverside park. Even though this would be far in the future (from 2022 to 2031) a number of Wellington street Merchants have appealed the Wellington Street park element of the Downtown Secondary Plan to the OMB.

Opponents contend that the cost of acquiring the land would be far too high, that another park is not needed so close to Royal City Park, and that many successful businesses would be displaced. Some have been in the same families for 30 to 40 years. Many of the business owners argued that moving to new locations would be very expensive, and that the uncertain future of their properties made additional investments in them risky. Despite the cost of an OMB hearing, they decided to go ahead with their appeal which may not be settled for a long time. Other aspects of the Downtown Secondary Plan such as intensification and encouragement of high rise structures were met with approval from numerous downtown businesses and developers.

Transportation Planning

Results of several earlier transportation planning studies are included in the September 2012 consolidation of Guelph's *Official Plan* (OP). Here only the major principles guiding transportation and land use planning will be addressed. Guelph's *Official Plan* recognizes that land use and transportation planning and demand are inextricably linked. However, finances and citizen involvement both have the potential to alter considerably recommendations on land use and transportation planning contained in any *Official Plan* or secondary plan.

Construction of the Wellington Street interchange with the Hanlon expressway began in October 1998 and it opened in July 2001. It connected Wellington Street west of the expressway with the Silvercreek Parkway into downtown Guelph. The interchange cost $13.2 million and opened a year later than expected because of a design flaw that resulted in several months of delays and a lawsuit against the Ontario Ministry of Transportation. The final price was above the budgeted cost by $3.2 million.

In addition to the cost issues, the project generated considerable controversy, including discussion about whether it was necessary, about the environmental damage that it would inflict on the Speed River and its impact on local traffic patterns. Until recently, it was the only controlled access interchange on the Hanlon. On April 30, 2012, construction began on the Laird Road interchange which was partially opened during the week of November 11, 2013. It was fully opened on November 29, 2013, in a public ceremony attended by local officials and Guelph Member of Provincial Parliament, Liz Sandals.

For many years, Guelph and Kitchener residents have lobbied for a new highway to replace Provincial Highway 7 between the cities. After many years of speculation, the new highway was approved by the Liberal government in 2007.

In 2012, premier Dalton McGuinty promised that construction on the project would begin in 2015. By then, all the necessary land had been purchased and construction began. In 2007 the total cost of construction was estimated at $300 million which will undoubtedly increase. Controversy about this project included arguments that it was not necessary, that it would increase greenhouse gases,that it would harm delicate ecosystems and that widening the existing road would be an excellent solution. The approved four lane, controlled access route is north of the existing highway.

Traffic Calming

Guelph Council has wrestled with traffic calming since 1998 when speed humps were installed on Dufferin Street. At that time there were 13 neighbourhoods, representing 25 streets on the waiting list for traffic calming. Since then councils have dithered, changed their minds, listened to vocal opponents of traffic calming, passed and rescinded various calming measures and finally adopted a policy. It took 5 years before the council of the day could agree on a consultation and calming policy without changing it at subsequent meetings. The closure of the old iron bridge crossing the Speed River at Norwich Street in 1998 (when it was designated as a heritage site) effectively calmed traffic that formerly used it as a shortcut from Woolwich Street to Eramosa Road.

In 2003, Council finally adopted a new traffic calming policy. After much lobbying by persons and groups for and against various types of calming, they decided that a number of calming measures could be used after extensive consultation in the neighbourhoods involved. Calming would not apply to arterial roads or four lane roadways. Detailed criteria were set up to determine citizen participation and appropriate calming measures. Many possible calming measures were considered for various streets but only a few were implemented. The link below takes one to the city's 20 page document explaining the measures available and listing costs:

*https://**guelph**.ca/wp-content/.../policy_**Traffic**Management.pdf*

Vertical traffic calming measures, which include speed humps, raised crosswalks and raised intersections were approved by city council in October 2003, but were to used only as a "last resort". Subsequent efforts to remove speed humps and alter other aspects of the policy failed. By 2005 Council was still arguing about calming measures, including four way stops and curb "bump outs". Unfortunately, residents on the streets being considered often opposed calming measures supported by others on the same street. Ultimately, Council had to decide which view to support.

After the initial speed humps on Dufferin Street in 1998, humps were installed on King, Queen and Arthur Streets in 2008 and on Exhibition Street in 2009, while controversy continued about their safety and effectiveness. As recently as 2012 some residents of Ontario Street wanted the "Bump Out" at Tytler School removed, but their petition was denied by Council. At one time or another, the Guelph Fire Department, Ambulance Services, organizations for the disabled, Guelph Accessibility Advisory Committee and many citizens opposed traffic calming as "unsafe", "dangerous", a "nuisance", "hazardous to one's health", "bad for the environment", "likely to ruin vehicle suspensions", etc. etc. One objector threatened to take the city to Supreme Court because speed humps "would damage his disabled wife's back." Ultimately, and after almost 15 years of dithering, Guelph Council adopted and retained a Policy on Traffic Calming. Not surprisingly, none of the dire consequences predicted by opponents seem to have occurred.

Cycling Plans

Guelph's *Cycling Master Plan* was created to guide the

development of a cycling network throughout the city. It is intended to encourage cycling to reduce traffic congestion and related emissions. Guelph's new *Official Plan* directed the *Cycling Master Plan* to develop a safe, efficient, convenient and sustainable transportation system for all forms of travel including cycling and walking. The OP stated that the city would ensure that pedestrian and bicycle networks were integrated into transportation planning. They must provide safe, comfortable travel for pedestrians and cyclists within existing communities and in new developments. They should also provide linkages between intensification areas, adjacent neighbourhoods and transit stations, including, where feasible, dedicated bike lane space for cyclists on the major street network.

To fulfil these objectives, the city prepared the *Bicycle Friendly Guelph Initiative*, which proposed improvements to Guelph's cycling infrastructure and culture. It envisioned tripling the cycling share of daily travel by improving the cycling network, enhancing road safety, and fostering improved attitudes among cyclists and motorists about sharing the road. Guelph wants to become one of Canada's most bicycle-friendly communities by providing a safe, attractive and practical cycling environment. It intends to triple the number of daily trips by bicycle in ten years by providing events and rewards for cycling and satisfaction with cycling opportunities. However, the *Official Plan* also attempts to promote a livable City by encouraging all modes of transportation including transit, bicycle and pedestrian movement. It recognizes that the automobile will continue to be the primary mode of travel for residents and businesses in Guelph. Growth in the Eastview area will eventually require a new north-south highway east of the city to connect Highway 401 and Highway 7. The OP also recognizes the need for a new road link between Kitchener and Guelph. It contains a number of proposals for road widening and new roads within the city. Details may be found on-line on Guelph's website:

http://guelph.ca/uploads/PBS_Dept/planning/OP/full
%20September%202012%20consolidation.pdf.

On Tuesday 19 February 2013, a city committee approved a cycling master plan which could add 280 kilometres of new bicycle lanes by 2022, and 30 kilometres of existing trail paved for cycling commuters. The new bike lanes will be created while arterial roads are being reconstructed or remarked during the next 10 years. The plan will require the elimination of parking on Downey, Eastview, Grange, Starwood and Stevenson streets. They were initially intended to be four-lane routes, but since development has not occurred as predicted, one lane in either direction which are normally used very little has been allocated to parking.

The new bike lanes are already in the 10-year capital forecast for upgrades but will have to be approved by council during regular budgeting. The new master plan is intended to make cycling a convenient, attractive and accessible form of transportation in Guelph. The Stone Road Cycle Track which is a separated route for cyclists between Edinburgh Road and Gordon Street has had 290 per cent increase in cycling since it was installed a few years ago, excellent evidence for the addition of new bicycle lanes.

In October 2013 a City Staff report detailed the possible costs of a comprehensive bicycle lane master plan that could cost up to $13 million. It includes the addition of about 36 kilometres of on-road bicycle lanes during road-widening construction. The addition of these bike lanes to road projects will constitute about 20 per cent of total construction costs. Widening roads for bike lanes will cost about $9.7 million over the next 10 years but in the proposed 2014 capital budget, only $1.7 million has been allocated. Another 78 kilometres of on-road bicycle lanes over the next 10 years will be created by marking the pavement without widening roads. This work will cost $450,000 over the next 10 years.

A capital budget account for the construction of off-road paths for both bicyclists and walkers anticipates paving sections of the city's primary trail system to create a continuous on-road, off-road network. A total of $3 million has been allocated for this work. The cycling master plan identified sections of Woodlawn, Stone and Edinburgh roads as appropriate locations for this type of multi-use boulevard trail. The total cost of the Woodlawn Road boulevard trail would be about $2 million and the trails on Stone and Edinburgh roads will cost about $1 million. Adding a separate bike lane outside the curb on the section of Woodlawn between Nicklin Road and Silvercreek Parkway is estimated to cost $800,000. It would cost $1.2 million to complete the Woodlawn Road path from Silvercreek Parkway to Elmira Road, with construction of this section potentially beginning in 2015. A separate capital account was created to allocate $150,000 in 2014 for the study of the primary trail system. This would identify which sections of the primary trail system could be paved, develop a functional plan to align the trails, and prepare an estimate of the cost of their construction and annual maintenance.

Niska Road Controversies

Niska Road has long been a fast and easy route from southern Guelph to Wellington Road 124 and the Waterloo Region or Cambridge. At the Speed River, it traverses the former Kortright Waterfowl Park on a one lane Bailey Bridge built in 1974. As southern Guelph has become built up, the road has become more popular with commuters and also more thickly lined by the homes of affluent citizens. Since 2002 it has been the focus of controversy about its future and a problem for City Council.

One group of people, mostly commuters, would like to see the Bailey Bridge replaced by a permanent two lane bridge and the road improved. Another, primarily local residents, would like to keep the existing bridge as a traffic calming measure or convert it to a pedestrian bridge and close the road. Both groups have submitted powerful arguments to the committee studying the issue and to City Council.

In 2012 the city decided to seek provincial funding for the replacement of the one-lane Niska Road Bridge from a new $51-million provincial program for critical road, bridge, water and waste water projects in 2013 and 2014. In 2013 the city hired consultants and set up a working group to plan for the bridge replacement, but in 2014 it learned that no Provincial money would be available for that purpose. The issue has been complicated by the closing of the Kortright Waterfowl Park and its return to the Grand River Conservation Authority. The landscape around the bridge is historically significant, beautiful and was settled by some of Guelph's original pioneers who travelled on the old pioneer road to this area. Proponents of keeping the existing bridge or closing the road packed meetings in 2015 to discuss the future of the bridge.

Meanwhile the city's capital budget listed a $2 million line item for a Niska bridge replacement in 2015 and 2016. It also recommended reconstructing and providing operational improvements to Niska Road. It did not mention restoration at cost of approximately $800,000, or the neighbourhood's preferred solution to either retain the one-lane bridge, or to close the road to cars with a bike/pedestrian bridge only. An environmental assessment will have to be conducted to determine the effect of replacing the bridge.

In 2015 the controversy continued. Opponents of the new bridge made the following arguments. Slowing vehicles would discourage traffic from Wellington Road 124 through the residential neighbourhood on a narrow collector road that was not designed to carry regional traffic. Slowing traffic would also protect wildlife crossing the road along their migration corridor on the Heritage Speed River and former Kortright Park. Proponents argued that the road and existing bridge were unsafe, caused accidents and slowed necessary trips from Guelph to Road 124. In the words of one commentator:

In the end, it comes down to what we value in our city? Is it getting from point A to B as fast as possible? Or is it recognizing the irreparable damage that could occur if a two-lane bridge is built and Niska Road is widened through an area that forms an important cultural heritage landscape that is unique in the City of Guelph. You decide?

Guelph City Council has voted to proceed with a two lane bridge, but opponents are planning to appeal.

Guelph Central Station

Guelph's new Inter modal Transit Terminal was first proposed in 2002. It was designed to consolidate intercity bus, local bus and railway services into one facility. At that time, the downtown terminal for Guelph Transit buses was three blocks away at St. George's Square. A feasibility study initiated in 2004 suggested that it would be more convenient and efficient to consolidate all services on Carden Street. This would not only facilitate easy transfers, but it would also remove smelly idling buses from the heart of the city.

Guelph City Council endorsed the Carden Street location and the concept design in 2004. The project received federal and provincial infrastructure stimulus funding in 2009. Detailed design and stakeholder consultations were conducted and construction began in April 2010. The task was projected to cost $8 million, of which $5.3 million came from Provincial and Federal Infrastructure Stimulus Funds. In July 2010, the historic Canadian National Railways steam locomotive 6167 was moved. The 320-tonne locomotive travelled 100 metres on the back of a flatbed trailer with 96 tires to its new resting place across the tracks. This short trip cost $275,000, a sum considered reasonable by those who laboured for years to restore the engine to its original condition.

The opening of the bus portion of the station was to be delayed from October 2011 to May 2012 to allow time for the renovations of the railway station building to be completed. Unfortunately, this has not yet occurred. After the demolition of the original Greyhound Terminal on the site, Greyhound had to move its terminal to a temporary location at 17 Wyndham St. South, where it remains. The building is small and inconvenient for those desiring to transfer to rail or city bus services.

Meanwhile, Guelph Central Station (also known as Guelph Central GO Station) became the main inter-modal transportation terminal in Guelph. It is used by Guelph Transit buses, Aboutown Bus and GO Transit intercity buses. Greyhound cannot use the facility until the renovations of the railway station are completed. Guelph Central Station is also served by GO Transit intercity trains and Via Rail. It is located at 79 Carden Street and includes the historic Guelph Railway Station, as well as the site of the former Guelph Bus Terminal. The name "Guelph Central" was chosen with input from the community and the transit service providers using the new station.

As usual in Guelph, the new location was severely criticized by numerous individuals and organizations. Senior citizens felt that it was too far to walk to the central area where buses had historically stopped. The Square had been very convenient to a number of banks, merchants and medical services. Some downtown merchants were convinced that the removal of buses from St. George's Square would reduce pedestrian traffic and hurt their businesses. Many did not like the new location beside the railway and a wide street where it was cold and windy. Guelph Transit drivers were pleased about the new washrooms in the bus facility, but were upset that there would be no lunch room for them until the station renovation was complete.

The project encountered additional problems. Red tape and bureaucratic bungling at the Provincial and Federal level delayed the promised renovations of the historic railway station. It took many months to transfer ownership from VIA which signed a deal in December 2010 to sell the train station to the city for the token amount of $1. The city finally took ownership of the station in May of 2013 and started the procedure of designating the building under the Ontario Heritage Act. Getting ownership transferred to the city was a long and complicated process that ultimately required a federal government order-in-council.

The former VIA station was designated in 1993 as a heritage railway structure under the federal Heritage Railway Stations Protection Act. A condition of the transfer of ownership to the city was the signing of an agreement between the city and the Ontario Heritage Trust. It described the exterior and interior features of the train station that must be protected. It also specified that any future proposals for changes would require the approval of both the city and the Ontario Heritage Trust. Unfortunately, VIA removed its agents from this building in 2013, making it difficult for people who do not use the Internet to obtain tickets.

Before the city begins renovations, it must wait until the train station is vacated by a telecommunications company that has a lease to use the premises. Eventually, VIA Rail, GO transit and Guelph Transit will use the building. Despite the fact that plans have been made and an architect hired, renovations have not yet begun. The cost of building the new transportation centre on Carden Street was shared among the three levels of government, but the entire estimated $1.2 million price of renovating the Via station will be paid by the city. The renovations will include a break room for Guelph Transit drivers, a Greyhound ticket booth, a VIA Rail ticket booth, new washrooms, and more seating. Tickets for Guelph Transit, while not yet official, may be sold via the Greyhound booth in the renovated station. Lack of finances to complete the job delayed the final station tender procedure. Renovation documents will be released for tender in late February or early March in 2016. The city is hoping to start the renovation in April 2016 and expect the work to be completed by the following April in 2017.

Guelph Central Station partly opened in May 2012 after moving railway tracks, building bus shelters, bus and train platforms and making Carden Street a one way street. This three year $10 million construction project dragged on much longer than expected and was delayed because of an error made in manufacturing the glass walls for the station's bus shelters. Three-sided "wind screens" were to be installed before Guelph Transit's transfer point moved from St. George's Square to the new station on Carden Street. However, the error delayed the glass walls until July.

Until July, the roof canopies provided little shelter from wind-blown rain. Three-sided frames with glass walls were eventually installed around the benches, with the side facing the buses remaining open. Accounts from users after the glass walls were installed indicated that with any amount of wind,rain still penetrated the shelters. In the winter, waiting for buses for more than a few minutes is "brutal" since the open shelters provide little warmth or shelter from blowing snow. Guelph Transit began to use the station in 2012 followed shortly by GO Transit buses. GO Train service started serving Guelph Central in November 2011 and VIA Rail continued during the construction.

GO Kiss and Ride Facility

GO Transit's $11 million kiss and ride and tunnel underpass project, connecting Farquhar Street to Guelph Train Station was delayed by several factors. First, an occupancy permit for the Kiss and Ride and tunnel had not been obtained on time. The Presto transit card readers and an automated ticket vending machine had not been installed. The elevator was not yet operational. This delay was because of a widespread backlog caused by an elevator workers strike in the spring. Finally, a concrete walled tunnel opened on Sept. 22, 2013. It allowed commuters to be dropped off at a paved lot off Farquhar Street and walk underground to the train platform. The Carden Street railway platform was repaved and can accommodate a 12-car train, whereas previously it could accept only 10-car trains. By the time this was written, the elevator was operational and the tunnel was being used by GO and VIA commuters.

Parking Master Plan

In May 2013, City Council received a report on a new *Parking Master Plan* for the city. It could include apps to pay for on street parking, two hours of free parking downtown and more on street parking in new locations. By 2031, the number of downtown residents and employees is expected to increase to 8,500 and 7,500 respectively and the *Parking Master Plan* will address this population growth. The report was prepared with a consultant and includes data obtained at two public information meetings that took place on Feb. 26 and April 16, 2013.

The report contained 13 guiding principles for the *Parking Master Plan* study. They included ensuring that the revised parking system reinforce the economic development of downtown, that all parking spaces are used efficiently before additional parking facilities are built, and that the parking system be designed, planned and operated in a transparent manner. All components of the new strategy must be consumer friendly. The report proposed the possibility of continuing two hours of free parking per day downtown, of converting some parallel to angle parking, and providing parking payment technologies such as a mobile phone app. The current level of on-street parking is already at capacity, and off-street parking is approaching its limits.

Subsequently,city staff proposed to make the city's parking operation self-sustaining, and projected additional revenue over 20 years for each change. This additional revenue would total $59.7 million over 20 years. They suggested the following: paid on-street parking in the downtown; $17.3 million; full cost recovery from city employees for parking spaces that they use; $13.7 million; increases in permit, hourly and Saturday parking rates; $10.1 million; downtown parking fines moved from the city's bylaw to its parking operations; $6.6 million; a pay & display system at all parking lots, eliminating staffed parkades; $5.8 million; a permit program in neighbourhoods surrounding the downtown for street parking by both residents and non-residents of those streets; $3.2 million and a new levy on Urban Growth Centre property owners; $3.1 million. These proposals are subject to approval by City Council. On June 18, 2014, Council acknowledged the ongoing *Parking Master Plan* community discussions, but decided that a 350 space structured parking project is required in the immediate term, and that the project initiation be identified in year one of the 2015, ten year Capital Budget for consideration. Free two hour parking continues in the CBD, but some councillors and merchants would like to have it replaced by parking garages. The controversy continues.

Guelph Transit

During the last few years, Guelph Transit has experienced some major managerial difficulties. In July 2013 Guelph Transit's general manager Michael Anders was let go. Apparently privacy and legal reasons prevented the city from saying whether Anders was fired or resigned. Anders joined

Guelph Transit in late 2009 after several years as market research director for the Toronto Transit Commission. In 2010, a major study of Guelph Transit recommended many changes in routes and service. During Anders' management of Guelph Transit, bus transfers moved from St. George's Square to the new Guelph Central Station on Carden Street. At the same time, bus routes were reconfigured, resulting in a record number of complaints from riders. Anders offered a public apology to riders for Guelph Transit's poor service. New schedules during peak times had a significant impact on the number of missed connections. Despite a year of major changes in 2012, ridership exceeded seven million for the first time but revenue was below budget projections.

In September 2013 Guelph Council learned that Guelph Transit's supervisor of mobility services, Bill Richardson had been fired from Hamilton Street Railway with a $200,000 severance package. A workplace arbitration ruling concluded that he had lied to a supervisor about sending pornographic emails to a female employee. The City of Hamilton was ordered to pay the woman $25,000 in damages. On December 11, 2013 the City of Guelph appointed of Phil Meagher to the position of general manager of Guelph Transit. He had been acting general manager since early August after Anders departed. In April of 2014, Bill Richardson sued the City of Guelph for his "high handed and callous" dismissal. He asked for $85,000 in lost wages and $50,000 for stress and other damages caused by the dismissal. Richardson reportedly had come to Guelph after being highly recommended by two Hamilton city managers. The legal action has not yet come to trial. Meanwhile, Guelph Transit is considering feedback from riders before implementing major route changes once again.

University Transit Hub

In 2011 the University greatly improved the bus pick-up

location in front of the University Centre. With more travellers expected to use transit services to and from the University, Guelph Transit improved its service to nine routes, with frequency increasing to one bus every 15 minutes. Four new Guelph Transit bus bays and new bus shelters were built south of South Ring Road on the east side of the loop.

To improve pedestrian safety, new walkways and crossings with activated signals were installed on each side of the South Ring Road and University Centre main entrance intersection. Also, new concrete sidewalks were added from Christie Lane to connect with Winegard Walk on the north side. GO Transit increased its weekday bus service as well. Vehicles will enter and exit P42 only from its west access to Christie Lane. Greyhound and Aboutown, which provides bus service to and from Hamilton, continue to use current stops in the bus loop. Vehicular access on the north end of the bus loop will continue to be restricted to buses and emergency vehicles.

COMMERCIAL PLANNING AND WALMART

The OP sets out the location and regulations for various types of commercial areas. They are as follows: Mixed Use Nodes, Intensification Areas, Neighbourhood Commercial Centres, and Service Commercial Areas. Only the general principles regulating commercial activity are presented here. Details may be found in the OP.

Mixed Use Nodes are developments on one or more properties on both sides of an intersection of major roads within a "node". They are intended to serve the needs of residents living and working in nearby neighbourhoods, employment districts and the whole city. A mixed use node is a well defined focal point grouping complementary uses in close proximity to satisfy several shopping and service needs at one location. If possible, uses are connected by local roads and parking. They are generally located at major intersections and have space for additional uses.

Intensification Areas are intended to promote the intensification and revitalization of existing well defined commercial nodes to use land efficiently by grouping complementary uses in close proximity. This will improve the possibility of satisfying shopping and service requirements in one area.

Neighbourhood Commercial Centres contain one or several commercial buildings within a compact node. They are intended to serve the shopping needs of residents living and working in nearby neighbourhoods and employment districts. Compatible institutional and small scale office uses may also be permitted. Medium density multiple unit residential buildings and apartments may also be permitted if the principal commercial function is maintained.

The Service Commercial Land Use Designation provides

locations for highway-oriented and service commercial uses that do not normally locate in the CBD because of site area or highway exposure requirements. It may also include commercial uses of an intensive nature that may conflict with residential land uses. Retail commercial uses in these areas are limited to protect the continued viability of the CBD.

Schedule 1 of the OP, *The Land Use Plan*, displays the locations where each of these commercial zones exist or would be allowed. Despite the OP, developers proposing new or enlarged commercial areas have appealed city policies and decisions to the OMB, resulting in variations to the regulations in the OP. The Walmart debate and subsequent appeals to the OMB illustrate this point graphically.

On July 25, 2005, Council approved a Staff Report outlining recommendations for changes to the commercial planning approach in the City that provided flexibility and the ability to respond to "Big Box" proposals. Not everyone was pleased with its recommendations, especially opponents of Walmart. One critic made the following comment:

> *In its Commercial Policy Review recommendations -- approved by council -- the city planning department, aided by a consultant from Toronto, has quietly decided that Guelph should have the equivalent of four huge commercial "power centres" with as many as two dozen big-box stores. There will be no carefully planned integration with housing. No walkable, linked development. No creative, made-in-Guelph designs. Just the same big, ugly, noisy, traffic-intensive, parking-lot heavy, treeless, soulless architecturally-hideous development that has ruined countless other cities before us.*

The Walmart Debate

On June 9, 1997 city council voted to reject power centres (big box stores) on land zoned industrial at the corner of Woolwich St. and Woodlawn Rd., and on land zoned institutional on Stone Road. Walmart, through its developer 6&7 Developments and Hammerson Canada triggered an OMB hearing by appealing the city's decision not to rezone these areas. More meetings, legal manoeuvres and OMB hearings resulting from this appeal continued until the May 2004 council meeting when the Quarrie council approved Walmart's rezoning request. The battle between Walmart and its opponents became a classic example of citizens fighting a multinational company intent on changing the *Official Plan,* local planning regulations and by-laws. It became both nasty and expensive for Walmart, the city and the citizens opposing Walmart's plans.

During the first seven years of OMB pre-hearings after council's 1997 decision, the following parties were involved: 6&7 Developments (Walmart's developer), the University of Guelph (owner of institutional land), the Bay (owner of Zellers), Armel Corporation (owner of the west end shopping centre where a large Zehrs store is located), the City of Guelph, and the Ignatius Jesuit Centre of Guelph (which would be beside the new Walmart). Residents for Sustainable Development in Guelph (RSD) was formed to represent those opposing the Walmart development at Ontario Municipal Board hearings. The group's position was always that it opposed the location of the proposed development rather than opposing Walmart as a corporation. When the OMB hearing on the Walmart development finally began, only three parties participated: 6&7 and the City supporting the proposal, and RSD opposing. Some of the other original parties had their own OMB hearings and others settled differences, leaving the Walmart issue to be settled separately.

Council Approval And OMB Hearings

The city council led by Mayor Kate Quarrie was so determined to bring Walmart to Guelph that it voted to pay a city lawyer to support Walmart's position at the OMB. The following voted in favour of the motion: Mayor Quarrie; councillors Baily, Billings, Birtwistle, Ferraro, Furfaro, Hamtak, Moziar, and Schnurr. Opposing the motion were councillors Burcher, Downer, Kovach and Laidlaw. As a result, approximately $250,000 of taxpayer's money was spent on legal fees for the OMB hearing in 2004. The vote was a perfect reflection of the left/right split on council. During the 2005 budget process, it was proposed that a further $50,000 be set aside to pay for a hearing of RSD's appeal of the Board's decision. The $50,000 was approved, with the same councillors supporting the expenditure.

At all the OMB hearings, RSD argued that there were a number of areas with appropriate zoning and designations on the OP available for a Walmart store. It soon became obvious that Walmart desired only the Woodlawn/Woolwich location because it owned 6 & 7 Developments which had purchased the land in question. Despite numerous arguments from opponents that other equally viable locations were available, Walmart insisted on locating at the Woodlawn/Woolwich site. RSD argued consistently for any other location, citing traffic congestion, proximity to two cemeteries and the Ignatius Centre, and the availability of other sites as reasons to locate elsewhere. They sent many letters and emails to Walmart executives proposing locational solutions, but seldom received replies or even acknowledgements of their correspondence. On several occasions, RSD invited Walmart, the city and the Chamber of Commerce to meetings to discuss the issue without success. An excellent report by Ben Bennett, *Secrets, Lies and No Replies* http://www.not-there.ca/secrets.PDF contains copies of all the correspondence and a detailed account of the issue.

The Guelph Preservation Action Committee, (GPAC) which also opposed Walmart's application, was formed in January 2005. It attempted to obtain a copy of an unsolicited petition that Walmart claimed contained 9000 signatures supporting its location in Guelph. It had been entered as evidence in the August 2004, OMB proceedings as Exhibit 22. Despite numerous attempts to acquire this document, Walmart ultimately declined, citing the privacy of those signing the petition as the reason for not making it available. Apparently, the OMB had retained only the first page for its records and returned the remainder to Walmart, so GPAC never did see the original. GPAC collected more than 12,000 verifiable names (with addresses and signatures) for their petition opposing Walmart at Woodlawn and Woolwich. RSD asked Walmart to produce a proper petition with 40,001 verifiable names, signatures, addresses and postal codes to show that more than half the adult population supported a store at the north end. It suggested that the ideal solution was for Walmart to build two 75,000 sq. ft. stores in the west end on Armel lands and in the east end on Watson Road land where a Zehrs was proposed. All these suggestions were ignored by Walmart.

OMB Approval

After a long OMB hearing beginning in 2004, on January 3, 2005, the OMB ruled that Walmart could build its store on the 6&7 site at the corner of Woolwich and Woodlawn. Not to be deterred, RSD launched an appeal on January 12, 2005 with the Divisional Court of Ontario. It would focus on the Charter arguments from the OMB hearing highlighting conflicts in compatibility between the proposed development and the religious uses at Ignatius Jesuit Centre. After an adjournment and a change of location, Divisional Court granted RSD leave to appeal. On August 12, The Divisional Court of Ontario denied the appeal by RSD against the OMB decision allowing a Walmart store in Guelph's north end. Thereafter RSD planned to appeal the decision to the Ontario Court of Appeal, but it refused leave to appeal.

Court Appeals

In January 2006 an application was filed with the Ontario Superior Court of Justice alleging that the by-law allowing Walmart was illegal and in violation of the Canadian Charter of Rights and Freedoms. It alleged that commercial activity would directly and substantially interfere with the religious beliefs and practices of individuals of many faiths who use the Ignatius Jesuit Centre and adjoining lands. Section 273(1) of the *Municipal Act* stated that any person can apply to the court to have a municipal by-law quashed for illegality. A final chapter in this drama was written when the multi-faith initiative to protect sacred lands in Guelph from major commercial construction sought leave to appeal a decision released April 5. This decision allowed intervener status on its Charter of Rights appeal to the developer, 6&7 Developments Limited. At this point, Ignatius and its supporters dropped their legal action and settled with 6&7 Developments.

Final Settlement

The settlement fully resolved a number of issues, including additional visual and noise mitigation through the use of berms and extensive plantings and landscape alterations. The Director of Ignatius agreed that they will not see any buildings or hear any additional noise that might be generated by development at this location. The latest proposal would result in significant plantings along the boundary between the development and the Marymount Cemetery/Jesuit lands, including numerous mature cedar trees and the establishment of a "Living Wall,"of growing willows.

RSD claimed that wherever Walmart located in Guelph, the

tax revenue would be the same, as would number of jobs created. Had Walmart accepted city council's decision rejecting the power centre at Woodlawn and Woolwich, and opened a store in one of the areas zoned commercial, it could have located in Guelph seven years ago. Therefore it lost seven years' worth of sales. At the minimum agreed sales rate of $505 per square foot, a 135,000 square foot (12,542 sq. m.) store would have generated $477,225,000 in sales, or almost half a billion dollars! In addition, for every year Walmart was not operating, another $68 million in Guelph sales would have been lost. The city also failed to collect approximately $1 to $2 million in taxes because of the seven year delay. In addition to lost taxes, the city spent almost $1 million on lawyers' fees during the Walmart hearings. The cost of staff time and effort has never been calculated. The moral may be that it is very difficult for any municipality to oppose an international corporation with almost unlimited legal and financial resources.

This is but one example. Similar but shorter battles were fought about Home Depot on Woodlawn Road, Canadian Tire on Stone Road and commercial developments on the former Lafarge Lands (see above). Some were resolved relatively easily while others were almost as difficult as the Walmart issue. In almost all cases that went to the OMB, decisions favoured developers rather than citizen opponents.

A Possible Commercial Development

In contrast to the situations above, residents in the Grange Road/Starwood Drive area of Guelph's east end feel that they have insufficient retail opportunities. For 13 years, Loblaws has owned the only land parcel large enough for a supermarket at the intersection of Starwood Drive and Watson Parkway. Despite incentives such as locating a branch library nearby, Loblaws has no firm plans to develop this site. In 2002, Council approved an application for a large commercial plaza there, but nothing has happened.

Nearby residents continue to complain that they are under served and must drive long distances to shop for groceries and other items. Given its other successful stores in Guelph, Loblaws seems content to leave this site vacant until demand increases considerably. Meanwhile, there is nothing that the city can do to force them to develop their land. It is ironic that some residents have fought vigorously to keep developments out (usually unsuccessfully), while others have fought just as vigorously to attract commercial development, also without success!

ECONOMIC PLANNING

The Sleeman Centre, Eaton Centre, Quebec Street Mall

Guelph's hockey team, the Guelph Storm, moved to the city from Hamilton in 1991. It played in the old and cramped Memorial Gardens until a new arena was built. The *Guelph Sports and Entertainment Centre* was opened in 2000 and cost $21 million. Like so many other major projects in Guelph, planning and finding a location for the arena took many years and much discussion. A number of locations were considered before it was built on the site of the former Eaton's store. The 5000 seat arena was built there after the city purchased the former Eaton Centre Mall from ING Barings for $1.7 million in 1998.

The city entered a public private agreement with a company called Nustadia in 1998 to build and operate the Guelph Sports and Entertainment Centre for 30 years. Guelph contributed half the cost of the project and also guaranteed a $9 million loan for capital costs, which was to be paid back by Nustadia. Unfortunately, Guelph's agreement with Nustadia failed because Nustadia could not keep up its interest payments. In 2001 the city had to assume a $10 million "senior" loan plus the $9.5 million "subordinated" loan that the city was already paying because Nustadia failed to make a June 1 quarterly payment of $181,250. The city paid $3 million during four years to make Nustadia's payments on its bank loan.

Nustadia attributed its cash shortages to a number of factors, including the failure to generate anticipated restaurant and food court revenue and lower than projected ticket sales from Guelph Storm hockey games. The company expected 3,500 people per game but the average was closer to 2,800 in 2000/2001.In 2005, after a four year reprieve, the city took over ownership of the Guelph Sports and Entertainment Centre because as had been negotiated, Nustadia walked away from the deal with no financial consequences. The City of Guelph assumed its $10 million "Senior" loan, plus $3.5 million in payments and the $9.5 million "subordinated" loan that it had guaranteed. In Spring 2010 the City upgraded the Sleeman Centre. The upgrade included adding a video score clock with four video replay screens as well as two LED rings at the top and bottom of the scoreboard.

The demise of the Eaton's store in 1999 resulted in the sale of the mall to the city, which renamed it the Guelph Centre. The back wall of the Eaton's store was torn down, and the space was rebuilt as the Sleeman Centre. The remaining portion of the former Eaton Centre became the Old Quebec Street Mall, which opened in 2003. This Mall was designed as an historic town's main street and an indoor version of a traditional market. The distinctive interior design has a high skylight roof, exposed bricks, with hanging plants and banners surrounding it to create an historic atmosphere. This was influenced by the limestone and brick buildings in downtown Guelph. The mall is designed to resemble old Quebec Street with outdoor store fronts as it was before the mall was built. A number of medical suites occupy the upper level and there is a large parking garage. Unfortunately business in the mall is not as healthy as expected and a number of former stores and business there have closed, at times to be replaced by others.

Downtown Revitalization

The historic Gummer Building, the Victoria Building and the Stewart Drugs Building on Douglas Street and St. George's Square were all damaged by fire in April, 2007. The Skyline Group purchased the buildings and preserved their facades and other historical features. They then created a modern, ecologically sensitive commercial and residential complex in the centre of Guelph.

The six-storey building at 1 Douglas Street combines main floor retail, second and third floor office space, and residential apartments on the top three floors. A fitness facility in the lower level is available to all residential and commercial tenants. These renovations filled the major gap in the square created by the fire and blend well with the surrounding heritage architecture.

Facade Improvement Grants

In September 2011, City Council approved matching grants totalling almost $125,000 to help a dozen downtown merchants and property owners to improve their building façades. This was the second year of the program which includes matching grants of up to $30,000 for façade improvements, and matching grants of up to $5,000 for feasibility studies. These studies will help businesses and property owners to determine whether building renovations or upgrades are physically and financially feasible.

Approved projects are generally located in the historic sections of downtown and range from $1,000 to $171,000 in construction value, representing everything from signage replacement to full façade restoration. An *Official Plan* amendment enlarged the area covered by the city's *Community Improvement Plan* for the downtown. The money would be used for painting, cleaning, replacing signs, repainting and other repairs to downtown buildings. Details of the *Community Improvement Plan* are discussed in the section on Brownfield redevelopment.

Guelph Innovation Centre

Innovation Guelph, which was established in 2010 by the Guelph Chamber of Commerce has expanded its roster of mentors to eight. Its new "Fast Lane" program for small and medium-size enterprises will support innovation and growth in the manufacturing sector. Since 2010 it has assisted 450 companies with business advisory services, and maintains about 100 active clients monthly. Its team of business mentors has facilitated the creation of more than 200 new jobs and has helped its clients to retain an additional 300 jobs. Innovation Guelph is now a key player in the development of the Guelph region's local innovation economy.

Industrial Growth

Guelph's manufacturing sector has been relatively healthy during the last few years. Two outstanding examples are Linamar Corporation and Hitachi Construction Trucks. In 2012, Hitachi embarked on Guelph's largest business expansion by doubling its manufacturing space on Woodlawn Road to increase production and employment levels. Würth Canada, a new Guelph facility in the Hanlon Business Park will include a 26,000 square foot (2415 sq. m.) state-of-the-art office building and a 75,000 square foot (6968 sq. m.) distribution centre. The company moved its Mississauga operation to Guelph.

In 2002, Skyjack became part of the Linamar Corporation, a diversified global manufacturing company of highly engineered products. Linamar has more than 18,000 employees in 44 manufacturing locations, 5 R&D centres and 15 sales offices in 12 countries in North America, Europe and Asia. It continues to expand overseas and in Guelph. Many other Guelph industries in the agricultural, technical, beverage, electrical, metal fabricating, chemical, machinery, plastics, transportation equipment and a number of others continue to thrive. The University of Guelph is the city's second largest employer after Linamar. A number of government agencies also provide employment opportunities.

HANLON BUSINESS PARK RESISTANCE

2002

One of the most contentious issues to be addressed in Guelph between 2000 and 2015 was the development of new industrial land. For many years municipal politicians worried about the disproportionately large percentage of Guelph's assessment revenue derived from residential properties. City staff and almost all Guelph councillors were determined to attract more industry, and with it assessment revenue, by providing land on which new industry could be persuaded to locate. Most of the possible sites in the north and west of the city were privately owned and very expensive while the large Guelph Correctional lands in the eastern suburbs were owned by the province which had not yet decided their ultimate role. In 2002 a number of economic studies proposed some solutions to the assessment problem, leading to protracted debates and ultimately some violence and a "sit-in" in southern Guelph.

It soon became apparent that the largest tracts of city-owned property lay in the southern Hanlon Creek Watershed; an area designated as environmentally sensitive and beloved by naturalists and environmentalists. The debates began in earnest with the release of a Four Year Economic Plan in 2002. It suggested economic priorities and some areas where new businesses might locate. Some of its recommendations were as follows:

> *The document, meant to set out a strategy for the economic development department (and by extension, Guelph) for the next three years, is far reaching.*
> *It contains nine objectives sub-divided by 22 objectives and further broken down to 56 "activities", from attending trade missions to developing a south-*

end business park. Some were:
to develop "employable lands" on a large parcel of
property purchased by the city this year west of the
Hanlon Expressway and develop a marketing plan for
the new business park
to act as the lead agency in promoting Guelph's life
sciences and agri-food research and development
park
The city wants to be one of the top two Canadian
centres - and among the top five in North America -
for life science, including agriculture, food and
veterinary research and business development.
Guelph has already got a good international
reputation in life science thanks to research and
development efforts at the University of Guelph, but
the city will be pushing for investment by related
businesses in Guelph.
Locations for such ventures will be reserved in the
new (Hanlon)business park that Guelph has planned.
Last summer, the city purchased about 400 acres of
land on the west side of the Hanlon Expressway.
About half will be usable after environmentally-
sensitive lands are protected.
Beginning with the development of a master concept,
the city will move onto pushing for Official Plan and
zoning bylaw amendments for the project and then
begin site development. The city wants to mix
corporate office and industrial uses, something rarely
done in the past.

In her 2002 State of the City address, delivered at the annual meeting of the Guelph Chamber of Commerce in October, Mayor Karen Farbridge made the following comments about plans for the new industrial lands:

The 2001-2004 plan reflects the city council's new
commitment to beefing up the economic development

department,

In 2001, we had four land sales in the Hanlon Business Park that totalled a little over 12 acres -- similar to Kitchener and Waterloo but significantly less than Cambridge and Brantford which were up around 100 acres each. For 2002, we have closed land sales totalling 6.126 acres. In addition, 2.974 acres are in the zone change process and are expected to close before year end.

However, this is only part of the picture. While other municipalities are running out of serviced industrial land, Guelph is moving to be in a position to capitalize on the market with the new Hanlon Creek Business Park adding more than 400 acres to our inventory. Combined, Kitchener, Cambridge and Waterloo have approximately 150 acres of serviced, or soon to be serviced, industrial land available.

More residents were finding employment outside the city during the last decade or so although 73 per cent of residents still find employment within the city. Employment rates, labour force and employment levels all increased between 1996 and 2001.

The Hanlon Creek Business Park on the west side of the expressway "will be a SmartGuelph showcase," Farbridge said.

Adding 420 acres of serviced employment land "set in a premium natural setting along the Hanlon Express-way," will support the existing Hanlon Business Park while increasing the potential for "life science cluster development."

Guelph is pushing to be recognized as the top life science, agri- food and environmental centre in Ontario, one of the top two in Canada and one of the top five in North America, she said.

"With 60 ag-biotech companies, 24 research centres, one renowned university and over 6,000 jobs in the sector, we are well on our way to achieving this goal."

2003

Chamber of Commerce president Ian Smith said that to involve Guelph's traditional base with new industry and to create corporate and research and commercialization facilities, city hall is planning the Hanlon Creek Business Park, which ultimately is expected to create thousands of new jobs for the city. Smith saw the campus-like business park across a highway from the similarly-named Hanlon Business Park becoming, in part, one of the city's life sciences hubs. Life sciences, he suggested, have strong growth potential for Guelph. In fact, his chamber, city hall, the University of Guelph and Guelph Partnership for Innovation (a networking group) are working together to bring a life sciences centre to Guelph to commercialize discoveries in emerging fields like biotechnology, genetics, agrifood technology and biochemistry.

A column in the Guelph *Mercury* made the following points about the area being considered for the industrial park. Ultimately, many people felt this way and the Hanlon Industrial Park became one of the most contentious issues in the history of Guelph:

> *"The Hanlon farm is quintessentially Guelph - an oasis in the midst of the urban environment of southwestern Ontario. Community planning, attention to the environment, love for nature and fellow man continue to be the underpinning values of those who plan for this city's future, coupled with very progressive attitudes toward research, science, education and economic development."*

Soon after this column was printed, the *Mercury* published details about the proposal under the following (somewhat prescient) headline: "Hanlon Creek Business Park to be hot spot in the future."

Jim Mairs, manager of city hall's economic development department said that a 650-acre plot of land on the city's south side, immediately west of the Hanlon Parkway will be the location of many new jobs and would be the "city's future." The industrial, corporate and research and development business park, in a campus-like setting, would be a long-term initiative that ultimately will offer businesses four million to six million square feet of space and ultimately employ 3,000 to 5,000 people. He anticipated that the city would sell on average 40 to 50 acres (16 to 20 ha.) a year. When green space, roads and other amenities and other amenities had been accommodated, some 420 acres (170 ha.) could be sold.

The new park, on land annexed from Puslinch Township in the early 1990s was required because the supply of potential industrial space in the city was low. It is across the highway from the 365 acre (147 ha.) Hanlon Business Park, which had less than 40 acres (16 ha.) available, all in small parcels of which the biggest was 47 acres (19 ha.) South of the Hanlon Business Park on the east side of the parkway 1,000 additional acres (405 ha.) were suitable for development, but this would occur many years in the future.

The new Hanlon Creek Business Park is a five-minute drive from Ontario's major Highway 401 corridor and recognizes the changing nature of employment. It is divided into three zones; one for corporate headquarters, a second for research and development companies, particularly in the information technology, environmental protection and agrifood/biotechnology sectors, and a third for the continued growth of advanced manufacturing firms. There are extremely good opportunities to attract agrifood, life sciences and other biotechnology firms, with Guelph already boasting a solid reputation as the home to leading agricultural companies, the University of Guelph and the headquarters of the Ontario Ministry of Agriculture and Food.

2004

The proposal for a new business park in the sensitive Hanlon watershed generated considerable debate both within council and among citizens. Environmentalists, potential neighbours and those just opposed to growth lined up against it. Several organized groups lobbied against the park, but the major opposition occurred after council finally approved its establishment.

2005

In February 2005, the *Mercury's* headline became the first of many to reflect the intense conflict ultimately generated by the new business park: *"Business park plans get nod despite neighbours' opposition."* The new Hanlon Creek Business Park was approved by city council in spite of opposition from nearby residents. Because of wetlands, vegetation, wildlife and other natural feature only about 370 acres (150 ha.) of land at the site could be developed for industrial use. The environmental, social and economic requirements and impacts all would have to be considered and addressed before the site could be developed.

Several residents from the Kortright Hills said that they accept the industrial development but had many concerns about how this site was going to be developed. They might choose to fight council's approval decision at the Ontario Municipal Board. Many worried about traffic on Downey Road. To alleviate neighbourhood concerns, council placed a number of restrictions on the development. There would be a 300-metre buffer zone between the residential area of Kortright Hills to the north and the industrial land to be developed. Any warehousing facilities on the two northerly blocks would be indoors, and the parcels could only be used for light industry. Council asked staff to form a liaison committee including three members elected by the Kortright

Hills neighbourhood to work with staff as they develop the industrial park. The city also agreed to work with Cox Construction to find a route for trucks hauling aggregate, because the company would not be able to use its current route. Council voted to support the draft plan for the park, which had been years in the planning stage and was originally slated to open in 2002.

After city council rejected a proposal to ban manufacturing and warehousing operations from an area close to their homes, a neighbourhood group planned to appeal the approval of the Hanlon Creek Business Park to the Ontario Municipal Board. As time passed, neighbourhood opposition to the park increased. One opponent stated that "a review of the 2004 State of the Hanlon Creek Watershed report reveals that the city has allowed incremental encroachment by other development on the buffers of the provincially significant wetlands in the Hanlon Creek watershed. One would expect that the city would go above and beyond what they have asked of private developers in order to protect this ecological jewel." "What was supposed to be a corporate business park designed with large open spaces that respected and protected the ecological functioning on the property, has now morphed into a generic manufacturing and industrial sprawl that could pollute the Downey and Admiral Wells, our groundwater, the local stream, and destroy fish habitat and other natural resources."

By March, additional opponents had weighed in with statements such as: "Business development" at the expense of critical wetlands, old-growth maples and wildlife habitat makes absolutely no sense and to hide poor policy behind an "employment" strategy is laughable. It makes no sense to "give" inadequate buffer zones or wildlife corridors to this development as a "solution." A real strategy would be to look at what we know will become unused because of the economic slowdown, not to push through a controversial development as "employment lands."

2006 – Approval

By 2006 residents were pleading to save old-growth trees. An Ironwood tree in the proposed business park dated back to the time of Columbus and five old-growth trees were discovered in a hectare-size grove in the southeastern corner of the park. A 500-year-old hop hornbeam tree appeared to be the oldest in Wellington County. Such interventions and discussions continued until the residents' association and the City agreed on specifications for the proposed park.

In June, mediation by the Ontario Municipal Board (OMB) resulted in a "win-win" situation for the parties involved in the dispute. "Virtually all the areas the (Kortright) association had identified prior to the appeal have now been addressed," said Eric Gillespie, the lawyer for the group. "Many people feel that this clearly demonstrates that the city, the developers and the residents have made a very real commitment to being leaders in drinking water protection," he stated.

In early November, Mayor Kate Quarrie indicated that the Park could now go ahead and stated: "This helps to ensure the city has a sufficient supply of employment lands, and reinforces the message that Guelph is open for business," in a news release. Strategically located for targeting both Canadian and US. industrial uses and consumer marketplaces, the Park was expected to attract both new business wishing to relocate and existing local businesses desiring to expand.

2008 - Continuing Controversy

A Guelph Urban Forest Friends (GUFF) spokesperson

appealed to Environmental Advisory Committee members to ensure that the city not only "retain a hop hornbeam tree that's more than 400 years old," but also preserve as many trees as possible in the development, including expanding a heritage maple grove along Forestell Road to save some trees of historic significance. "GUFF believes the trees in this grove should be evaluated for their heritage values," said the spokesperson whose organization advocates for larger local urban forests. The author is uncertain whether either a 400 or 500 year old tree actually existed in the area.

2009 - Escalation of Opposition

Headlines in the *Mercury* reflected the escalation of opposition to the Hanlon development by various groups: "These are all going to be destroyed". "Developing business at cost of trees, wetlands not worth it, group says; city says steps taken to protect natural areas."; "Environmentalists pepper city staff over Hanlon site; Loss of trees, threats to water are key concerns." "Buffers dramatically reduced in size". Many additional issues were raised with the city's Environmental Advisory Committee which questioned staff, consultants and listened to citizen delegations.

Specific questions were asked about buffer zones around sensitive areas, wildlife amphibian culverts and crossings, the future route of Laird Road and the location and management of stormwater ponds. Buffers had been reduced dramatically in size since 2000. Original 30-metre buffers protecting the shrub-dominated wetland protrusion in the southeast were reduced to 15 metres. Buffers in the western portion of the site, which originally ranged from 30 to 100 metres, were all changed to 30 metres. The city's environmental planner stated that while some 1,700 trees would be cut to make way for industrial buildings, another 2,500 trees and almost 5,000 shrubs will be planted to compensate. The city's environmental engineer asserted that no sewage lines would run through the environmentally sensitive area and that low impact development techniques -- rainwater harvesting and green roofs among them -- are recommended in construction.

A senior biologist with Natural Resource Solutions Inc., the consulting firm that's monitoring and collecting data for the city, said that it will follow Ministry of Natural Resources guidelines if any at-risk or endangered species are found. The company is monitoring for the Jefferson salamander (none have been found so far) and the western chorus frog, which has been found, although in already protected areas. Guelph Urban Forest Friends voiced concern over the trees that would be lost with the development. They were also concerned that the public hadn't had a chance to speak directly to city council on this matter. The Director of the Wellington Water Watchers raised his group's concern over Guelph's water supply. Once roads and parking lots are paved, there will be considerable runoff, thus reducing the ability to recharge Guelph's aquifer, the source of the city's drinking water.

The Jefferson Salamander

By May 2009, additional reservations had been raised about the Hanlon Business Park. The environmental group Land Is More Important Than Sprawl (LIMITS), and the Western Canada Wilderness Committee both urged the city to protect the Hanlon ecosystem,to protect old growth trees, to develop requirements for developers to recharge storm water back into the ground and to ensure maintenance of a headwater tributary of Hanlon Creek, classified as a coldwater stream. And then the issue of the elusive Jefferson Salamander was raised.

The Jefferson salamander, so rare that it's protected by the federal *Species at Risk Act*, is not often seen. It lives in

Carolinian forests, briefly breeds in fish-free ponds each spring, and hides in holes during winter and times of trouble. All those habitats exist naturally on the proposed business site. Yet, not a single Jefferson Salamander has yet been confirmed as being in the area. They're not visually identifiable and none have ever been identified (in the area) by the ministry of Natural Resources. A DNA test is required to definitively identify the Jefferson Salamander. Unfortunately, the the Jefferson Salamander looks almost the same as the more common spotted salamander, known to inhabit Guelph.

The city consulted several experts, including those from the University of Guelph to ascertain whether any of these rare and exotic Jefferson Salamanders lived in the area. After much debate and thorough exploration of the area, none were found. Nevertheless, activists and city officials spent long hours debating the changes required to protect the salamander if it did exist in the area. Many opponents of the business park became very emotional about this issue which was covered extensively in the local press. The debate raged on, even though the Ontario Municipal Board had approved 75 environmental and preservation conditions on the Hanlon Creek development. In addition, each building or business to be built on the site would be subject to an individual site plan review. No sewage lines were to go through the environmentally sensitive area and low-impact development techniques such as rainwater harvesting and green roofs were being recommended for all construction. Despite all the debate and assurances from the city, opposition to the business park continued and increased.

The Occupation

Opponents of the Hanlon Creek Business Park occupied the site on 28 July, 2009, halting construction work on land that they considered environmentally significant and fragile. They vowed to maintain their occupation of the land until the city stopped the project and agreed to leave the land to nature. Drexler Construction had begun work on a new service road there, clearing a stretch of land several hundred metres long from McWilliam Road to a tiny tributary of the Hanlon Creek. The company was also contracted to install a culvert at the tributary. At the site, protesters called the work a scar on the land and said that it was the impetus behind the occupation. They hung a banner reading "Stand for our Future, Ally with the Earth" on the side of an idle excavator, and set up an encampment near the tiny stream. They carried enough food into the site to feed a crowd, preparing for a long siege.

About 30 protesters arrived at the site in early in the morning. Their numbers increased as the morning progressed. Many had their faces obscured with handkerchiefs and sunglasses. A seven-man Drexler Construction crew had arrived just before the protesters and had not yet begun working. The arrival of the protesters,who surrounded the excavator at the site, halted the work. It was still at a standstill late in the afternoon. Another group of protesters sat or stood all day at the entrance to a trail into the construction site, blocking access.

City reaction to the occupation was swift. Mayor Karen Farbridge said that the city had no intention of halting development of the long-studied and carefully planned business park. She said that Guelph's economic future depended on the business park, which was being built in a manner that was environmentally responsible. Traditional manufacturing was not the focus of the park, she added. The aim was to have a concentration of life science and environmental technology enterprises occupying the site. The city would not condone illegal activity on the site or at city hall. Guelph Police officers were stationed along Downey Road where they monitored the protest and awaited directives from the city. A Guelph Police spokesperson said the police presence was to ensure that the protest remained peaceful.

A notice of trespass was delivered to protesters on July 29, giving them 24 hours to move from the construction site. They were also given the option to set up an alternate protest site elsewhere on the property. After four days, the occupation included an evolving tent settlement at the site. A spokesperson for the protesters said that plans were underway to host nature walks, a potluck dinner and a series of musical performances there on Saturday. A survey of neighbouring homeowners indicated broad support for the actions of the protesters, even though most believed that the business park would go ahead. Many were quoted in the press supporting the protesters who had created a "really caring, socially sharing community,"observing sustainable camping methods, and had constructed a composting toilet.

The environmental activists occupying the site went court to fight an injunction filed by the city requiring them to leave. The notice of the injunction gave them only three days to prepare a defence. On some days there were up to 50 people on the site. The group said that they have no intention of leaving. They wanted the city to abandon its plans to turn the Hanlon Creek lands, with its centuries-old trees, a variety of bird species, reptiles and amphibians, into industrial lands. During the week, about 100 people came to the Hanlon Creek lands and some provided food and vegetable donations. Protesters who appreciated all the local support, remained certain that the court would support their position.

On August 4, a Superior Court judge allowed the occupation of the planned Hanlon Creek Business Park to continue until the tenth, under certain terms. The Judge's order would allow no more than 30 activists and five press representatives at any given time on the Hanlon Creek lands. The protesters would be allowed to remain in the area where they had installed tents, a shade structure, a log tower, a kitchen, a composting toilet, a hand washing facility and first-aid station. While protesters remain on the property, the City of Guelph could send workers to repair silt fences and perform water analysis. Surveyors would also be allowed to replace any survey stakes pulled out. The judge was impressed by the peaceful protest and hoped that the issue could be resolved through negotiations.

The City's "Notice of Action" served to activists included the following:

An interim, interlocutory and permanent injunction restraining the defendants:
From entering the Hanlon Creek lands.
From obstructing or interfering with roadways known as McWilliams Road, Downey Road, Laird Road and the Hanlon Parkway.
From obstructing access roads, roadways or access points leading into the Hanlon Creek lands.
From preventing city employees, agents, contractors, subcontractors, etc. from using the access roads, roadways or access points to enter and exit the property.
From obstructing or interfering in any way with the city and its contractors' work relating to the construction of the Hanlon Creek Business Park, within the Hanlon Creek lands.
An order that the city and its contractors can use reasonable force to remove any barricade, vehicle or property from the lands and access points.
An order that the city and its contractors not be held liable for any property damage arising from any use of reasonable force to remove property.
Damages of $5 million for conspiracy, interference with economic relations, inducing breach of contract,

trespass, nuisance and intimidation.

City Victory?

Justice Douglas Gray granted the city an injunction on August 13th requiring the protesters to leave the site. He also granted the protesters a limited injunction preventing the city from doing work on a culvert and road for 30 days. This was to allow Natural Resources Minister Donna Cansfield to decide whether a stop-work order should be issued, since what appeared to be a dead Jefferson Salamander had been found on the site. A ministry spokesperson said that it was gathering all the facts surrounding the business park development.

The small group of anonymous protesters who had occupied the Business Park left a trench about half a metre deep across the road, which blocked entry to vehicles. Lengths of large black pipes were strewn about, also blocking access. A makeshift bridge over a small stream led to the former campsite which was littered with bails of straw in the form of partially assembled fort beside a log tower three metres tall flying a black flag. The former campsite contained a homemade fireplace, wooden bench, pieces of lumber and rough-hewn logs. Someone had scribbled "irrepressible" in marker on a portable toilet and a construction sign lay where it was tossed on the ground ("hard hats, safety shoes must be worn"). Protesters asserted that they had left the site in better shape than when they entered, and a number of neighbours expressed support for the important, peaceful protest.

On August 27, Minister of the Environment, Donna Cansfield decided that construction could go ahead with certain restrictions to protect the Jefferson Salamander. The city received a Federal Government announcement stating that $621,294 was being granted to the city for the Business

Park. Michael Chong, Wellington-Halton Hills MP, announced the funds as part of a $1.4 million investment from Canada's Economic Action Plan to stimulate the area's economy. The funds, provided through the Community Adjustment Fund, would go toward culvert construction, the first phase of the business park. The city had committed $20 million for the proposed industrial park, which included the land purchase, environmental monitoring costs and the current contract with Drexler Construction Ltd. When all servicing is completed, the total project cost would be about $32 million. Because the city learned of a trench being re-dug off McWilliams Road, police kept the area under surveillance.

Late in September, two of the former protesters decided to sue Guelph police for "being used as a political tool to repress dissidents." Julian Ichim of Kitchener and colleague Kelly Pflug-Back each filed "notices of action" for $30,000 in damages, plus associated costs. The pair said that they would seek $10,000 for defamation, $10,000 for breach of their Charter rights and $10,000 in aggravated and punitive damages. If the two win the pending lawsuits, they will donate the money to cover any legal defence needed by other activists in future. Guelph police stated that they would await the court's decision on the lawsuit.

By the end of October the city had received permission from the Ministry to continue site preparation in areas where the Jefferson Salamander would not exist. Meanwhile, the owner of Drexler Construction accused the activists of intimidation at his home and the activists threatened to sue the press over its reporting of this event. Many letters to the editor and press releases by all parties involved kept the controversy, which would be revived again soon, in the public eye.

A Nasty Confrontation

On Thursday October 29, the mayor hosted a sod-turning ceremony to mark the progress that had been made in the Hanlon Business Park. This provided an outstanding opportunity for the protesters to once again publicly display their displeasure with the "desecration" of a pristine wilderness in the south of Guelph. They did so with a vengeance as noted in the *Mercury* headline on the thirty first that read "*Vitriolic hatred' at Hanlon protest*". About 30 local dignitaries and City Councillors arrived at the site to be greeted by about 75 angry and hostile protesters chanting "Fuck you scum" and other insults. Many were dressed in costumes or had obscured faces. A number of guests inside the buses feared for their safety as protesters rushed the vehicles, pounding and spitting on the windows, and shouting insults. Some of the guests worried that the police on the site would not be capable of protecting them, but no physical violence ensued.

After the ceremony, the war of words continued with councillors calling the protesters "anarchists" and protesters writing that "anger was justified." They claimed that the city avoided public input, deceived the opponents of the Business Park, overlooked widespread opposition and used legal action against opponents as a form of intimidation. Others wrote in an email that "Too much life is being destroyed every moment;" "The Hanlon Creek Business Park (HCBP) is just one example of the destruction of the vital resources that sustain us. We all need this earth, we all need water to drink, and disgusting projects like the HCBP are not only causing great harm to our water, but they are also killing so much life." Guelph police reviewed video tapes of the protests but didn't lay any charges.

More Legal Action

On Sept. 2, 2009, protesters had delivered a letter to the home of Drexler Construction's owners which warned Drexler not to take part in the construction and indicated that opposition to the project was growing. Drexler felt that the letter threatened his safety and that of his family and complained to Guelph police. The police then released a statement saying that "attempts to intimidate or extort are criminal acts and will not be tolerated by this Police Service," but did not mention the names of those who delivered the letter. Nevertheless, Kelly Pflug-Back paid a visit to the Guelph Police headquarters on Fountain Street on November 23, accompanied by about 10 supporters to serve legal papers to the police. These were not accepted, but subsequently were received by the Police Services Board.

Pflug-Back and and co-plaintiff Julian Ichim, both sought $30,000 in damages for alleged "defamation, Charter of Rights and Freedoms violations and aggravated and punitive damages". They took exception to a police news release related to the incident, which they felt misrepresented their letter delivery to Drexler as a criminal act of intimidation. According to their statement of claim, the media release was "inflammatory, unreasonable and does not accurately reflect the facts as they occurred." Pflug-Back said that anyone openly involved in the Hanlon Creek business park protest would have their character tarnished by such a media release, even though they were unnamed.

The plaintiffs argued that the news release caused distress, a loss of reputation and disruptions in their lives. Police Chief Rob Davis said that the unusual aspect of the case was that no one was identified in the investigation or named in a police press release, yet Pflug-Back came forward and identified herself and Ichim. "We never published their names, so I don't know how we've attacked their credibility or their character." Davis said that the courts would decide on whose interpretation was correct and whether the activity was lawful or unlawful. Ultimately the charges were dismissed. At the end of November, the protesters held a week long rally to encourage support for their cause. They made the point at a noon hour rally that many environmentalists understood and supported their position.

2010

In March, the protesters filed their defence against the city's suit against them. They asserted that the city's $5 Million claim was a legal bullying tool intended to intimidate them. The statement of claim, filed by the city and the land developer in February, asserted that the defendants entered the business park lands last July 27, halting construction. The document stated that the defendants conspired to blockade the entrance and to trespass to prevent the plaintiffs and their contractors from entering the property to complete construction of the business park. "The actions of the defendants were undertaken for the purpose of harming, and have in fact caused harm to, the plaintiffs," said the amended statement of claim. "Alternatively, the defendants knew or ought to have known that their actions would cause harm to the plaintiffs and were directed toward the plaintiffs."

The protesters responded that they "entered and in some cases remained on the land from time to time to prevent serious and irreparable harm to the land, to the environment, to endangered species, to residents of Guelph, to the city's property, and to the city". "The actions of the defendants and occupiers were necessary to prevent this harm." In February 2012, the city dropped its claim which had cost the taxpayers $60,000 in legal fees. Spokespeople for the protesters stated that it had always been a "SLAPP" (Strategic Legal Action Against Public Participation) designed to stifle dissent and frighten the protesters. The city denied this allegation.

Hanlon Creek Development Begins

Environmental activists failed to make an appearance as earth movers began work on infrastructure and building sites in the new business park. Neighbours were pleased that a quarter of the land would be preserved as parkland, but were somewhat sceptical about that promise. In July, a private security firm, Royal City Security began to patrol the site and asked persons walking there for identification. City officials said that they did not want anyone loitering around the site. At the north end of the construction site, a sign stated "Authorized Entry Only" in bold red letters. "This property protected by guard dogs," it warned. By then a number of former protesters had participated in the G20 riots and some of them had spent considerable time in jail, preventing them from protesting again in Guelph.

2011- 2012

By February 2011 a university expert questioned whether the Jefferson Salamander had ever existed in the Hanlon Creek area, since neither salamanders nor their eggs had been discovered there. In early July of that year, a judge ordered Julian Ichim and Kelly Pflug-Back to pay court costs for their defamation suit against the Guelph police. The judge wrote that the evidence was clear that the identity the plaintiffs was made public entirely through their own efforts in calling a press conference and attending at the police station. "Had they not so identified themselves the public at large would have no idea of their identity." The lawyer representing Ichim and Pflug-Back said that "The claim wasn't about the money, but it was about the perceived injustice of this police press release." By November, ground had been broken for the first building in the park.

The City's $5 million claim against the protesters remained on the books until February 2012 when it was withdrawn, thus ending the legal saga of the Hanlon Creek Business Park. An editorial in the *Mercury* stated that a case could be made that the lawsuit was strategic. It originated during a high stakes game of political football with a group that had significant support as well as substantial opposition. "If it wasn't designed to limit public participation in a certain variety of protest, it certainly was delivered just before the five seemingly tireless activists in this matter - and several of their peers - pulled back on conspicuous advocacy efforts that might further delay development efforts at the site." Local radical activists suggested that the lawsuit had discouraged them because of the economic intimidation that they perceived it to represent.

Hanlon Business Park Progress

A February 2014 report on the progress of the three-phase Hanlon Creek Business Park was disappointing. The first phase of the park attracted Würth Canada and Granitworx which employ only 315 people. With 63 per cent of its land undeveloped, the first phase of the Park was expected to generate more than 3,700 jobs. So far, employment has fallen far below this target. The next two phases of the development were to generate 4,300 jobs. The first of these is fully serviced and awaiting projects,while phase three has not yet been serviced. Employment estimates for the business park were developed for the city's 2010 employment lands strategy.

The report does not include costs incurred by the city to develop the park but does show that the city sold $11 million worth of land in the first two phases of the park. The changing characteristics of many industries, where automation requires fewer employees, may force the city to revise its calculations of possible job creation. Hopefully, the city's "break even" point for the first phase of the Park will occur by the end of 2017.

Numerous foreign firms have toured the city's available employment land in the last several years, but global economic volatility has been an impediment to attracting them. Several visited the city and the business park and appeared ready to make acquisitions here and then at the last minute declined because of conditions in their home countries. Development at the business park has generated $132,000 in new annual property tax, $900,000 in one-time development charges and $42,000 worth of building permit revenue.

In August 2014, Council endorsed a city staff proposal to develop the third and final phase of the Hanlon Creek Business Park.

THE HOWITT PARK – LAFARGE LANDS CONTROVERSY

The following headline in the Guelph *Mercury* on June 16, 2004 *"Guelph 'oasis' faces development threat; Lafarge Inc. 'aggressively trying to sell' 54-acres of land off Silvercreek Parkway,"* marked the beginning of a battle over planning and land use between local citizens and a developer that ended only in 2014.

Lafarge Canada Inc. ceased their quarrying and asphalt manufacturing operations on a 54 acre (22 ha.) triangular parcel of land off Silvercreek Parkway South more than a decade ago. Since then, trees have grown and wildlife has returned. It became "a really great example of a naturalized landscape that's just been left alone." The site, which Lafarge has been attempting to sell for years, might become easier to sell because the city no longer insists that Silvercreek Parkway be extended south, which would require a developer to build an expensive overpass or underpass to cross rail lines. Lafarge therefore created a detailed presentation about possible utilisation of the land and planned to solicit proposals from developers.

Neighbours, who for years had used the vacant land as their private park were understandably upset when development proposals were revealed. They had enjoyed the little stream, dense woodland and undulating terrain for everything from hiking to dog walking to picnicking. For some the opposition was pure NIMBY; for others it was a case of preserving a natural area near their homes, and for others it was an abhorrence of possible Big Box sales outlets in Guelph. As is almost always the case in Guelph when any land use changes are suggested, a group was formed to oppose the proposals for the Lafarge lands. Thus the Howitt Neighbourhood Residents' Association was born. By 2005, the Association was well organized and began to hold parties and information sessions for those interested in the development proposals. A number of members pushed to designate the area entirely residential, but this would be uneconomical for the developer.

By 2006, the Howitt Neighbourhood Association was pleased to discover that proposals for the Lafarge lands did not conform with the Planning Department's Commercial Development Review. This had suggested new commercial nodes on the four corners of the city and did not identify the Lafarge property within its Commercial Policy areas. In July, City council opposed including the Lafarge lands in this commercial policy when it voted on the review. Nevertheless, the developers argued that this was not a problem since their plans included major residential components as well as retail uses. In September, Woodbridge-based land development firm, Rosewater Management Group confirmed a deal for Silvercreek Guelph Development Ltd. to purchase the vacant, triangular, 53 acre (21 ha.) site near the Hanlon Parkway and Paisley Road from Lafarge for an undisclosed amount. They would become the developers.

Access to the property soon became a major point of contention. The Ministry of Transportation of Ontario (MTO) would not allow direct access to the Hanlon Parkway so other options had to be considered. The remaining reasonable possibilities for the necessary second route to and from the development were either reopening Silvercreek Parkway North and building an underpass, or extending Inkerman Street and funnelling traffic along residential streets. Neither of these options satisfied the Howitt Park Neighbourhood Residents' Association.

The developers desired to open Silvercreek North, build the underpass, but not open Inkerman Street. They felt that the high cost of this option would not threaten the viability of their development. A past estimate of $20 million for the cost of reopening Silvercreek North and building an underpass or overpass at the Canadian National Railway main line seemed high. Rosewater hoped that it could be done for less. Opponents pointed out that Paisley Road and St. Joseph School would be greatly affected by increased traffic from Silvercreek North if it were reopened.

Before the municipal election in 2006, local newspapers polled candidates and received replies suggesting that infill projects such as the Lafarge property would be a significant issue. The Provincial *Places to Grow* legislation mandated intensification in older built-up areas which would be determined by provincial regulations. Candidates urged local growth management strategies to provide municipal guidance according to Guelph's wishes rather than as a response to Provincial directives. The Lafarge property had challenging access and environmental constraints. It bordered a large residential neighbourhood and the impacts of infill developments on residents would have to be be mitigated. Sound urban design, traffic control and appropriate buffers would also have to be be incorporated. People agreed that the development must be sensitive to, and maintain the character of the neighbourhood.

By 2007, no plans had yet been approved, but neighbours were concerned about the state of the vacant property which had been littered with garbage. Piles of asphalt shingles, yard trimmings, bags of household garbage, dismantled appliances and mattresses had been dumped on the land, which remained a popular dog-walking area and playground for neighbourhood children. By May, the developers had become impatient with the City's slow response to its plans and threatened to take the city to the OMB to force a decision. In July they did just that.

In December, Silvercreek Guelph Development (Rosewater) launched an OMB challenge against what it claimed was council's "refusal or neglect" to rezone the Silvercreek Parkway South land from its current industrial zoning, to zoning that would be needed for a mixed-use commercial development. Their development proposal included a shopping centre on the west side of Howitt Creek which was excluded from the commercial policy passed by city council in July 2005. It allowed commercial developments of a similar large size to be built in four areas in the city's northern, southern, eastern and western outskirts.

Early in 2008, representatives of the developer outlined a revised plan, but residents' concerns about traffic, access and the effect on the neighbourhood were not addressed to the satisfaction of the neighbourhood association. The developer provided estimates of peak traffic volumes, but wasn't able to estimate full-day volumes. No information was available on the amount of through traffic that might travel between Paisley Road and Waterloo Avenue if Silvercreek Parkway North were extended south to join Silvercreek Parkway South. Opponents intended to present their concerns at a March meeting where they would attempt to reach a compromise with the developer.

Although an application for developing the former quarry, which became an asphalt plant and a then vacant field was filed more than two years earlier, March 2008 was the first time it came to Council. Even though the decision was now to be made by the OMB, Council "mimicked" a public meeting to gauge public opinion so it would know residents' opinions when making its decisions on the application. The developer planned to create a "main street experience" on Silvercreek Parkway. The two largest big-box stores would be located well away from the street, rather than trying to "pretty them up" to make them part of this streetscape. The developers would dedicate land east of Howitt Creek to the city for a 14 acre (5.6 ha.) park with trails. Its uses could include dog walking and a winter skating area. Part of the area east of the creek would occasionally flood during storms and provide flood plain storage capacity.

By May, Armel Corp., a major local developer, and 6&7 Developments Ltd., which developed the site of Walmart, both opposed the Lafarge proposal and attained party status at the OMB hearing. The city's opposition was because the proposal did not conform with the city's *Official Plan*. It also had technical concerns about the plan to build an underpass under the rail line and about details of drainage on the site. Throughout the summer, the OMB held mediation sessions and by the end of January 2009 had reached a compromise that satisfied the Howitt Park Neighbourhood Association. The City of Guelph, the Howitt Park Neighbourhood Residents' Association and Silvercreek Guelph Developments Limited, agreed to request that the OMB approve a mixed use employment/commercial and residential development on the site.

After the five-month negotiation and mediation process, proposed *Official Plan* and zoning amendments were agreed to permit:

• *A main street area for restaurants and other services along Silvercreek Parkway between Paisley and Wellington Streets;*
• *A business park, residential community and park on the east side of Silvercreek Parkway;*
• *Retail/commercial uses on the west side of Silvercreek Parkway on lands bounded by the Hanlon Expressway, to be phased in over six years to minimize impacts on existing retail/commercial businesses.*

The proposed development would be subject to a number of detailed conditions including a requirement to construct an underpass under the CN Rail Line to make Silvercreek Parkway a through street between Paisley and Wellington.

The Howitt Park Neighbourhood Residents' Association stated that they had wanted to develop something that would be acceptable to the applicant and acceptable to them, and this was finally achieved. The tentative settlement still required OMB approval.

The revised plan, with the support of the Howitt Park Neighbourhood Residents' Association, was supported by Guelph City Council in 2009 through Minutes of Settlement that included modified amendments to Guelph's *Official Plan* and Zoning by-law to accommodate the revised mixed-use development. Armel Developments opposed the appeal made to the Ontario Municipal Board by Silvercreek Guelph Developments Limited at a 22-day hearing. Together with the Howitt Park Neighbourhood Residents' Association and Silvercreek Developments Limited, the City was successful in demonstrating to the Board that the re-designation of the property, so that it could be developed as a mixed-used node.

On January 13, 2010, the Ontario Municipal Board ruled in favour of the company plans to build 245,000 square feet (22,761 sq. m.) of retail space, including a big-box store, and more than 300 units of residential development on the former Lafarge lands along Silvercreek Parkway South. The proposal, which was opposed by fellow developers Armel Corp., was the subject of a lengthy hearing during summer and fall of that year. The decision read in part:

> *Through mediated sessions, Silvercreek Guelph Developments Limited modified its proposal to address the concerns of City Council. These modifications included a significant reduction in the retail floor space and restrictions of the location, size and phasing of this space. The changes also included the introduction of business park, residential components, and lands to be dedicated to the City for*

parks, trails and infrastructure such as stormwater management and roads. Holding zone provisions are also included to ensure that the infrastructure upgrades are completed.

Armel was the sole holdout, basically because the commercial area proposed, which might include a Costco outlet, would be in direct competition with their commercial development at Imperial and Paisley Roads, which includes the large Zehrs supermarket. By 2011, the site had not yet been developed and some opposition continued. A number of trespassers who continued to want the land returned to nature used the site, sometimes littered and ignored the visible "no trespassing" signs. Users of the land had moved signs and cut fences to gain access. Meanwhile, the owners attempted to keep their fences and signs intact until development could occur.

By February 2012, the land had not yet been developed, but some detailed transportation plans which posed additional potential problems had been made. A small number of residents would have to change the way they leave their homes if the plan to reopen Silvercreek Parkway south of Paisley Road were adopted. Residents of the dead-end section of Silvercreek and on a dead-end side street referred to as "Old Paisley" would keep their dead-end streets, but they would only be able to get to and from those streets by making right turns. Because the city's plans routed Silvercreek below the railroad tracks through an underpass, the road could not simply be extended. Instead, a service road would be created at the existing grade to give the homeowners access to their driveways. After eight years of planning, hearings, opposition, conflict and compromise, the Howitt Park, Lafarge Lands saga might nearly have ended.

In June of that year, Armel Corporation applied for

permission to locate a large Costco store on their lands in the west end near their Zehrs development at the corner of Paisley and Imperial Roads. Local residents felt that if a Costco were built west of Elmira Road, across from the Zehrs site, there would be major increases in traffic in the area. They planned to mount spirited opposition to the Armel plans. At the same time, Rosewood Corporation which had planned to develop the Lafarge site also objected to the Armel proposal because it might hurt their efforts to secure an anchor tenant.

In January 2013, Silvercreek Developments Guelph submitted a revised proposal for the Lafarge site to the Planning Department. They had hoped that a Costco big box store would anchor its retail development on the Lafarge site, but Costco had chosen a site west of the west-end Zehrs Store on land owned by Armel Corporation. That development was approved by city council in October 2012. As a result, Silvercreek sought a number of changes in the agreement which was approved by the OMB in 2008 between it and the neighbourhood and city. Silvercreek wished to alter the layout, number and size of retail stores to be built near the Hanlon Expressway on the former Lafarge site. The stores would all be smaller than those in their original proposal. A new market analysis would be provided to assess the impact of the revised plan on existing retailers. The timing of building permits would also be altered to reflect the deletion of the proposed big-box store.

A supermarket would replace the big box store, and office space would be north of a new city park, while housing would be south of the park. Retail development was all to be located on the west side of the Silvercreek extension, between Silvercreek and the Hanlon Expressway. The developer also wanted to be allowed to shift 10,000 sq. ft. (929 sq. m.) of the allowed 245,000 square feet (22,761 sq. m.) of retail space to be near the "market square" which would be a pedestrian-oriented section of the development surrounded by service-commercial space, which could include restaurants, banks and florists.

OMB Approval for Lafarge Lands Development

In December 2013, eight years after a developer first proposed commercial buildings on the vacant 54-acre site, the former Lafarge Quarry lands were finally approved for development. The city is preparing to connect the two ends of Silvercreek Parkway, which will provide a new north-south link for drivers, and access to buildings on the site. The road will service the development and provide a north-south connection linking Paisley Road and Waterloo Avenue. The CN mainline tracks south of Paisley Road now separate the north and south parts of Silvercreek Parkway, so an underpass will be built beneath the tracks when the roadwork is undertaken. The $7-million cost of the underpass will be shared equally between the city and the developer, Silvercreek Guelph Developments Ltd.

The total cost of the roadwork for the development is estimated to be about $14 million, including the underpass. The city will pay a total of $5.5 million, with the developer contributing $8.5 million. An environmental assessment and railway approvals for the underpass and roadwork have been obtained by the city. Hopefully, the Silvercreek extension will be open to traffic in 2015. City council passed a motion approving *Official Plan* and zoning amendments requested by the developer to allow changes to development plans that could result in a supermarket being built on the site. The changes approved by council allow different building sizes than were stipulated in the mediated settlement, as well as a wider range of commercial uses on the site. The changes also removed timing restrictions on development of the site. The revised plans include office space, housing and a new city park, but it is uncertain whether a supermarket can be attracted to the site. The agreement allowed one 145,000 sq. ft. (13,471 sq. m.) big box store to be built, with a restriction that it be either a warehouse membership club, or a home improvement retail warehouse.

THE NEW GUELPH MUSEUM

Another interesting and controversial issue that occupied politicians in Guelph between 2000 and 2014 occurred because by 2004 the Guelph Civic Museum had outgrown its building at the intersection of Dublin St. and Waterloo Ave. Fortunately, a solution had become possible with the abandonment of the Loretto Convent beside the Church of our Lady on "Catholic Hill. The convent had been vacant since 1996 and while Bishop Macdonell officially closed as a high school in 1995, it remained in use for a few years by the Wellington Centre for Continuing Education. Both buildings were owned by the Roman Catholic Diocese in Hamilton which had declared that they were not worth saving, applied for a demolition permit and decided to tear them down. However, since Heritage Guelph had different ideas, an eight year saga began.

Heritage Guelph declared the convent part of a composition and skyline that characterize the "Church of Our Lady Mount" and is an important part of the history of Guelph. A city heritage planner declared that a tour of the convent and recent studies indicated that while the convent is old and needs upgrading, it was sound and not in derelict condition. Council decided to delay issuing a demolition permit for the convent to support Heritage Guelph staff in additional talks with the diocese. It would also direct staff to review the city's demolition control bylaw, which does not protect heritage buildings.

The bylaw, passed in 1989, requires council to approve the issuing of all demolition permits related to residential properties in Guelph. The goal of the bylaw is to maintain the city's housing stock, and generally councillors considering an application under the bylaw want to see a plan to replace any residential buildings being lost. The *Planning Act* states that when a demolition control bylaw is in place, "no person shall demolish the whole or any part of any residential property in the area of demolition control unless the person is the holder of a demolition permit issued by the council." If city staff believed that the convent was subject to the demolition control bylaw and council refused to issue the demolition permit, the diocese could file an appeal to the Ontario Municipal Board, which has the authority to order that a permit be issued.

Even though the Hamilton diocese had applied for a demolition permit in February 2004 to tear down the buildings, diocesan officials met with about 100 people at an open house in April. They submitted numerous ideas for reuse of the convent, which had been built in 1856. Father Dennis Noon, parish priest at Church of Our Lady, said that a decision to delay demolition came after discussions with Heritage Guelph. The diocese decided to delay demolition until the city completed a feasibility study of reuse options.

By August, pressure to save the Loretto Convent had increased. Space to expand the museum at the Dublin site was limited and museum officials were hoping that city council would reconsider the Loretto convent as a new home for the facility. Museum officials estimated that the cost of renovations and relocating the museum there would be comparable to expanding at its current location. The chair of the museum's board urged council to consider seriously the Loretto convent as a new site for the museum. With the Loretto convent facing demolition and the Catholic diocese open to having the building used as a museum, the museum board urged the city not to dismiss the convent site as a new home for the museum.

By September, Council had appointed Alastair Summerlee, President of the University of Guelph, to Chair a task force to study the feasibility of using Loretto Convent as a museum. The Guelph Museum Board had been offered $5,000 from Royal City Realty to perform a feasibility study on reuse of the convent. The new task force was made aware of the offer. In January, the task force suggested that council should proceed immediately with the heritage designation for the building regardless of the outcome of discussions. Opinion was divided on whether public money should be used for any convent project, but even those who opposed the use of public funds were supportive of retaining the building.

In April, the task force reported that the convent was an ideal site for the museum in terms of location and prominence in the city. A museum was also the most attractive option for the diocese because it is consistent with the activities of the Church of Our Lady. Museum relocation committee chair Ian Brown said that expansion of the museum at its current site would cost about $2.6 million, compared with $2.8 million to move the museum to the convent. An added incentive was that the convent had 45 to 50 parking spots, compared to the museum's eight.

By 2006, the first phase of the museum feasibility study included a technical assessment of the convent building, including the masonry and roofing. The existing two-storey addition on the west side of the convent (which includes a sun porch) would be demolished, along with additions to the third and forth levels which have no historical significance. They would be replaced by a "non-combustible," three-storey, flat-roof addition and basement, including a new five-storey exit stair with access to all existing and new floor levels.

Plans suggested seven galleries (including a local artist gallery and the existing children's and John Galt History galleries), three programming areas, a future conservation laboratory, exhibit preparation area, and storage for textile and furniture artifacts. There would be curatorial, research and archive space for the museum, which officials say has long been bursting at the seams. Some exterior windows would be replaced to match existing windows, which would remain. The convent interior would be completely retrofitted and would be barrier free.

A civic election in November resulted in major changes on city council. The previous council had prepared for moving the Civic Museum to the Loretto Convent by saving that building from the wrecking ball but had not allocated any funds for the move. In its first year the new council voted that the $12.7 million project should go ahead if $6 million in funding could be secured from other levels of government. As a result, lobbying and local fund-raising began in earnest. Since the museum proposal had been before council for years, several councillors argued that funds should be provided and the move completed before 2011. In a debate about the capital budget forecast, several speakers noted that the Catholic Diocese might not wait five years and that the convent building could deteriorate if there were a long delay.

2007

Councillors continued to suggest that the museum be moved to the convent building before the 2011 date scheduled in its budget. Katherine McCracken, director of Guelph Museums stressed that having the museum next to the Church of our Lady would greatly increase its viability as a tourist attraction. A major incentive to proceed with the move came when Cambridge MP Gary Goodyear announced in early March that the Federal Government would provide $1 million toward the project. Even better news came when MPP (Member of Provincial Parliament) Liz Sandals announced a few days later that the Provincial Government would pledge $5 million to renovate the convent. In late 2007, the city entered a 50 year lease with the diocese under which it pays no rent, but assumes about

$40,000 in annual operating costs to maintain the building.

2008-2009

Discussion of plans for the museum move and fund raising efforts continued into 2008. The city said that another $500,000 would come from the sale of the old museum, and a similar amount from fund raising. Early in 2009 preliminary plans for the renovations were made public. They showed a glass extension on the east wall of the Loretto Convent building. There was acknowledgement that the convent building wasn't even really visible until 2004 when the old high school on the site was torn down. Now that it's visible Guelph residents seem quite attached to the view of the convent on the hill. On the other hand, museum employees and some citizens had become very fond of the Dublin Street building and were sad to see it being abandoned.

Not everyone was happy with the expenditures entailed by moving the museum. Gerry Barker, a *Mercury* columnist and constant critic of city council, listed the financial commitments made by council and suggested that it reconsider these expenditures which he felt could not be afforded by already overburdened taxpayers. His list of projects included the following: the Wilson Street parking garage (almost $15 million), the Carden streetscape project in front of the new city hall and Guelph Civic league offices ($8.7 million), the Loretto Convent/Guelph Museum (projected taxpayer cost $6.7 million), the downtown library and parking garage ($55.5 million preliminary price tag) and the new city hall (projected to cost $52.3 million), not counting the lawsuit with the original builders of the new city hall, legal costs or the old city hall conversion to a judicial centre.

By the end of the year, city officials were revising their plans to move the civic museum into the former Loretto Convent when construction bids were over budget. Katherine McCracken, director of Guelph Museums, said that bids were about $2 million higher than the budgeted $12.7 million. If the project did not proceed, the city risked losing $6 million in provincial and federal grants which were dependent on the project being significantly underway by Spring 2010. The city began to review the project with its architects in an attempt to identify savings. Some landscaping work, for example, could become part of a later community fund raising campaign. The interior of the convent, much of which had been divided into very small rooms was completely stripped during demolition, making design work easier for the architects.

2010

By the middle of 2010, plans for the new museum were well under way. The existing 30,000 item collection had been crammed into space only one-third the size of its new home. With $100,000 raised so far, another $400,000 was to come from a public campaign that began in April under committee chair John Valeriote. Retired Lawyer Hugh Guthrie became the Honorary Chair but died peacefully at his home in Guelph on June 28, 2010, after a brief illness. His estate contributed $200,000 to the campaign. The new museum's archives will be known as the Hugh Guthrie QC Archives Room. By the end of the year, the $12.7-million redevelopment had received $5 million from the province, $1.5 million from Ottawa and $5.7 million from the municipality. Local fund raising continued into 2011.

2011

By early in the year, John Valeriote, chair of the museum's capital campaign said that: "It has been tremendously successful, and continues to be". The campaign, which had already raised more than $700,000 was scheduled to end soon. By March, local fund raising had provided $772,000 toward the new museum.

By May council decided to sell the former museum building to cover a cost overrun in the construction of the new Civic Museum in the Loretto convent building. Without the proceeds from the sale, the city would have had to issue additional debt to cover the projected overrun of between $500,000 and $700,000. Additional fund raising to cover the cost of landscaping was being discussed. By the end of the year, museum staff hoped that museum's collection could be moved from its current home on nearby Dublin Street the and the new building could be open to the public early in 2012.

2012

By January 2012, museum director Katherine McCracken was particularly pleased with the feel of the new facility. She had worried about having too many modern materials inside the historic old building, but the new glass and old stone complemented each other rather well. An interactive childrens' gallery would tell stories of children through different eras, but would not be too "high tech". Being next to The Church of Our Lady which is the number one tourist attraction in the city was an added bonus for the new museum.

On February 25, 2012, the new museum finally opened to the public and received rave reviews from most visitors. Standing on "Catholic Hill" beside the Church of our Lady, it had become "an engaging community space where people can discover the history and stories that make Guelph, Guelph" according to director Katherine McCracken. Its construction was a triumph of good sense and hard work by many members of the public and by politicians who had endured seven years of "nay-saying" and criticism from people such as former councillors Rocco Furfaro, Peter Hamtak and David Birtwistle. When on council and thereafter, they had led the opposition with words such as: "I don't see the value of the property. . . The building is a money pit. . . The convent is falling down." Fortunately subsequent councils and hundreds of citizens who donated money to the project saw the future differently.

The former Guelph Civic Museum building on Dublin Street was sold and has been converted into a community arts centre with rental spaces for local artists and artisans.

THE CENTRAL LIBRARY: NO PROGRESS

For a number of years, Chief Librarian Norman McLeod had been concerned that the central library at the corner of Paisley and Gordon streets had outgrown both its building and location. Inside the library, space was cramped, storage areas were overflowing and there was too little space for users. Outside, the parking lot could not accommodate peak-use parking. Furthermore, the building was getting old and needed repairs. The matter of replacing the 35 year old library had been discussed before, but in August 2000, City Administrator David Creech suggested to Council that it spend $50,000 to hire a consultant to recommend a site for a new library.

During discussions about a location for the new library, several councillors suggested that it be moved to the Guelph Centre mall which was owned by the city. Opponents maintained that the floors in the building could not support the weight of library books and retaining ownership of the mall would mean that the city would have to lease retail space to other mall tenants. Soon the question of library relocation became inextricably linked to the future of the former Eaton Centre Mall.

The mall had been purchased by the city 15 months earlier as part of a deal to build its new sports and entertainment centre. By September, a firm based in London, Ontario wanted to anchor the mall with a speciality food market and an athletic centre, while a local firm envisioned an outdoor pedestrian mall through the middle of the existing mall, with a new streetscape of shops, offices and 90 housing units on two upper floors. The estimated real value of their bids for the mall ranged from $500,000 to $825,000. During these discussions, which finally ended in a sale and reconstruction of the mall, the library was ruled out as a viable tenant and the site search continued.

By April 2002, Council had agreed upon a concept plan for a new library, but no site had yet been selected. A library relocation study recommended that the city plan a 65,000 square foot (6039 sq. m.) library and examine costs for a short list of potential sites for the replacement of a library about a third the size it should be for a city of 100,000 people. Currently, there were 600,000 visits a year to the existing 33,000 square foot (3,066 sq. m.) library. A new library with an estimated $11 million cost could be be put into Guelph's five-year capital forecast. The cost is about the same as what was going to be put aside to re-engineer the Eastview landfill site which had been scrapped. A report suggested that the library should definitely receive priority over the proposed $14 million Civic Administration Centre. Because of the space shortage at City Hall, city staff were being accommodated in nearby office space that might otherwise remain empty, thus relieving the pressure for a new Civic Administration Centre.

By September 2003, Council had made progress on the library site. After a three-hour debate, it authorized staff to investigate putting the library into the old downtown post office and extending it into the Baker Street parking lot. It then authorized city staff to negotiate with Canada Post about purchasing the downtown post office and agreed that the post office and Baker Street lot were the preferred location for a new main library. This site was selected from four downtown sites on a short list that was approved by city council in December 2002. The initial design would have a Wyndham Street entrance into the building through the heritage facade of the post office building. The interior of the building would be gutted to adapt it to its new use. The irregularly shaped library building would be three storeys high and cost about $17.3 million. This would be offset by an estimated $1 million from the sale of the current library building on Norfolk Street.

This design could also include a five-storey parkade that would accommodate 570 cars, to be built next door to the library. Before the site was finally selected, city council would have to authorize purchase of the post office and approve the design and budget. A gruelling debate followed the consultants' report. Some city councillors did not want to spend the money on a new downtown library. Councillor Rocco Furfaro felt that Guelph did not need a new library and could not afford it. Councillor Dan Schnurr said that Council must consider solutions that didn't involve "throwing money at it to build another Taj Mahal. It is time for us to say no to some of these things. We can't afford it." Others stressed that nothing had been decided except the location for a new library.

In November, the library issue became part of the election campaign between Karen Farbridge and the challenger Kate Quarrie. In a statement released by Quarrie, it was asserted that the city under Farbridge had been hiding capital budget figures. Quarrie said that the city's debt had "doubled" in one month in a news release in which she suggested that the Farbridge administration was not "transparent" on financial issues. Farbridge countered that Quarrie had altered financial documents and misrepresented their dates. Farbridge said that the new library and Civic Administration Centre were contained in the capital budget forecast approved by council last winter, but they were "annotated." The annotation ensured that these two projects would not proceed until a funding strategy had been identified and the projects were approved by council, which hasn't happened yet. With the defeat of Farbridge by Quarrie and a number of her supporters in the election, the library controversy bubbled up again in 2004.

During that year, a number of delegations to Council provided evidence that the city needed a new library while others urged that the old Post Office be the site. On a visit to the main branch's children's library for story time a child noticed a large crack in the wall. There was too little space to hang up coats, the room for the event was dimly lit and the bathroom was "grossly inadequate." A third of the books were too high for a child to reach, while others were so tightly packed on the shelves that they were difficult to remove. Because all seats were taken or not a suitable size, the child had to read her book on the floor. Other delegations stated that the library was well beyond replacement age.

After receiving a letter from Kate Quarrie in June stating that there was no urgency to acquire the post office building, since the new library project was moved from 2006 to 2008 in the city budget, the Library Board replied that they preferred the Post Office as a location for the new library. By December, some councillors wondered whether the library should be located in the planned new Civic Administration building on Carden Street. This was despite the fact that Council had chosen the Post Office site in 2003. Eventually it was decided that the new Civic Administration Centre would not be large enough to accommodate the library.

On Jan. 17, 2005, Canada Post moved all its operations from the old post office at 138 Wyndham St. to its new building at 250 Woodlawn Rd. W.; a state-of-the-art facility. Federal officials informed Guelph that the city would have the right of first refusal on the vacant building. However, City council declined the opportunity to buy the former Wyndham Street post office, causing the Guelph Public Library Board to search again for a new location for its main branch. In a 9-4 decision on February 8 council voted to ignore a staff recommendation to negotiate with Canada Post to purchase the building, and then voted 8-5 to advise Canada Post that the city has no interest in the property for municipal purposes. Several councillors spoke out against Council's move, but hard-core right-wing supporters of Kate Quarrie justified their decision. They cited the cost and suggested that the Post Office should have been considered for the location of a provincial offences court. Needless to say, the Library Board, the Chief Librarian, city staff who were ignored, and many citizens were outraged by what they considered to be a foolhardy and short-sighted decision by a dysfunctional council.

In an editorial on February 5, the *Guelph Mercury* criticized council for its rash decision. It went on the state: "Had the city purchased the post office, it could have used the space for city staff until the library is built in 2009. Instead, council chose to continue paying more than $300,000 per year to rent space on the corner of Wyndham and Macdonell streets. A council poised to cut funding for arts, culture and social programs cannot afford to rent space it doesn't need." This and numerous letters to the editor following the decision reflected feelings in the community that many members of City Council voted against the purchase because it had been proposed by the previous Farbridge administration. This mean and vindictive attitude had pervaded city hall from the beginning of the Quarrie term and seems to have biased other votes by councillors.

By the end of March, Wellington County had decided to purchase the old Post Office. In the words of one County Councillor: "I supported the purchase because I thought Guelph city councillors were out of their minds for not buying it." Wellington County Council then purchased the building in 2005 and assessed the City of Guelph $ 2.7 million for its share of renovation costs to cover joint services administered from the building. Some estimated that this decision cost the city $2 million more than if they had purchased the Post Office building. It also left Guelph without a location for a new library. At the end of April 2007, Wellington County unveiled its new offices in the renovated building, revealing the extensive work that went into converting the space to accommodate social services offices and to restore the building to its original glory, uncovering mouldings and black marble pilasters for all to see.

Later in 2007, a new staff report to Council once again recommended a Baker Street site for the new library. Staff also suggested that frontage on Wyndham Street would be very beneficial for the library. They also raised the issue of combining the library project with a parking facility nearby on the Baker street site. This would ensure maximum use of parking spaces on nights and weekends as well as during weekdays. Because Kate Quarrie's council left the Baker street parkade in limbo on tied votes, the parking lot remained free to be used for the library and a parking building.

The new library was scheduled for 2011 in the city's 2007 capital budget forecast and was budgeted at $17.3 million, but some councillors thought that it should be built sooner. By 2008, the new council had considered several alternative sites for the new library and rejected plans for a parking garage on Baker Street. They then selected that location for the new central library, a parking garage and condominiums. Expropriating a number of properties along Wyndham would give the library a main-street presence.

In February 2009 city council approved the staff-recommended conceptual design for the new library and Baker Street redevelopment that would eliminate four Wyndham Street properties. It also made a commitment to help displaced businesses find new suitable locations. This was directed primarily at Ray Mitchell and his Family Thrift Store, which was described by six delegates and some councillors as a cultural and community fixture in Guelph's downtown. Council planned to compensate for lost businesses and the 30 low-rent apartments above the four commercial spaces that would disappear. Except for

Mitchell's family store, much of the commercial space had become vacant during the year, when it became clear that removing the buildings might be an option for the development project. City staff estimated that it will cost $360,000 to demolish the Mitchell building which the city purchased for $1.25M.

The conceptual design for the new library complex included a 90,000-square-foot (8,362 sq. m.) library on three floors and about 400 public parking spaces. The desired privately-developed 200 to 300 residential units and about 20,000 square feet (1,858 sq. m.) of commercial space were not included in the $55.5 million preliminary cost estimate. The design concept with frontage on Wyndham Street was designed to become a "north anchor" for the downtown.

A Major Setback

In October 2009, City council removed both the library and a proposed south end recreational complex from their capital budget. In a period of financial uncertainty, both projects were pushed further into the future. Meanwhile, owners of the buildings to be expropriated were becoming dissatisfied at the slow progress after their tenants moved out. Some felt that they should be compensated for lost business and no rent as their structures remained vacant. By 2010 city officials knew the location of the new main library, but cost, final design and timing of the project remained to be determined, while money to acquire property for the library was unavailable.

By 2011, two upper Wyndham Street buildings where the city planned to build a new main library were to be demolished, beginning in October. The vacant land could then be used temporarily as a 45-space parking lot. City council approved the parking lot plans in 2010, but demolition didn't happen then because chimney swifts were discovered in a chimney there. The provincial Ministry of Natural Resources was concerned about loss of habitat for endangered species like the chimney swift, and suggested that replacement habitats be provided. In January 2012 the demolition of two city-owned buildings on Wyndham Street finally occurred, making space for additional off-street parking. However the city's 10 year capital budget forecast still didn't include a library. The land had been cleared, library plans had been made, but no money had been committed to what many in Guelph consider to be an essential project. In August 2010 a new parking lot, accessible from Baker street was finally opened where the demolished building had stood. Discussion about when to build the library and other uses for land continued.

THE CIVIC ADMINISTRATION CENTRE: A LEGAL SAGA

In early 2000, Guelph City Council began to discuss the possibility of closing the historic city hall and either building a new facility or moving operations to the former Eaton Centre Mall on St. Georges Square. At that time City Administrator, David Creech stated that renovating the mall for city hall purposes would "pale beside the cost of building an administration centre on the Memorial Gardens site." Having outlived its usefulness, Memorial Gardens which was adjacent to the old City Hall was to be demolished. By May of that year, Mayor Karen Farbridge suggested that there was no rush to replace City Hall, since the city had not yet sold the former Eaton Centre (renamed Guelph Centre). She felt that a decision about an administrative centre should not be made before the future of Guelph Centre was known.

Council continued to discuss a number of possible building projects such as a new central library and a new city city hall. By 2002 a number of alternative sites had been considered and Mayor Farbridge suggested that one of four options would see both a Civic Administration Centre and a new main library squeezed onto the Memorial Gardens site. If this option were not chosen, then Memorial Gardens should be taken off the short list of potential library sites, just as the former Eaton Centre and the Guelph Armoury were removed from the short list by city council in April of that year. Later in the year, Council decided that the new library would not be located on the former Memorial Gardens site. In December, Council decided to approve two major items in the 2003-2005 budget and a forecast for the following two years; a new municipal centre and a main public library.

Early in 2003, Council agreed that the limestone facade of the former Provincial Winter Fair Building, discovered under the siding of Memorial Gardens during its demolition, should be the exterior north wall of the new city hall structure. The city then began a design contest to select an architectural firm for the new City Hall. By June, five architectural submissions had been received and were to be made public that September.

A design by Adamson Associates Architects for the Civic Administration Centre to replace the Memorial Gardens arena next to the existing, crowded, 19th century City Hall on Carden Street was eventually selected. Of the five teams that submitted designs, only the winning team and one other were willing to provide a certificate signed by an independent expert saying that they could come within 10 per cent of the city's estimated budget specification of $154 per square foot for new construction. While the certificate isn't a legally binding contract, it's a "substantial" indicator of the firm's intent. The vote on the city hall design concept was 8-5. Voting against were Dan Schnurr, Rocco Furfaro, Gloria Kovach, Dan Moziar and David Birtwistle.

During the civic election in November 2003, Kate Quarrie and her supporters replaced Karen Farbridge and a number of former councillors. Given Quarrie's feelings about new municipal building projects, both the library and the city hall project came under intense scrutiny. During the election campaign, Quarrie stated that drilling new wells to provide additional sources of water should come before any new buildings. All major projects were suspended, to be discussed again only after the 2004 budget. Several councillors who had not supported either the library or the new city hall argued that all discussions with the architects be terminated, but council eventually agreed to delay such activities until the full financial implications could be determined.

By December 2004, council was to decide whether a redesign was needed for city's proposed Civic Administration

Centre. Central to the architectural redesign, which would cost about $40,000, was an historic wall from the former Ontario Winter Fair building that was found under the facade of the now closed Memorial Gardens. The original design for the Civic Administration Centre suggested 120,000 square feet (11,148 sq. m.) of office, public and leased space, with a large glass facade at the front of the building to protect the heritage wall. By removing the glass facade and decreasing the square footage of the centre, it might be possible to save millions of dollars.

In 2005, additional progress was made on the city hall project. A number of councillors supported the new civic administration building which would bring staff from several rented downtown buildings into one space, while the current city hall might become the permanent site of the city's provincial offences courthouse. However, a number suggested that the historic wall be demolished and recommended changes to the original design. In April council agreed have to city staff negotiate costs for new architectural designs to accommodate the changes. The administration centre was expected to relieve the space shortage for city workers, who were scattered in five downtown buildings which cost the city $600,000 a year to lease. A twin project, turning the current city hall into the city's new courthouse, was also being investigated.

In April, City staff were authorized to negotiate an agreement with Adamson Associates to proceed with the city hall design. The budget for the architectural fee totalled $1.4 million; $200,000 for phase one (program development and schematic design; $200,000 for phase two (design development; and $1 million for phase three (construction documents).

By June, council had decided on a new plan for the city hall and concluded that the Adamson proposal had been the previous council's project. The new concept, with a courthouse located in the existing City Hall, and city staff in the Memorial Gardens portion of the new building was this council's concept. By the end of the month, council had chosen Moriyami & Teshima Architects to redesign the building. In October, at a public meeting, these architects revealed their plans for a 120,000 square foot (11,148 sq. m.), $35 million downtown administration centre and an adjacent $8.7-million provincial offences courthouse.

Early in 2006, Memorial Gardens had been demolished and plans for the new Civic Administration Centre had been modified. The city notified the Canada Green Building Council that it would seek a silver rating for the new city hall under the LEED (Leadership in Energy and Environmental Design) rating system for green buildings. The project's design included a green roof made of living plants on 50 per cent of the roof surface. Green roofs absorb rainwater or delay runoff from heavy rains, thus reducing demands on the city's storm water drainage system.

In June the city accepted Urbacon Buildings Corporation's bid for the new Civic Administration Centre at $32.5 million. Architect fees, underground parking and various other costs increased the total to $37.7 million. Although that was $610,000 above the originally budgeted cost, it was more than offset by the demolition of Memorial Gardens costing less than budgeted. Good news came in February 2007 when the Province of Ontario agreed to provide $800,000 to protect Guelph's heritage by preserving the facade of the former Royal Winter Fair building which had been discovered behind a wall when demolishing Memorial Gardens. It would be incorporated into the new Civic Administration Centre complex.

By the end of 2008, it was becoming obvious that Urbacon was not going to meet the completion deadline negotiated with the city. The city claimed that the construction company was responsible for many delays while Urbacon blamed the city for issuing too many change orders. Finally in October 30, 2008 the City of Guelph hired a new contractor for its city hall project, Alberici Constructors Ltd. to finish the job begun by Urbacon. The site was sealed by Guelph Police and Urbacon employees were denied entry and told to clear their belongings from the site.

A month after being fired, Urbacon filed a $19 million breach of contract lawsuit against the city. The city responded a month later with a $5 million counterclaim against Urbacon and a similar suit against Aviva Insurance Company, which the city alleged was obliged to indemnify the city from damages. The city was then directed to deposit more than $3.2 million with the court as part of its ongoing legal dispute with Urbacon Buildings Corp. The money had been part of a "holdback" fund held by the city, but subcontractors on the project brought a motion seeking to have the city deposit the funds with the court. During construction, the city held back 10 per cent of payments, a standard approach to protect against potential liens. These holdback payments are typically paid out on successful completion of a project. Part of Alberici's responsibility was to work with the consultant team to prepare a list of deficiencies in construction that happened under Urbacon's supervision. Meanwhile, twenty subcontractors filed liens against the new administrative building for outstanding wages after Urbacon was fired. Nine subcontractors filed statements of claim against the city.

2009

Alberici Constructors Ltd. finally delivered their timetable which forecast that city staff would be moved in and interior work completed by the end of March. Their cost had not deviated too far from initial projections. With architects' fees, fixtures and other expenditures, plus $2 million to demolish the former Memorial Gardens, the latest commitment was $52.3 million. Local gadfly, Gerry Barker pointed out in his *Mercury* column that:

> "This project's costs have escalated from the original contract price of $42 million to $52.3 million, including the yet to be completed old city hall renovation. But wait, there's more. Council has decided to streetscape and do associated roadwork in the area in front of the civic complex for an additional $8 million. This doesn't even take into account possible court awards arising from that Urbacon lawsuit. Don't forget, too, the legal fees to defend the action, cost unknown."

His views tended to reflect those of a number of former councillors in the Kate Quarrie administration which was replaced by that of Karen Farbridge who was elected in 2006 and returned again in 2010.

Discussions in council again turned to the ultimate location of the Provincial Offences Court which remained in the former Eaton Centre. Some suggested that using the old city hall for a court would consolidate city staff in the new "Civic Square"; would allow the heritage features of the building to be restored and protected; would ensure the "prominence and dignity" of the facility; and would provide a permanent home for the court within a city-owned facility. While the cost of the court project was to be split evenly between the city and Wellington County, if it didn't proceed the city would pay $3.44 million and the county wouldn't contribute anything because a new court facility had not been provided.

On May 22 the City of Guelph announced that it had hired construction management firm Collaborative Structures Ltd. of Cambridge to convert Guelph's historic, 152-year-old city hall at 59 Carden St. into the new home of Guelph's

Provincial Offences court. The same company recently managed the renovation of the Dominion Public Building (Guelph's former post office) at 138 Wyndham St. N., now Wellington County's social services offices. The old city hall served Guelph from 1856 to 2009 and is a National Historic Site designated under the *Ontario Heritage Act*.

Renovations of the old city hall at 59 Carden Street started in May 2010 and revealed many of the building's original features such as tin ceilings, cast iron columns, windows, cornices and archways. Most were restored or replicated during the renovation process. Judicial chambers were located in a new addition at the rear of the building and allow barrier-free access to all courtrooms. The main courtroom features a barrier-free workstation for the Clerk of the Court on the same level as the Justice. Guelph's Provincial Offences Court began operation at 59 Carden on August 3, 2010 while work continued inside the building.

By September 2009, substantial progress had been made on the new Civic Administration building and it was officially opened on the nineteenth to praise from citizens and councillors. Citizens would no longer have to have to ascertain which of five buildings to visit to conduct business with the city. Formerly, city staff were scattered among offices at several downtown addresses. All were now consolidated in the new facility. It had also been decided that Guelph's new Civic Square would have an artificial outdoor rink and a changing pavilion.

2010

After the new city hall was finished, plans released by the city indicated that another building would be constructed next to an artificial ice skating rink in the new civic square. This "pavilion" would house public washrooms, lockers and benches in different sections behind thick tempered-glass walls facing Carden Street. Even though the city hall building had been completed, much additional construction was scheduled for the square between the new city hall and Carden Street. Unfortunately, numerous delays and endless construction noise, dirt and traffic made life very difficult for established merchants on Carden street.

By the end of the year, shop keepers on Carden street were divided in their assessment of the construction problems. Loss of parking as a result of all the construction downtown had been offset by the city's decision to offer two-hour free parking in the Wilson Street Parking Lot. Merchants said that the new square and streetscape were going to be even more beautiful than before work started. As construction dragged on through the winter and spring, some stores experienced major losses of business and reactions became considerably more negative.

In December, the city faced another legal challenge arising from the construction of the Civic Centre. In an email to the mayor, Irwin Seating Company asked to be paid $27,000 for manufacturing and installing the 151 seats. They suggested that they remove the seats since they had not been remunerated. Mayor Karen Farbridge replied that Irwin Seating Company's contract was with Urbacon and not with the City, so they should pursue payment from them.

2011

Having endured many months of construction in front of their shops, Carden street merchants were becoming increasingly discontent with the disruptions. The Hockey Shop's sales were "down drastically" from September through November before rebounding in December when Carden Street was reopened for the winter. On some days you couldn't see the store because of high dirt piles on Carden Street. By May frustration increased because paving stones from the USA were delayed past the street completion date. An Endicott, N.Y., company that makes the bricks had been having difficulty filling the city's "big order," and the city has been "pushing" for delivery. Hopefully the New York firm would deliver some of the paving bricks in mid-June and the rest in early July. By June, several retailers suggested that the city should compensate them for lost business.

After almost five years of disruption because of construction, one merchant was very close to laying off employees. Meanwhile, heavy rain had been slowing the necessary underground work. As a result a merchant began to play very loud music while another sent an email comparing city staff to the Three Stooges. It included a photo of the famous comedy trio and a suggestion that it depicted a city manager and "his expert team of planners" working on Carden Street construction projects. The email was sent to members of city council, to several city staff members, including the named manager and to some downtown businesses. In response, libel notices were issued on city letterhead by city solicitor Donna Jaques, asking that blog post be removed and that the sender email all recipients apologizing for the comparison. After considerable public outcry about the city's heavy-handed response, the libel notice was withdrawn and Mayor Farbridge spoke with the aggrieved merchant.

Carden street problems continued through the summer, especially when dirt covered the road. It was often closed, parking was not available and heavy machinery rumbled through the new civic square. New businesses were especially hard hit and the Carden Street Café closed on January 8, 2012. The owner of this iconic Guelph restaurant where many musicians including Jane Siberry got her start, attributed its demise to the Carden Street construction. The café also had a strong link to Hillside Festival with the two providing a venue for talented up-and-coming performers.

Fortunately for employees, after construction had ceased, a new restaurant opened in its place.

By June 2011, several city councillors had suggested that Carden Street merchants be reimbursed by the city for their business losses. They felt that those on Carden street had suffered more than any other merchants in downtown Guelph. Their street had been closed completely at times, work had dragged on far longer than expected and construction in the adjoining civic square had caused a great deal of noise, dirt and disruption. By July, some disgruntled merchants considered launching a class action suit against the city but in September, Council agreed to allocate $175,000 to be split equally for use by each of the 34 affected businesses on Wilson Street and Carden streets and part of Wyndham Street North, with each getting $5,000. The street still had not opened in August, but the city promised that one-way traffic would begin on August 13. On Sunday, December 18, Carden Street was finally completely re-opened to allow two-way traffic between Wilson Street and Wyndham Street, much to the relief of local merchants.

The Civic Square and Rink:Success!

During this period, City council had decided on more ambitious plans for a civic square in front of the new city hall. Additional delays occurred because the city re-tendered the contract for a pavilion with washrooms, change rooms and benches in front of city hall. The square would then include a skating rink and summer water feature funded primarily from fund raising and infrastructure stimulus dollars from the Federal and Provincial governments. The Nicholas Lambden Memorial Children's Foundation contributed $400,000 to the project, helping to make its construction possible. Nick was the boy who lost his life on an outdoor rink in 2007 so his parents supported the new rink in his memory. Late in 2011 when it opened, the rink became very popular, and in just a few days it quickly became the community gathering place that had been missing in Guelph's downtown.

By the beginning of 2012, reaction to the new rink and square was both positive and negative. Users and some Carden Street merchants were very pleased, making comments such as: "It's really nice to have an outdoor skating rink for kids. You can go whenever you want." and "To see Carden Street bustling again is pretty satisfying."The Hockey Shop Source for Sports on Carden Street had people stopping in to rent and buy skates. The owner asserted that "we have been blown away by the use it is getting" as pedestrians and skaters returned to his store. Others were not quite as happy because skaters and market patrons filled all Carden Street parking spots on Saturdays but did not patronize some local stores. They felt that skaters didn't notice the stores across from the square. Undoubtedly this problem will decline considerably when the ice has melted. By March break a warm spell closed the rink and we will have to await additional reaction from Carden Street merchants.

By summer 2012, the splash pad in the rink area was operating. It immediately became a magnet for children and their parents, especially during the hot days of June and July. It attracted many new people to Carden Street, but some merchants continued to complain that "splashers" were monopolizing parking spaces that should have been used by shoppers. Others attempted to attract the influx of additional people to their shops and restaurants. Clearly City Hall Square has been an outstanding success and now movies will be shown there in the evening. Whether this attraction hurts or benefits Carden Street merchants remains to be seen. Meanwhile, the vision of those promoting the square and new city hall seems to have been fulfilled.

Continuing Disputes with Urbacon

However, the city hall saga had not yet ended. The city and Urbacon Buildings Group   participated in two days of voluntary mediation in fall 2012 in an effort to resolve Urbacon's $20 million breach of contract suit against the city, and the city's $5 million counterclaim. Guelph filed a similar suit against Aviva Insurance Company, which the city alleged was obliged to indemnify the city from damages. The city alleged that it fired the builder because Urbacon repeatedly failed to meet the latest project completion target. In its lawsuit, Urbacon claimed that the delays were the fault of the city, citing hundreds of change-work orders issued by the city during the construction project. Deciding whether the city's work orders contributed substantially to, or caused the construction delays would seem to be the crux of what could become expensive litigation.

The City-Urbacon lawsuit was originally scheduled to be heard in Guelph's Superior Court on January 7, 2013 and run for three to four weeks. Eventually it was heard in Brampton at the Ontario Superior Court of Justice. It began on Jan. 22 and continued until late March with some gaps. Several supervisors with Urbacon testified that they were often at the site by 6 am., even on Saturdays and Sundays. They asserted that they had done everything possible to complete the project as agreed, but were constantly presented with change orders from the city. These interrupted the flow of the work and added many small projects to the ongoing construction so the building could not be completed as contracted.

Delays in the construction schedule meant that work often started and stopped abruptly and would be done weeks, sometimes months later than anticipated. In September

2008 Urbacon workers were denied entry onto the construction site by police. They were given four hours to move their belongings from site, but police would not open the gate, so they passed things over the fence. Accounts by Urbacon witnesses suggested that the city had taken draconian actions when replacing Urbacon with Alberici Constructors Ltd. and had not treated Urbacon fairly.

The city was directed by the court to deposit more than $3.2 million with the court as part of its ongoing legal dispute with Urbacon Buildings Corp. This was part of a "holdback" fund held by the city, but subcontractors on the project brought a motion seeking to have the city deposit these funds with the court. During construction, the city held back 10 per cent of payments, a standard approach to protect against potential liens. Such holdback payments are typically paid out on successful completion of a project. Because of disputes on the city hall project, which came to a head in the fall of 2008 when the city fired Urbacon, the holdback was not released by the city and would not be released until lawsuits were settled.

During January and February 2013, Superior Court in Brampton heard testimony from both Urbacon and the City of Guelph. Guelph's lawyer claimed that Urbacon worked on things that weren't required for Guelph's new city hall to be "substantially complete," causing the builder to miss its deadline to finish construction of the complex. In a meeting with Moriyama & Teshima Architects, Urbacon said that it would need an additional 45 to 60 working days past its Aug. 15, 2008 deadline because of several critical changes requested by the city, which meant that construction wouldn't be finished until Oct. 20, 2008.

Two weeks before the project was terminated there were concerns about Urbacon's construction schedule. Moriyama & Teshima Architects wanted an updated schedule that kept track of lost time due to delays, but it became more difficult since additional work was constantly being added to the project. By the beginning of the court case in 2013, the City of Guelph doubled to $10 million the amount it was seeking in damages from Urbacon Buildings Group Corp. The only issue to be determined was whether Guelph had the legal right to end the contract and order Urbacon off the site. The $10 million being sought by the city was a counterclaim to the $20 million that Urbacon demanded from the city.

In an opening statement, Urbacon lawyer Marco Drudi claimed that the evidence received from the city was questionable and alleged that many of the issues that Guelph wishes to dispute were absent from the notice of default. Lawyer Derek Schmuck, representing the city, said that he presented Urbacon with five binders containing 346 documents, hand-picked from the thousands of documents of correspondence between the city and Urbacon since 2006.

Drudi focused most of his opening statement on whether cancelling Urbacon's $42-million construction contract was justified. He said that the main issue was the time at which the project would be substantially complete. When the project was terminated on Sept. 19, 2008 the focus shifted to the roughly $500,000 in deficiencies. By then, Urbacon had spent two years on the project and was roughly 45 to 60 days from completion. An extension was negotiated that would have made the building completion by mid-August instead. This deadline was later extended to early September to accommodate changes to the design. On Sept. 19, 2008, the city terminated the contract and Urbacon was ordered from the site.

Burlington's Alberici Constructors Ltd. was subsequently hired to finish the city hall project, while Cambridge's Collaborative Structures Ltd. was retained to renovate the former city hall. Two days of mediation in September failed to resolve the dispute.

The trial became very complex, with arguments about interim billings and progress reports. Urbacon claimed that many critical changes occurred during the last third of the project and that these late changes disrupted the schedule. As subcontractors began interior work and completed finishing work, new issues were raised and more answers were needed. The roughly 600 requests for information submitted by Urbacon throughout the project were deemed excessive by the city. Urbacon's lawyer claimed that Urbacon could not meet the deadline because the city also requested a last-minute change involving the installation of the Novec fire suppression system. The city countered that there were change orders because the sub-contractors were not performing and didn't like to work during the winter. The trial dragged on after a two week break and a verdict was not expected until October 2013.

Judge's Ruling on Urbacon Suit

At the end of March, 2014, Judge MacKenzie ruled that the City did not have the right to terminate the contractor hired to build City Hall and Guelph's Provincial Offences Court, despite the City having done so with the best interests of Guelph taxpayers in mind.

April 10, 2014

Guelph will pay $6.635 million to Urbacon Buildings Group Corp. to settle the City Hall construction company's wrongful dismissal case out of court. In addition, Guelph's legal costs in the case are already $2.23 million. The city said that there are sufficient funds in reserves to finance the settlement. By reaching a settlement out of court, the city avoided additional legal costs. The money will come from the city's capital financing and not result in an increase in property taxes. Marco Mancini, CEO of Urbacon stated that it is pleased that, notwithstanding the issues that separated them, Urbacon and the city were able to come together and resolve their disputes.

Judge MacKenzie suggested that city staff exerted too much influence over the consultant, Moriyama and Teshima, whose job was to liaise between the city and Urbacon as a neutral party. He also found Murray McCrae's testimony to be less than credible. McCrae was the manager of corporate properties who oversaw the project for the city, and he was the city's prime witness at trial. His actions "culminating in the notices of default and termination created a seismic shift in the contractual liability landscape. This shift fatally undermined Guelph's position that its termination of Urbacon was justified in the circumstances," wrote the judge in his decision.

ROWDIES IN THE CENTRAL BUSINESS DISTRICT

During the last few years, downtown Guelph has seen a major influx of bars and large drinking establishments. As retail business have relocated or closed, developers have taken advantage of vacancies to create new spaces where bands can perform and alcohol can be served. A number of these occupy very large areas and many sell food as well as alcohol. Zoning by-laws enable the city to control some aspects of the local "bar scene" but unfortunately are ineffective at controlling the number of patrons using these facilities. As a result, Guelph has become a favourite drinking destination for local students and for many customers from other communities. The problem of rowdy drinkers, particularly on Thursday, Friday and Saturday nights has become a prominent topic of discussion by citizens and politicians and a major enforcement issue for Guelph's Police services. As the years have passed, the problems seem to have increased despite numerous attempts to control the number and behaviour of the drinkers. The following discussion highlights the major issues and attempted solutions to this continuing quandary.

Guelph Police services established a special Core Patrol as a pilot project in 1997 after a task force of city and police officials and merchants discussed approaches to deal with rowdyism, fights and vandalism caused by 3,000 bar patrons spilling out onto downtown streets during peak bar hours. During this project, a special team of officers was dedicated to downtown. This project was extended in various forms thereafter, but results were mixed as the number of bars and drunks continued to increase. By 2001, a "universal barred list" was to be circulated among bars to keep out hard-core undesirables who fought with police, sexually harassed wait staff or became violent with other patrons. The initiative was developed after a meeting among eight downtown bars, including the big ones (Van Gogh's Ear, the Palace, Club

Denim) the Guelph Police, the Downtown Board of Management and liquor licence authorities.

Then a plan to establish a "zero tolerance" approach to offences in the downtown was developed by the Guelph Police unit in charge of downtown policing. Problems identified in the downtown were panhandlers, drinking in public, urinating in public, rowdiness, large crowds as the bars close and lack of transport to remove people after the bars closed. Littering of food containers from late night food vendors, graffiti and other property damage, skateboarders, and a growing street level drug trade exacerbated the problem. The evidence of drunks' complete lack of consideration was often evident on Saturday mornings in the form of scattered half-full food containers and vomit on sidewalks, the smell of urine on the sides of buildings and occasionally broken windows. In addition to being very unpleasant for pedestrians and merchants, cleaning these messes and controlling drunken crowds was becoming very expensive for the city, as was replacing broken windows by merchants.

Fights, assaults, robberies, noise and mess were blamed on downtown bar patrons, many of them University of Guelph students, and indirectly on the bar operators. On the other hand, crowds of drunks during the summer are often as large as when the university was in session, leading to the conclusion that out-of-town patrons plus non-university youth contributed considerably to the "rowdy" problem. As the years passed, additional remedies were attempted to control the situation.

By 2002, downtown bars began taking other measures. They generally agreed to stop serving large pitchers of beer near closing time. This should reduce the last-minute binging and prevent patrons from lurching onto the streets with their brains swimming in alcohol and bladders bursting.

The bars were also not allowing patrons to purchase large rounds of alcohol late at night. Such initiatives were a result of regular meetings among bar owners and managers, the Downtown Board of Management, Guelph Police and officials from the Liquor Licence Board of Ontario.

2003

Downtown Problems and Solutions

In 2003, Guelph Police, University of Guelph and Guelph Transit met "to try to work out some of the final details" of who would pay for policing, and the initiation of late night buses running from downtown to the university. A zoning review in response to an application for two new bars suggested that they be limited to 380 square metres. Existing bars would be grandfathered, a status automatically given to uses in place before new zoning rules are passed. Since the mid 1990s, the number and sizes of bars in downtown Guelph continued to expand, so that approximately 5,000 people could be accommodated within the core area at licensed sites.

Increasing late night crowds continued to stress police resources. At a trial in 2003, police officers and bar staff described an especially tense Friday night after the last day of exams in 2002. A rock thrower in a crowd of 400 to 500 people at about 2:30 that Saturday morning was identified by an employee outside the nightclub, Van Gogh's Ear. The judge also noted that the problem of students passing out in flower beds and urinating on public buildings is quite different from the challenge posed by the hardened crowd of drug users and gang members from Toronto and elsewhere, who consider Guelph a good place to party. It was suggested that there would be shootings and stabbings in Guelph's bars as crowds continued to increase. During the first six months of the year, Guelph Police used 40 "levels of force" during 34 incidents, and officers pointed firearms seven times, each of them for the purpose of self-protection and arrest. They also drew a firearm once to prevent the escape of a robbery suspect. No Guelph Police officer had discharged a firearm in the line of duty that year.

One observer made the following comment: "It's not like we're the Niagara Region, touting all the local wineries, or even Kitchener, with its annual beer and brat fest disguised as a heritage event. This is sedate little Guelph, a peaceful university town that used to train farmers, for gosh sakes. How did we get to the state of having too many bars, emptying their inebriated patrons out into the street at 2 a.m., who in turn empty themselves into the street shortly after, leaving a toxic cocktail of partly digested Chinese food and urine-soaked doorways to greet the morning's downtown shoppers. And we have to wonder why people would rather shop at the mall? Instead of having a nice place where young people can learn that you can enjoy a drink and have a pleasant evening with friends without getting sloshed, we have got a dark and unfriendly place where underage trainee punks can get lessons on boorish inebriated behaviour." Clearly the problem was becoming worse and called for more drastic counter-measures.

A commentator suggested that Guelph police would have to change their tactics to control drunken crowds, especially when they were greatly outnumbered and facing gangs that disregarded their authority. With close to a 10,000 seat capacity in the downtown core and two new bars on the way, Guelph's downtown attracts local people and those from outside the city. Many bars in downtown Guelph continue to over-serve their patrons with few being cut off from alcohol while others take a short walk to the next bar to continue drinking. Remedies could include a much higher level of coordination between police and staff of downtown bars, increased visibility of officers to defuse situations, and a permanent task-force to develop a long-term plan to address the issues that have been reported in the local press.

Another commentator suggested that instead of the police deploying a heavily armed and very expensive tactical unit to control crowds, pub owners should pay for crowd control by off-duty officers as happens at festivals and other large gatherings. Guelph Councillor Cathy Downer proposed that cameras be installed since police cannot see half the fighting, public urinating and defecating, yelling, screaming and assaults. Guelph Police were not so sure that camera-based security was a good idea. Responses to incidents recorded by cameras would be reactions to crime when there should be efforts to prevent crime. And there was the question of who would monitor the cameras. Others worried about surveillance and privacy issues. Earlier bar closings were also suggested.

By the middle of the summer, tougher measures were instituted. These included banning unruly bar patrons from all downtown bars; issuing fewer warnings in favour of more tickets, arrests or charges; staging more bar blitzes to deal with overcrowding, serving to intoxicated patrons or minors, or breaking the smoking bylaw. Police told bar owners to expect more blitzes and more officer visibility in September. Then University of Guelph's 17,000 students (including 1,100 more first year students than last year) would swell the ranks of downtown's estimated 6,000 bar patrons. Police were also working with bars to create one "banned person" list. (*Estimates of downtown's bar capacity varied widely in news reports during 2003*). Guelph Police posted notices at all drinking establishments indicating that they would be checking identification, and no tolerance will be shown to under age drinkers using fake or borrowed ID. Bars will continue to give fake or borrowed identification (usually a driver's licence) to the police.

The Magic Bus

On April 4, 2003, student organizations at the university began free Friday and Saturday service from downtown to the campus after bar closings. This was an extension of the University of Guelph Magic Bus programme that picked up students in front of City Hall every half hour on late nights and Sundays. During a spring pilot project, cab companies "were hopping" with all their cars being utilized, even when the free buses were operating, so they did not suffer lost revenue. Occasionally drunken riders became rowdy or carried food onto the free buses but such behaviour was discouraged by drivers and police. This service relieved pressure on besieged taxi drivers but seemed to do little to discourage drunken rowdies in the core. In October, another large club opened, contributing additional bar seats in the core.

In 2004 a new Guelph Transit route began to run Friday, Saturday and Sunday mornings from 1 a.m. to 4 a.m., after the success of the Magic Bus, which previously shuttled university students from downtown to the campus. That service was not operated by Guelph Transit, but by students at the university and the Downtown Board of Management. At one time Guelph Transit did offer a late-night service, which was scrapped because of all the vandalism. By September 15, with only one weekend of operation, the new late-night bus service was being judged a success by Guelph Police. On the other hand, the Amalgamated Transit Union Local 1189, suggested that drivers were worried about vandalism and the possibility of violent situations occurring on the bus because passengers had been drinking. Safety features such as silent alarms to summon the police were suggested to alleviate their concerns, but were determined to be impracticable.

Drivers' fears were validated in October when a driver was

assaulted and ten University of Guelph students were beating each other with hockey sticks, golf clubs and beer bottles on the street. Early in November the University late-night bus service was suspended indefinitely after a rider punched a driver in the head several times early Sunday morning. The bus service, paid for by the university's student government and operated by Guelph Transit, included a shuttle between the university and downtown, and a bus from the university into the city's residential areas. Shortly thereafter the students began their own late bus service until the issue of Guelph Transit drivers' safety could be addressed. In December another GTC driver was assaulted for refusing to take a passenger beyond the end of his route. The perpetrator was subsequently arrested and charged with assault to which he pleaded guilty.

Problems in the core continued as a bar patron lost the sight in one eye as the result of a brawl among other drinkers. A thrown bottle missed its intended target and struck the 20-year-old Guelph victim. He was rushed to Guelph General Hospital, and then transferred to Victoria Hospital in London where he underwent two operations, which couldn't save the sight in his eye. Local bar owners expressed remorse and anger at this violent and stupid act which encouraged the city to take additional measures against drunken rowdyism.

Early in February, the city announced that it would extend the moratorium on new bars. By this time there was enough capacity in licensed establishments in the core area to serve close to 10,000 people, not including the River Run Centre and Guelph Sports and Entertainment Centre with a total combined additional capacity of almost 8,000. Despite the one-year moratorium on downtown drinking establishments, a number of new establishments were allowed in April 2003 because they had applied before the ban took effect. In April 2004 the moratorium on new downtown drinking establishments was extended for another year to allow the city's planning department more time to study ways to combat excessive night-time rowdiness. The new bylaw did not affect the numerous existing bars in downtown Guelph, where indoor capacity is 1,300 patrons at Club Denim and 600 at the two next-largest, Van Gogh's Ear and Trapper's Alley.

A legal loophole had allowed establishments to connect to neighbouring bars as well as to bars above the first floor, exceeding the legal limit. The bar ban encountered some opposition from owners of establishments that did not serve alcohol late at night and generated considerable discussion about other ways to contain and control Guelph's rowdy night life. The city had become a bonanza for bar owners with huge drinking establishments downtown, many of which have little more decor than a barn or abandoned warehouse. Councillors and business owners generally agreed that Guelph, with its thinly-spread police force must somehow curtail new big-box bars. Discussions also continued about the best methods to protect bus drivers from rowdy riders. The city's finance and administration committee discovered that it costs the city $279,000 annually to clean up the downtown core and another $134,000 for extra police patrols on Thursday, Friday and Saturday nights. The committee asked city staff to find ways of incorporating those costs into the business licence fees for bars and restaurants. This suggestion was rejected by restaurant owners who noted that they were not responsible for drunks scattering food late at night.

By the end of the year, the planning committee passed recommendations to reduce new licensed establishments to 190 people and 230 square metres, and to restrict bars to the first floor of buildings. Current regulations, adopted in 1996, allowed bars too occupy 380 square metres with a maximum occupancy of 500 people. However city staff noted that only one municipality (Ottawa) of nine surveyed had size restrictions for bars.

2005 - 2007 Continuing Problems

By 2005 no solution had been found to control bar sizes and councillors continued to argue about how much should be charged for licencing fees. A small business owner pointed out that his fee is as much as that for a bar with 500 seats and that several licencing categories should be established to make fees fair to all. As the year wore on, attention was diverted to the problem of public urination. With no municipal urinals and thousands of drunks with brimming bladders pouring out of pubs after 2:00 am. walls and alleys and even streets had become substitutes for appropriate urinals. After much heated debate about the concept of public "pissoirs" and even more debate about their location, council considered a pilot project to ascertain whether such facilities would be used, but took no action for several years. Additional debate occurred because the design of proposed urinals would not easily accommodate women. Despite the seriousness of the issue, council's debates on the matter became almost comical.

Before urinals were considered seriously, the city was advised to pass a new bylaw to control public urination. Police Chief Rob Davis said that officers had been ticketing people for urinating and defecating in the city's core, only to have charges eventually thrown out in court because the current bylaw covered only highways and bridges. He recommended that the city follow the lead of Waterloo, which passed a bylaw prohibiting any "fouling" (spitting, urinating or defecating) of city owned and privately owned land, vacant land, highway, road, sidewalk, pedestrian way, water feature or boulevard.

While pissoirs were being discussed, the issue of the safety of drivers of the "Magic Bus" emerged again after continued rider rowdyism. Some drivers had food thrown at them, others were verbally abused and others were spat upon. Many doubted whether the cameras that had been installed in late night buses were really helping since they didn't seem to deter bad behaviour among drunks. One driver ferrying riders from the University of Guelph to the downtown called for assistance after several passengers refused to quiet down and one allegedly reached over the driver to open the bus door. Meanwhile, taxi drivers also felt threatened.

The issue of taxi cabs was discussed at police services board meetings, when residents complained that they have had to deal for years with the noise of drunken bar patrons congregating near the Surrey Street office of Red Top Taxi. The police services board had passed a motion to ensure that employees were safe, allowing taxi companies to lock their office doors at night while still providing service. Bar patrons, however, continued to congregate at the office, banging on the door and causing noise problems for nearby neighbours. This problem was not caused by the taxi company, but is a consequence of so many bars being together in such a concentrated area, leaving the nearby residential areas and the police to deal with large groups of students trying to get back to campus on weekends.

It appeared that 2,000 to 3,000 people needed transportation out of downtown at the weekend and that the existing arrangements were not working. This prompted police and city staff to draft a proposal to install three late night taxi stands downtown; one on Carden Street near city hall, another south of St. George's Square on Wyndham and a third on Macdonell near the Greyhound Bus Terminal. By 2007, City council had approved a plan to set up these late night downtown taxi stands to resolve noise complaints from people living near taxi company offices. Once the taxi stands were established, Red Top Taxi would no longer pick up passengers at its Surrey Street office, but erect signs directing people to the taxi stands. It was hoped that the stands would make it easier for people to get a taxi, as it reduced the necessity to call a taxi or go to a taxi company office or flag down a taxi.

Unfortunately, the taxi stands did not solve Guelph's late night pick-up problems. Some drivers continued to pick up patrons on the street instead of returning to the stands while taxis continued to be "swarmed" as soon as they stopped. Many drivers were still afraid that they or their vehicles would be damaged by out-of-control drunks wanting rides. Some proponents argued that more stands would be a good solution, but the controversy continued. Drivers had had doors kicked in and regular riders living downtown now had to find a taxi at a stand instead of phoning for a pick-up.

Meanwhile the "pissoir saga" continued! Guelph police had been cracking down on people from the weekend bar crowd, who felt that downtown doorways and alleys were appropriate locations at which to relieve themselves. They were issuing $240 fines to anyone caught spitting, urinating or defecating on sidewalks or in alleys, but no new facilities to accommodate full bladders had been constructed.

Outdoor Patios and Longer Bar Hours

By 2007, discussion had turned to the prospect of additional outdoor patios and longer drinking hours for bars. The Night Life Task Force that had been formed in the spring of 2007 to address late-night bar and food seller issues continued to consider options. Several individuals including restaurant owners and the Downtown Board of Management felt that Guelph's collection of sidewalk patios attracted a diverse crowd of people from different age groups, which has a positive impact on the core. Longer hours would bring additional people in the evening and create a really vibrant culture downtown. Patio owners were required to clear the decks at 11 p.m. and are allowed to operate only from April to October. A recommended pilot project would extend patio service until midnight, with a closing time of 12:45 a.m., and allow them to operate year-round. While it remains to be seen what volume of traffic there would be at a mid-January patio, more understandable is the impact of an extra hour of drinking. On the other hand, the police said that they had enough on their plate without worrying about rowdy people who might confront other customers sitting on patios and minding their own business. They felt that 11 pm. was late enough for patios to remain open.

The debate continued for some time. Proponents of longer hours argued that there is a distinguishing factor between restaurants and bars. Those who would frequent patios allowed to stay open would not simply sit and drink alcohol. Most of the restaurants that have patios in the downtown attract those who want a drink or two with a quiet meal, but do not intend to get drunk. Bars that that attract drunken rowdyism must be targeted, starting with staggered closing hours. Making sure that thousands of people partying downtown don't all spill out onto the streets at the same time is a better step to take than keeping people who want to have a nice meal with a drink from doing so past 11 p.m. During this debate, a new Irish Pub which had support and opposition was proposed for downtown. It eventually opened.

In 2008, the debate about additional bars and special levies on those open after midnight continued. There were suggestions that only those establishments that are open after midnight should be subject to a special fee. However, it has been difficult to identify, with any degree of certainty, which business establishments are contributing to the current rowdiness. A bar stool tax had been proposed but was not supported by bar owners, although some suggested that only the big bars should pay. Opponents of the tax argued that their business had already been hurt by no smoking regulations and the admission of younger students to university. One councillor proposed more litter bins downtown, or building round-the-clock restrooms. Bar owners were unambiguous that they were already overwhelmed by various levels of government regulations, but felt that those who weren't already doing so could contribute by employing their own cleanup crews on Sunday morning sidewalks.

Municipal Affairs and Housing minister Jim Watson said that he was concerned about newspaper reports of drunkenness, rowdyism, vandalism, fighting and assaults, including a December column titled, "People won't want drunks on their doorsteps." He gave one piece of advice to the city, urging it and the University of Guelph to combine to help curb drinking and rowdyism by students. Students living off campus could be invited to an annual neighbourhood dinner at a community centre and to discuss their rights as students and responsibilities as good citizens "not to have out-of-control parties or yelling at two o'clock in the morning." After a front window at Wimpy's was smashed, there were renewed calls for a downtown crackdown. At the same time, downtown residents continued to complain about nighttime rowdiness, broken windows, the occasional brawl and chicken bones and leftover noodles, both fresh and partly digested, lining city streets on weekend mornings. The Downtown Guelph Business Association passed a resolution opposing the levying of fees on specific types of businesses, which it called "differential taxation."

Ultimately, city council decided to embrace a "co-operative" approach to late-night downtown problems, rather than trying to pass extra policing and cleanup costs onto bars and restaurants that are open after midnight. This meant that extra costs estimated at about $174,000 annually; $125,000 for policing and $49,000 for cleanup services by city staff, would continue to be paid through the city's general tax base. After considerable debate and a tied vote, council decided that these expenses would be covered from the regular tax base.

2009 – The Year of the Urinals

Considerable debate accompanied a staff proposal to introduce an "open-air urinal" in the vicinity of Macdonell and Wyndham streets "to evaluate its effectiveness and to assess public acceptance of this type of public facility." Evidence from Britain indicated that they had been effective but that they were not always appropriate for women. Guelph's police chief thought that women could use the outdoor urinals and supported a pilot project to test their effect on public urination. He added that the problem boiled down to the fact that some persons had no compunctions about "whipping it out"on the street and going right there.

Some suggested that the private sector must address this apparent service need in Guelph. They argued that "pay-per-potty" facilities could thrive given the present situation and lack of free toilet options downtown. Couldn't entrepreneurs market and maintain "late-night, portable johnny-on-the-spot loos?" They felt that this "beats the crude, public, coed alternative going before council for consideration." Others argued in favour of public open urinals, citing examples such as China, were urinals are often no more private than a trough running through the middle of an open room. Public toilets dot the streets of Paris, Amsterdam and Tokyo. Even here in Guelph porta-potties are used at every public event in the city; "they're at the edge of soccer fields and ball diamonds, and no one blinks an eye." Supporters of public funding pointed out that city police had issued $240 tickets 131 times under the anti-fouling bylaw in the past 12 months, That's $31,440 paid by the "pee-ers" themselves; far more than the $700 to $1,200 a week the city expects to spend during the summer urinal trial.

Others argued that the "booze barn owners" should pay the bill for toilet facilities for bar patrons. Why not mandate that alcohol be removed from the tables after last call but that the doors must remain open and washrooms accessible until the downtown empties? Debate raged about who should pay for pissoirs, whether women would or should use them and whether they were really necessary. Given that there are no public toilets in downtown Guelph and that bar facilities are not accessible after they close, council decided to go ahead with their "pilot pissoir project" in the summer of 2009. Downtown Guelph Business Association executive director Jennifer Mackie supported the trial. She noted that the trial period would help the municipality to decide whether public urinals should continue to be provided next year before public washrooms were built. One councillor stated that "We're going to count the litres," adding that every one collected in the urinals is one less befouling sidewalks and alleys.

Urinals were installed in September, and during their first three weeks, the units collected more than 2,400 litres of urine. The estimate is that this volume of urine represented about 6,000 trips to the pissoirs, removing a considerable amount of urine from walls, sidewalks and alleys. A lot of urine in the trial was collected while bars and other businesses were open, but much more probably entered the pissoirs' tanks after restaurant and bar washrooms in the core had closed. Despite their apparent success, critics of the urinals disliked their appearance, location and smell while others continued to complain that they were unfair to women. Many breathed a great sigh of relief when they were removed in November.

Discussion of urinals continued in 2010 when the experiment was not continued. Public toilets were to be installed eventually by the rink at the new city hall and museum. There was unanimity that the city needed twenty-four hour, seven day a week toilets, but there was no assurance that this would happen. Supervision was a major factor as was its potential cost. It had not yet been decided whether toilets would also be installed at the new Carden Street transit hub.

In addition to core problems, residents of the university area pointed out that they too suffered from student rowdyism. "What about those 'crazy kids' when they get dropped off by the buses at the university and come wandering through the neighbourhoods shouting, singing, swearing, puking, dropping food containers, knocking over mail boxes, stealing lawn ornaments and otherwise having a wonderful time?" Meanwhile, police had cracked down on core offenders. They followed through with charges against party animals in the downtown's wild-west entertainment district. Infractions were costly, with public urination and littering costing offenders $365 per conviction. Being drunk in public lightens the wallet by $65. Underage drinking comes with a $125 penalty, as does carrying fake identification or guzzling open liquor on the sidewalk.

Despite the pissoir experiment and police crackdowns, weekend nights downtown continued to be rowdy. On Saturday morning food, containers, vomit, urine and wrappers continued to foul sidewalks before street cleaners arrived. Problems continued into 2011 and 2012 despite all the efforts of council and the police. Several new restaurants opened, a popular coffee shop tripled in size and fights in bars resulted in several injuries. In one instance an offender was charged and taken to court; in another, a lawsuit ensued. The president of the university expressed his concern and dismay at the behaviour of a "small percentage of students". Police tried handing out candy suckers to revellers as a way to approach them in a non-threatening way. This may not have stopped any rowdiness, but it did give police a pleasant way to interact with students. The safety of cab drivers remained an issue that had not yet been resolved.

There was one bright spot in 2012. After major problems on St. Patrick's Day 2011, the city was ready for trouble on the same day in 2012. It took extra precautions, but was surprised when things went very well in 2012. There were armies of young people dressed in green traipsing throughout the south end of the city, but there were also many young people hosting up to 30,000 guests at College Royal. St. Patrick's Day kept the local police busy, beginning at 10:10 a.m. with a noise complaint. Nevertheless, the campus was teeming with happy families enjoying College Royal and the "bad scene" of 2011 was not repeated in 2012. Downtown continued to evolve as an application was made for a grant to assist the former Diplomat Hotel to become a modern "Boutique Hotel". This renovation and a number of new or improved restaurants should improve the "tone" of the area.

In August 2012, as part of a five week pilot project, city council decided to ban cars from parts of Wyndham and Macdonell streets from 10 pm. till 4 am. on Thursday through Saturday nights to make it easier for police to control the crowds leaving bars. This was also intended to reduce the possibility of collisions between cars and pedestrians. Portable toilets appropriate for both sexes (rather than open pissoirs) were to be installed in the parking lot beside the Sun Sun restaurant to accommodate late night revellers. One unit will be able to accommodate persons in wheelchairs. The city's share of these costs would be about $10,000.

A very large police presence was planned with downtown patrols being augmented by officers from other parts of the city. Bus and taxi transportation out of the "party area" were to be improved, with taxi stands patrolled by private security guards at Cork and Wyndham Streets and on Fountain Street across from the police station. Rather than being city employees, the security guards would be paid by the Downtown Business Association. It was hoped that they would be able to protect cab drivers who had experienced major problems with the last taxi stand experiment. Better regulated taxi stands should also reduce the frequency of drunks attempting to hail cruising taxis. The university late night bus would now depart from the new central bus depot on Carden Street. It was hoped that these measures would reduce "jostling" leading to fights among people on crowded sidewalks and empty the core more quickly. Some taxi drivers remained afraid and sceptical about the taxi stands but agreed to try them with the new security in place. As with all other initiatives or experiments, these measures met with opposition from some councillors, citizens and business people.

On the weekend of 7 to 10 September, the experiment worked rather well. Many students gathered downtown but few incidents were reported. Some taxi drivers continued to pick up people who flagged them down rather than using the taxi stands. The private security at the taxi stands prevented any problems for those who did use them. The portable urinals in the parking lot seemed to reduce public urination on streets and in alleys. A number of drivers either ignored or didn't see the no parking signs in the restricted areas and had to retrieve their vehicles from a parking lot to which they were towed without charge.

On October 7, 2013 a city staff report on the results of Project Safe Semester said that it was not necessary to explore the possibility of a bar stool tax to help fund policing downtown's late night bar scene. Project Safe Semester was a pilot initiative begun in 2012 with police, Downtown Guelph

Business Association, bars, the city and the University of Guelph cooperating to make downtown Guelph safer and more orderly during the first five weekends of the university school year.

A staff report on the first Project Safe Semester in 2012 called it a "resounding success." The report showed that in 2012 the crime rate in downtown Guelph dropped 44 per cent over the same period in 2010, when there was no special initiative in place. The Late Night Task Force agreed that the pilot was a success and called for the continuation of the pilot project in future years. It did not recommend further exploration of a bar stool tax.

Project Safe Semester cost $25,000. The city paid $20,000 of that and the Downtown Guelph Business Association the rest. It included a more visible police presence, the closing of the busiest section of downtown to vehicles for several hours, portable washrooms and more orderly taxi stations and bus service. This initiative appears to have solved or at least greatly reduced rowdyism and crime during annual University Homecoming celebrations. In Fall 2014, the project was continued, a number of cars were towed and charges laid for public urination. Pissoirs had not yet been installed, but rowdyism had been decreased in the core. The program continued till the end of September. The question of public washrooms remained unresolved.

There has been some controversy about bus passes for University students. Each semester, students paid a total of $105.10 for an unlimited bus pass and late night bus services which ran on the busy weekends. The late night service provides a shuttle service of six buses leaving the downtown core throughout the weekend to ensure that students get home safely for an affordable cost. The city pays for three of of these six buses, while the CSA and student fees absorb the remaining cost of this service.

2014 More Discussion of Public Washrooms

The shortage of public washrooms in the downtown core has contributed greatly to an ongoing public fouling problem. Over the past two years, the sides of buildings that received the most urine were in the downtown. In 2013, officers responded to 85 urination calls on Macdonell Street, 71 on Carden Street, 33 on Wyndham Street and 9 on Cork Street. Nearly all urination calls took place between 10 p.m. and 3 a.m. In 2012, officers were called to 280 urinating in public complaints. According to police service data, Guelph Police spend about 64 hours a year responding to public urination complaints. Once again council is to consider an accessible, gender neutral public washroom for the downtown. Having users pay a small fee could help cover the cost of maintenance.

Public, portable washrooms were set up during the 2012 project safe semester campaign and the facilities were well received by the community. In 2009, the City of Guelph ran a pilot project involving pissoirs; temporary outdoor washrooms with an element of privacy in the downtown. While they were well used, the pissoirs were not accessible and women weren't able to use them. Porta-potties were seen as a better fit by the city. The number of public fouling offenses declined when these washrooms were in place. Washroom use is not necessarily about enforcement, but about their accessibility. It's not just that people don't care, there really is no place to go. The police chief, several councillors, media columnists and the Downtown Guelph Business Association all supported the construction of downtown washrooms. Despite all the discussion, City Council has not yet addressed this problem. How can Guelph be an important tourist attraction and accommodate nightlife without easily available public washrooms?

TERMITES: SUCCESSFUL ACTION

Termite infestations in Guelph were first detected in 1975 but city officials believe that they have been in the city since the late 1960s. The insects were found in an office building as it was being demolished near the intersection of London Road and Cardigan Street. The city then discovered other colonies in fence posts, wood piles and tree stumps along Cardigan St. near the Speed River. The infestation subsequently spread to other blocks. Three Termite Management Areas were designated, all on the north side of the City, encompassing 869 properties. By the late 1990s, the city had begun a termite control strategy which was budgeted for $69,000 in 1999 and $78,000 in 2000. In 1999, the city approved an area-wide management program directed by Dr. Timothy Myles, a renowned entomologist and head of the University of Toronto's Urban Entomology Program, through 2001. It used a novel method called Trap-Treat-Release. That project substantially suppressed the termite population and appeared to have achieved eradication on some blocks.

In 2002 Guelph began to collaborate formally with the University of Toronto to combat its termites. The university's method exploited the fact that termites have a natural instinct to clean each other. A trap was devised to allow scientists to capture some insects, cover them with a poisonous chemical and release them back into their nests. In the process of cleaning each other, the termites are poisoned. In 2007, the city hired Tim Miles as Guelph's new termite-control officer. Guelph council announced that it was taking a "proactive and leading-edge role" by hiring Myles, former director of the Urban Entomology Program at the University of Toronto. He hoped to eradicate Guelph's termite population with the safest and most environmentally sustainable methods possible.

Myles was quite familiar with the infestation in Guelph since he had worked with the city off and on for nearly a decade. Council earmarked more than $65,000 in the budget for his position, along with $25,000 to support public education and a termite-control program. City officials said that Guelph is the only municipality in the province with a full-time termite officer. The eastern subterranean termite, or *reticulitermes flavipes*, spread north from the United States in the early 20th century, reaching Guelph in the 1970s. About the size and colour of a grain of rice, it thrives in dark, moist places and bores into wood.

According to city records, the main termite zone was delimited roughly by Woolwich Street, Earl Street, Exhibition Street and the Speed River. A new infestation was discovered in a separate neighbourhood in the north end on 21 different properties in the area of Inverness Drive and Windermere Court. Someone in that area probably removed contaminated wood from the main termite zone allowing the termites to establish colonies in the new area.

2010

A new chemical, Zinc borate, received federal approval for use in Guelph in 2010. By then the city might have been winning its war on termites. According to a report submitted to the city's Planning, Building, Environment and Engineering department, the number of termites found in city traps decreased by 67 per cent between the first and second half of 2010. Tim Myles, the city's termite control officer said that this drop represented a "very dramatic" decline, adding that for the first time in five years, no new city blocks reported infestations."If we continue (to see) those kinds of results for a couple more years, we'll have very few termites left to trap," Myles said.

Myles and his two technicians trapped more than half a

million termites between spring and fall of 2010, coating them with toxic zinc borate and returning them to their colonies. When other termites tried to groom them by licking them clean, they were also poisoned. After a few termites have licked the poison, they transmit it to others through grooming. Before the province approved the experimental use of zinc borate, Myles had to use parasitic nematodes, which he said were less effective.

A total of 43 city blocks were classed as either containing host infestations or adjacent to host blocks. By far the largest concentration of termite activity was within a downtown enclave bordered by Woolwich, Clarence, Dufferin and Tiffany streets. Last year, new termite activity was discovered in dead trees along the Speed River near Marcon Street, a block south of Tiffany, on property owned by the Grand River Conservation Authority.

2012

The Guelph *Mercury* ran the following headline:

> *Gains made in termite war: Far fewer properties in Guelph dealing with wood munchers than in the past.*

In April, Myles sent a summary report to homeowners indicating that the areas with termite infestations had been reduced. There was no termite activity in the 3,100 traps in the Windermere area in 2011, so the boundaries were further constricted. Overall, properties with termite activity declined from 869 in 48 blocks in 2009 to 637 in 38 blocks in 2012. He suggested that the number of termites trapped had decreased by some 60 percent by the middle of the summer; a good result. In addition, considerable progress had been made in removing termite habitats in the city. It appeared that strict controls and the use of zinc borate had made major progress in controlling Guelph's termite infestations. The programme continues as traps are checked and renewed regularly. The objective is to eventually rid the city of this tiny, hungry, destructive insect.

HOUSING: CONTINUING CONFLICT

The topic of housing in its various guises has consumed many hours of discussion and debate among members of city council, builders, developers, planners, the Provincial Government and citizens of Guelph. Several major issues have dominated these discussions. First and possibly the most important is the problem of affordable housing in a city with many students and rapid growth. Among citizens, a major issue has always been the location of specialized housing such as group homes, student accommodation, shelters for the homeless or battered women, retirement homes and high-density apartments or row housing. Sadly, the initial reaction has almost always been NIMBY (Not In My Back Yard) to these and other development proposals. Recently, with the implementation of the Province's *Places to Grow* legislation, considerable controversy has surrounded the height and density of condo and apartment towers planned for the central area of the city. At times discussions of these issues at City Council have become very heated, as have relations between neighbours and those proposing specialized residential facilities

Growth and Affordable Housing

In a report to City council in 2000, Assistant Planning Director Jim Forbes warned that the rapid development of single family homes would make it difficult for low income families to find affordable accommodation. He recommended that the city adopt a long-term growth strategy to accommodate all types of residential requirements. The issue of the homeless was becoming more pressing as housing officials warned that Guelph and Wellington homelessness was going to become much more acute. They suggested that the homeless staying with friends and family might soon be out on the street. By December 2000 there were over 2000 people on the list waiting for subsidized housing, and affordable rental housing was very difficult to find. It was suggested that tax breaks were required to enable some to afford any kind of housing in Guelph. Many who did not qualify for subsidized units were paying exorbitant rents for substandard accommodation.

The Canada Mortgage and Housing Corporation's annual report on the rental market in Canada showed that Guelph was tied with Kitchener for the lowest vacancy rate in Southwestern Ontario at 0.7 per cent, up slightly from 1999's 0.5 per cent. Compared to Canada's 26 major centres, only Ottawa (0.2 per cent) and Toronto (0.6 per cent) had lower vacancy rates. Average rents for one-bedroom apartments in Guelph were up 6.4 per cent to $647 from $608 per month. The most dramatic shortage was in the most popular two-bedroom apartments. Of the 3,790 two-bedroom units identified in the survey of private apartment buildings with at least three units available, only 16 units were vacant when the survey was conducted in early October of 2000. Rents had increased but incomes had not. People on welfare were still trying to manage after the 20 per cent cut in in their payments ordered by Premier Mike Harris in 1995.

Sister Christine Leyser ran the Welcome-In drop-in centre on Wyndham Street and also operated the city's only emergency shelter, "Stepping Stone". She also filled many of the rooms at the Parkview Motel with homeless families. Her shelter was always overcrowded, but wouldn't be if permanent affordable housing were available. The housing allowance of $325 a month for a single person on welfare was much too low for Guelph. Not even a room was available for that amount of money. In 1997, Fresh Start Housing, an agency that helps people to look for housing, listed one-bedroom apartments at 90, 100 and 102 Silvercreek Pkwy. at $622 a month. In 1998, the same listing was $630 a month. That was also the year when the province eliminated rent controls. More recently a one-bedroom apartment in those buildings cost $800 and a three-bedroom unit was $1,100. It was clear that Guelph had a major problem with affordable housing which was getting worse. The housing manager of the Wellington and Guelph Housing Authority and the Guelph Non-Profit Housing Corporation said that some families remained on waiting lists for subsidized housing for five to seven years or longer.

Matrix Affordable Homes, the largest private non-profit housing corporation in Wellington County, had worked hard to create housing that Guelph's most vulnerable citizens could afford. The result was projects like the 70 unit Ecott Place on Fife Road and the 31 unit low-rise building, Goulden Place, on College Avenue. The last project built with help from the province was the Matrix building on the corner of Woolwich Street and Eramosa Road.

Guelph's *Official Plan* stated that the city must supply housing for all its citizens but downloading of social housing had the potential to bankrupt the city. With much of the housing crisis linked to populations at two large local institutions; the University of Guelph, which attracted a double cohort of new students in 2003, and the Homewood Health Centre which treats a large difficult-to-house population of people for drug and alcohol addiction or psychiatric illnesses, their large land holdings were good sites for construction of rental housing. A large section of university land, north of the Edinburgh Market on Edinburgh Road, was already zoned for high-density housing. There was also potential in a review of city bylaws. It was illegal for basement apartments to be located in townhouses but the bylaw could be made more flexible so that apartments could be allowed where townhouses met building and fire codes. Guelph's population was rising steadily, but rental housing stock fell from 6,691 units in 1999 to 6,611 in 2000.

The city's *Official Plan* stated that conversions of rental housing to condominiums should be discouraged when the vacancy rate fell below three per cent and should be prohibited when the rate is below 1.5 per cent. Many rental units had been lost when buildings were converted to condominiums. Unfortunately, major development corporations like Armel had applied for rezoning of land zoned for high density townhouses and apartments to single family homes, because builders were not interested in less profitable high density developments. The issue of affordable housing had become a major concern in the city. In her inaugural address, Guelph's new mayor, Karen Farbridge, called for a task force of councillors to attend a meeting being organized by members of the Wellington and Guelph Housing Committee's working group on housing and homelessness to address the city's housing policies.

The Mayor's "Smart Growth Initiative"

In 2001 Mayor Farbridge urged council to address what had become an urgent housing problem in Guelph. There were approximately 2500 individuals and families on the waiting list for assisted housing. Six hundred and sixty-four people were homeless in the Guelph area during a period of a year. One hundred and fifty to two hundred youth in Guelph and Wellington were without adequate shelter at any given time. Vacancy rates in Guelph were a third of the ideal minimum vacancy rate of three per cent. Fewer rental housing units had been constructed as builders preferred single family units that were more profitable than rental units.

Council approved an affordable housing position paper and action plan and was preparing policies and by-laws to participate in a new Federal/Provincial program. Therefore Guelph had to find the funds to participate in the new programme. The Federal Government provided $25,000 per unit in matching funding, but the province had committed only $2,000 per unit. These terms made it financially difficult for any municipality to participate in the new housing programmes. Other than through the creation of accessory apartments, the private sector had not met the need for affordable rental accommodation. The city initiated several steps to confront the problem because social housing became the responsibility of municipalities on January 1, 2001. Private developers continued to prefer to build single family units to apartments or town houses.

The Wellington-Guelph Housing Committee made a presentation to council suggesting that a caring and humane community must ensure an adequate supply of safe and affordable housing. Nevertheless, the 660 units then under construction at the University of Guelph would not come close to meeting the need when the double cohort of graduating high school students arrived on campus in 2003. Furthermore, the city could not supply housing for new employees who arrive in Guelph for jobs at entry-level wages. Council suggested that the *Official Plan*, then under review, "be reviewed in respect to rental housing, and that all development applications be viewed in the context of the overall goals for inclusion of rental housing throughout the city," rather than by one development at a time.

New federal funding would not solve the problem; once it was distributed to all the provinces it would create only 20 units locally. This was further complicated by the requirement that matching funds, which had not been offered be provided by the province. Even then the amount was not adequate to allow developers to break even. As a result, vacancy rates were extremely low; 0.7 per cent in Guelph and rents soared. Average rents in Guelph were up by six to eleven per cent. If any were available, it cost $960 more a year to rent a two-bedroom apartment than it did in 1998. Of 6,611 Canada Mortgage and Housing Corporation rental units in Guelph, a mere 43 were vacant. A three-bedroom apartment in Guelph had an average rent of $800. Half the households in the city had an income of less than $32,000. By CMHC standards, affordable rent for them would be $792.

CMHC tried to boost rental stock through its Residential Rehabilitation Assistance Programme (RRAP). The programmes involved forgivable or partly-forgivable loans to upgrade properties or convert non-residential properties into housing. Under that programme, Guelph and Wellington County were allocated $390,000 for 2000-2001. In Guelph $6,500 of that money was used. A similar plan for disabled housing saw only $26,000 of $200,000 used. The rental housing situation in Guelph was of critical proportions. Of 1,000 rental units in the city, only seven were available to rent. The Canada Mortgage and Housing Corporation put a healthy vacancy rate at 2.5 per cent. From Jan. 1999 to Aug. 2001, 2,269 households applied for rental units but only 13 were placed.

The author made the following comment in a letter to the editor in 2001:

> *Guelph has one of the lowest residential vacancy rates in the province and a severe deficiency of affordable housing. It is far more profitable to build mansions on large lots than to construct two-bedroom bungalows or moderately-priced apartment units. People come despite Guelph's high costs of accommodation. But if residential and industrial development continue as projected, we may not have to worry about additional growth. Growth is already threatening the very qualities that have made Guelph so attractive to so many for so long.*

Late in 2002, local housing officials welcomed the news that Guelph and Wellington County would receive 100 of the

3,200 affordable housing units allocated to Ontario in the first phase of a new programme funded largely by the Federal Government. The province had been criticized for offering only $2,000 per unit in sales tax waivers, leaving municipalities and others to come up with $23,000 to qualify for the full federal grant. By 2003, housing bids for which developers were seeking a $2,000 incentive from the province per unit were approved by the city and forwarded to the Ontario Ministry of Municipal Affairs and Housing. Some progress on affordable housing had finally been made, but the problems had not yet been solved. Matrix Housing and the Canadian Mental Health Association were the newest projects to be funded from the $200,000 set aside for Guelph in 2001-2002 to address urgent homeless needs. Another $85,000 was announced for Change Now's new overnight youth shelter, and another $6,000 for a Distress Centre phone line service to help those needing emergency shelter.

In 2004, when Guelph had 40,000 families, discussions continued and shifted more toward the affordability of rental units. Seventy per cent of the city's 13,570 rental units were built specifically for tenant occupancy but the remainder such as basement apartments and units attached to stores were part of a secondary rental market. Over the last few years only that secondary market had grown. The social housing manager for Wellington and Guelph Housing Services said that solutions like rent supplements and support services worked in the case of downtown Toronto's "tent city," a squatter site where homeless people lived until it was bulldozed by authorities and occupants moved into permanent, subsidized housing.

Four developments in Guelph and Wellington County were to receive federal and provincial money in 2004. One was an $189,000, seven-unit project at 32 Gordon St. sponsored by a Guelph unit of the Army, Navy and Air Force in Canada organization, and Matrix Affordable Homes for the Disadvantaged. The units were to be occupied by lower-income senior citizens and others, with about 30 per cent of tenants paying rent that would be geared to income. Others were 33 units at 747 Paisley Rd., sponsored by the Guelph Non-Profit Housing Corporation; and 44 units at 371 Waterloo Ave., sponsored by 805395 Ontario Limited.

Unfortunately, the housing problem persisted into 2005. Rent increases jumped 20 per cent above inflation in Guelph and Guelph-Eramosa Township. The vacancy rate increased and new housing was being built, but it did not address the needs of people paying more than 50 per cent of their income for rental accommodation. There were still about 2,000 households in Guelph and the surrounding county in that situation. On the other hand, apartment owners have had to pass on the rising cost of utilities and property taxes, all of which exceeded the rate of inflation.

In January 2006, the Canada Mortgage and Housing Corporation reported 50 new multi-family housing units in Guelph and Guelph-Eramosa Township, compared to 12 in January 2005. City of Guelph planning staff had already handled several applications for new townhouse developments and the opening of the housing units approved during the previous year was celebrated in 2006. The city's development plan for 2006 allowed for 1,287 homes to be built during the year. Of those homes, 855 would be detached, 106 would be semi-detached and 326 would be townhouses in the northwest, northeast and southern areas of the city. The city also wanted more development in and around the downtown area. Commercial and industrial development had outpaced residential development during 2005.

By 2007, city council was considering a slowdown of "greenfield" development" and more emphasis on infill as mandated by the Provincial Government. However, the president of the Guelph Development Association suggested that if this policy were implemented, the city would get "very little greenfield development and very little infill" development either. He felt that housing prices were likely to increase as a result of the stance taken by the new council. He said that the city was messing around with the marketplace, and that would have an impact by increasing prices because the supply would be substantially less than the demand. He suggested that council was trying to reduce the city's housing inventory and promote more high-density housing without adopting policies to make infill development easier to accomplish.

Infill development was difficult in Guelph because of opposition from neighbours who feared more traffic, less privacy and possibly shadows on their property. Developers could spend huge sums fighting neighbours' appeals at the Ontario Municipal Board, only to have the OMB reduce a development's density to the point where it wasn't economically viable. "Prezoning" of specific areas of the city for infill development, as well as clear policies to hear residents' complaints might help. Most neighbours would not accept even the minimum densities that *Places to Grow* imposed on the city. Nevertheless, developers agreed that the city was under pressure to curb urban sprawl because of the province's *Places to Grow* legislation.

Later in the year, Guelph Wellington M.P.P. Liz Sandals announced that the province would invest $700,000 to create 10 new affordable housing units in Guelph. This was part of the program that helped people to own their own home through down payment assistance. For many families, the real hurdle is raising the down payment. Because rents in Guelph are relatively high for the size of the city, particularly for a family-sized rental property, mortgage payments may not be much more than rental costs. Sandals asserted that this programme was a really good way of assisting working people with low incomes to own their own home.

In 2008 a project on Mountford Drive offered "payment-free loans" of up to ten per cent of a home's value, which were not due until the property was sold. Although a helpful programme, it was criticized because the loan was temporary until the property was sold. Nevertheless it did assist people to purchase houses. This policy was an example of the type encouraged by the *Places to Grow* legislation because it was within a built-up area of the city, contributed to the creation of a range of housing options, provided convenient access to transit and was served by adequate community and infrastructure services. Despite such efforts, Canada remained the only G8 country that didn't have a unifying national housing policy and the waiting lists for affordable housing were getting longer. The problem seemed insoluble.

Early in 2009, the Minister of Municipal Affairs and Housing announced that $704 million would be available to repair social housing units in Ontario. Another $365 million would be allocated to create new affordable housing units for low-income seniors and persons with disabilities. Another $175 million would help to extend the Canada-Ontario Affordable Housing Program. This was good news for Guelph, but the city did not know how much money it would receive. However, the programmes did have a positive effect. Total building starts in the city in 2010 were up nearly 82 per cent over the same period in 2009, with 218 dwellings being started in Guelph, compared to 120 during the same period in 2009. Most of the change was because of increases in townhouse and condominium development; both affordable types of homes. Some empty nesters were demanding smaller, more affordable dwellings, and retirees were downsizing to homes that required less maintenance.

Controversy surrounded a developer's intention to convert apartments to condominiums in 2011. Council was concerned that rental units at 55 Yarmouth Street would be converted, but the developer asserted that renters could remain and did not have to purchase units that would cost from $180,000 to $237,000, not exactly affordable housing. On the other hand,the building did remain residential. Nevertheless, 152,000 Ontario families remained on the waiting list for social housing in 2011. There wasn't much desire among businesses to launch affordable housing projects, which required government subsidies and must follow program criteria. But with government aid and innovative designs, some corporate sponsors did begin local affordable projects in the city. Housing construction in Guelph fell to a 10 year low in 2011 because of the poor state of the economy. Only 627 new residential units, including 256 single detached homes were built in the city in that year. The next-lowest total during the past 10 years was the 797 units built in 2009, which included 330 single detached homes, also affected by the slowing economy.

Developers planned to build 200 townhouse units in a Starwood Drive project in 2012. This east end area had become one of the fastest growing regions of Guelph and required a zoning change from industrial to residential. More affordable units were to become available when single-family homes to be built on 19.3 acres (7.7 ha.) on the western edge of the city will have considerably smaller frontages than originally planned. They will also be joined by semi-detached dwellings and townhouses. City council approved changes to development plans for the land at the city's boundary with Guelph-Eramosa Township. The subdivision draft plan originally approved in 1997 called for 97 single detached homes on the 19.3 acres (7.7 ha.) which now would accommodate considerably more smaller, affordable units.

Early in 2012, eighty seniors' residences opened on St. Joseph's Hospital land, alleviating but not solving a shortage of affordable seniors' housing in the city. The Federal and Provincial governments had put aside half a billion dollars to be spent on affordable housing in Ontario over the next three years. However. the County of Wellington decided to spend its share of the money on subsidies of existing housing, spread over the next 10 years. Guelph MPP, Liz Sandals said that it would have been better applied to developing more housing units to reduce the waiting list. The county had taken three years' worth of money and spread it over 10 years which meant that no one would be removed from the list of those requiring affordable housing. By the end of 2012, there were still many people needing affordable housing in Guelph and the problem did not seem any closer to resolution than before. Things might improve if the economy recovers or if other levels of government contribute additional incentive funds.

Housing Conflicts

The problem of where to locate specialized residential facilities has been a continuing issue in the city. Group homes, town houses, apartments, high density developments and infill projects have often generated major controversy. Even proposals for new subdivisions are opposed if someone thinks that they will increase traffic, "lower property values" or restrict residents' access to open space. Objections are also often raised by residents if a facility such as a skateboard park or new commercial use is proposed nearby. Debates on such matters at city council have often been long and bitter. A few of the most notable are discussed below.

Group Homes

Early in 2000 the Guelph Teen Housing Committee

purchased a home at 51 Bellevue Street for $300,000, raising concerns among residents who worried about the safety of themselves and their children. They asserted that Bellevue Street was the wrong place for a group home. They argued that there was a lack of regulations affecting group homes and that the house being renovated for a teen home was largely secluded and backed onto a wooded lot and ravine, encouraging "crime generating activity". Objectors asserted that teens in group homes were at high risk for crime, drug and alcohol abuse. They also said that residents had difficulty getting information on how the facility would operate and on protection to be offered to the neighbourhood. They argued that the teen housing committee was an "unproven board", and asked planning committee of council to delay registering the group home, but this had already been completed.

The chair of the teen housing committee replied to criticisms by saying that police do not send "troubled" kids to group homes. Teens, who for reasons such as abuse, cannot live at home would be allowed into the home only if they attended school. The age group was 16-21 and there would be a maximum of eight residents. This included two staff members, four permanent teenage residents and up to two residents on emergency shelter basis. The planning committee asked city staff to investigate the concerns raised by objectors and to look into possible safeguards for the community. In February, city council approved the Bellvue street group home application.

Another controversy erupted in 2004 when Matrix Affordable Homes applied to have the zoning changed so it could continue to operate Serenity House at 136 Grange Street as a lodging house, as it had since 2002. The facility housed homeless people and ran a recovery program for those with drug and alcohol addiction or who had been in trouble with the law. It had been operating illegally until the application.

Fear and anger were apparent among residents who opposed the facility. Some would not let their children out of their sight because of concerns about drug addicts and alcoholics living in the house. Others demanded to know how it could have existed illegally in its present location without the city taking action. A neighbour collected almost 300 signatures on a petition against the rezoning. Despite assurances that drugs and alcohol were not permitted, people had seen men consuming alcohol on the property and smelled marijuana.

Police representatives commented that they had had few complaints about residents of Serenity House and had found the staff to be friendly and cooperative. The courts had sentenced a number of teens to live at the house. Angry residents threatened sitting councillors that they would run against them if the application were approved. After a heated meeting, some councillors concluded that NIMBY was a factor for many opponents, but that even people living outside the neighbourhood did not want the facility to be located near them. Planning Department had not yet decided whether to support the application for rezoning. A resident who favoured the application and supported group homes stated that she was afraid to express such an opinion in the public meeting. A councillor suggested that the facility be rezoned as a group home which required round the clock supervision of residents, but Matrix was not interested in running a group home. The city refused the application and Serenity House shut down.

LODGING HOUSES AND STUDENTS

Early in 2001, council contemplated revising the lodging house by-law. The low vacancy rate for rental housing in Guelph was based on buildings with three or more units and did not include accessory apartments or illegal lodging houses. It was possible that the lodging house bylaw was driving houses with four or more unrelated occupants underground. If they were not registered lodging houses, they might not conform with building and fire codes. Unfortunately, many students lived in such accommodation and were not covered by the existing by-law. Residents in the Old University Neighbourhood worried about a student ghetto developing in their area. They presented a report about a survey that estimated that 27 per cent of university students living off campus reside in their neighbourhood, which accounted for less than three per cent of the housing in the city. A resident and a councillor recommended that the city set 1.5 students per household as the maximum to maintain a diverse balance in any neighbourhood. Others recommended more education of students about the importance of reporting unsafe housing.

The issue of student housing in the Old University Neighbourhood boiled up again in early 2002. In March members of the Old University Neighbourhood Residents' Association packed City Hall to denounce a proposal from the Guelph Campus Co-operative to redevelop a College Avenue property for a 150-student housing complex. Some residents claimed that the development was a lodging house complex in disguise. Of 12,000 University of Guelph students, 40 per cent lived on campus, 10 per cent lived at home and commute, 13.7 per cent rented in the Old University Neighbourhood. Thirty-six point three per cent rented elsewhere in the city. The Old University Neighbourhood Residents' Association appealed the seven to six city council approval of a 40-unit townhouse complex on a one-acre property bordered by College Avenue, Borden Street and Hales Crescent to the OMB. The project, proposed by Guelph Campus Co-operative to accommodate only students, would receive exemptions from the city's lodging house bylaw, which usually applied when more than three people in a home were unrelated.

When the issue went to the Ontario Municipal Board, an official with the Guelph Campus Co-operative told the panel that it had several housing projects in the city, including a cluster of homes which had a long waiting list for about 40 students on the development site. The neighbourhood's lawyer argued that the complex would not conform to the character of the neighbourhood because the density was too high. He said that the project was wrongly being exempted from the city's lodging housing bylaw to allow relaxed parking requirements and to avoid a minimum separation of 100 metres between dwellings.

The Campus Co-operative property included a large commercial building, and six homes that accommodated about 40 students. The redevelopment would include six blocks of stacked townhouses, with two, three and four bedrooms, focused on a central courtyard. There would be 150 students in 40 units. The lawyer for the neighbourhood argued that the application was designed to skirt the housing by-law and in reality would include 34 lodging houses, as defined by city rules, replacing four licensed lodging houses that existed the College Avenue development site. The hearing was also told that allowing the student townhouse project would open the door to more similar proposals.

Despite all the opposition, in a decision released early in October 2002 the OMB said that the 40 townhouse units proposed by the Guelph Campus Co-Operative were appropriate for its 1.3 acre (0.5 ha.) site fronting College Avenue, Borden Street, Moore Avenue and Hales Crescent.

Given the significant costs to all parties, which were estimated to be about $70,000, it was suggested that someone be hired in future to attempt dispute resolution, rather than going to the OMB. The hearing cost the neighbourhood a lot of money and it cost the co-op a lot of money. A neighbourhood resident who opposed the development commented that:

> *"Those who supported this housing proposal, including Mayor Farbridge, have helped Guelph toward achieving what so many other university towns have already accomplished - a solid residential neighbourhood whose sole occupants are students housed in illegal lodging houses run by absentee landlords. Other communities call them "student slums," or, as in Kingston, it's simply known as "the ghetto." I wonder what we'll call it - other than poor planning."*

Student housing has always generated controversy. Often it is accompanied by noisy parties, unkempt properties and littering. Proponents of the Co-op proposal applauded the addition of this rental housing for students. They suggested that it would free up rental units for some of the thousands of people on waiting lists for affordable housing in Guelph. Opponents argued that five nearby families had moved away upon hearing of the proposal and that the neighbourhood was being ruined for long-term inhabitants. Nevertheless, the Co-op proposal was finally approved.

New Zoning Proposals

The issue of rooming houses, lodging houses and accessory apartments has been discussed as long as owners have been renting rooms or houses to groups of unrelated people, especially students. It has been very difficult to define such facilities, to identify them and to create regulations that would survive legal challenges. Between 2002 and 2012, when attempting to create a definition of lodging houses that would be fair and withstand legal challenges, city council discussed and debated this issue many times.

Council eventually passed a resolution approving zoning bylaw changes for accessory apartments that would require an initial licensing fee of $100; a maximum accessory apartment size of 100 square metres (not more than 45 per cent of the main dwelling's floor area); a maximum of two bedrooms in the accessory dwelling unit; and a variety of servicing and property restrictions. Unfortunately, various interpretations of this by-law led to a number of difficult situations. A project at 142 York Rd. nearing completion became controversial in the surrounding neighbourhood which feared another lodging house in their neighbourhood. Advertising about the 24 unit project raised concern at City Hall that rooms were to be rented out in contravention of the city's lodging house bylaw. The developer argued that he was not advertising lodging house rooms and that the by-law was so vague that almost any group of four or more people who paid rent are technically required to obtain a lodging house licence.

Critics argued that the bylaw enabled city staff to arbitrarily decide when a housing unit was a lodging house. This created a serious deterrent to any Guelph developer who might consider building four bedroom rental accommodation in the city. Presumably officials would not lay charges where a mother and a father were sharing their rented home with their two teenage or adult children and all four were contributing to the rent. But according to the definition in the lodging house bylaw, that family would be defined as lodgers and their landlord would need a licence to operate a lodging house to rent rooms to them. A student living in a York Road townhouse called the by-law discriminatory when it forced his roommate to move out. At that time, Guelph had 40 licensed lodging houses, while Waterloo had about 1,000. Clearly the by-law had to be reconsidered and rewritten. Waterloo's by-law defined lodging houses as "A house where furnished rooms are rented to individuals" which seemed to be simple and could be enforced through zoning. The developer of the York Road townhouse argued that students could live in clean, bright efficient units there instead of in dingy illegal basements as many did at the time.

Controversy continued in 2003 as residents of vulnerable neighbourhoods worried about loopholes in Guelph's accessory apartment by-law. Many complained that it was not working and cited experience in Waterloo as a possible model for Guelph. Waterloo has had better success when regulating lodging houses, having almost 1,000 licensed. It was successful because it proactively enforced the bylaw using fire inspectors. In contrast, Guelph and London (which had only 20 licensed lodging houses) enforced only by following up on complaints. Waterloo also had less stringent regulations for smaller lodging houses and worked closely with the university, which could advertise only rental properties that were licensed. Waterloo also educated citizens and promoted its bylaw in the real estate community. There, up to six people could share accommodation in a house (three in each unit) with an accessory apartment without contravening the city's lodging house bylaw. In Guelph, the accessory apartment issue and the lodging house bylaw were considered together, since they are related.

The by-law continued to be contentious and a new employee of the university was appointed to discuss it with the city. Meanwhile, the owner of 124 York Road townhouses filed a lawsuit against the city arguing that the by-law was not enforced fairly. He argued that the bylaw must distinguish between lodging houses where rooms are rented out individually, and houses that are rented by a group of people. He also lost an OMB appeal against a city decision not to allow more than three people to live in each of his townhouses. His court case was delayed until later in the year. In November 2003 a meeting at River Run Centre heard the results of investigations of a committee studying the lodging house issue. At that time there were about 900 shared rental housing units in the city that could accommodate more than three unrelated people, but only 45 of those units had been registered under accessory apartment or lodging house regulations. As many as two-thirds of the unregistered shared units did not comply with one or more zoning regulation. The problem was that any enforcement campaign would greatly increase the cost of such accommodation.

Accompanied by frustration and complaints from people living near student accommodation, the lodging house by-law debate continued for several years. The city planned to change the definition of a lodging house to one which required stringent health and safety regulations and periodic inspections. A lodging house would become a dwelling where more than three people live together in a rental unit with more than four bedrooms. Despite all efforts to create a new and enforceable by-law, council continued to hear complaints from residents in the university neighbourhood and assertions that the situation was spiralling out of control. The 100 metre separation between lodging houses was not working and the new by-law had not yet been implemented.

After several more years of discussion and citizen complaints, council decided in 2010 to hire a consultant to assist in developing an enforceable by-law. To give council time to accomplish this, a one-year freeze on creating accessory apartments and lodging houses in much of Guelph was approved by council in early June 2010. This freeze would be repealed once a zoning amendment was passed, if there were no appeals to the Ontario Municipal Board. Under the existing zoning bylaw regulations in Guelph, lodging houses were permitted in single detached residential dwellings and were limited to five to twelve lodging units, partly depending on the availability of parking. New lodging houses were subject to a 100-metre separation distance from an existing facility.

By the end of July, city hall staff recommended that the maximum number of housing units in new lodging houses be reduced to eight from twelve as part of a new approach to shared rental housing in the city. These changes were being proposed to address destabilization threats to neighbourhoods because of the concentration of lodging houses. Staff suggested that a combination of zoning changes and a licensing program for shared rental housing would alleviate problems in neighbourhoods, while attempting to ensure that there were enough housing options for low-income people, including students. The proposed changes would deal with the location, density and intensity of shared rental housing. In addition to a lower limit on the number of units in new lodging houses, lodging houses would be limited to one kitchen, so that they could not have accessory apartments.

A proposed licensing program would regulate shared rental housing, including how many bedrooms could be rented. The licensing system would limit the number of rental bedrooms in two-unit houses to four. Existing lawful two-unit houses renting five or more bedrooms would have to reduce their number of rental units to four. Licensing lodging houses could address concerns about absentee landlords by requiring the licence holder either to reside there, have on-site management or a superintendent to improve accountability for tenant behaviour. Because a third of existing permitted units would become unlawful if they rented more than four bedrooms, the pressure to create more unlawful housing might increase. Hopefully new zoning and licensing would manage the shared rental housing business and reduce conflicts between such units and neighbours. Licensing rental accommodation would allow the city to impose conditions as a requirement for obtaining, continuing to hold, or renewing a license, which could include regular inspections.

If a lower limit on the number of units in lodging houses were approved, it would apply only to new lodging houses. About one-third of existing lodging houses had more than eight units, and they could continue to operate. There were currently 53 certified lodging houses in Guelph, concentrated in Ward 5, where over 80% of known lodging houses were located. Only 4% were owner-occupied. There were also about 1,500 registered two-unit houses which were distributed throughout the city. About 68% of them were owner-occupied. On average, 100 new accessory apartments were created annually in Guelph. Known legal shared rental housing properties accounted for only 2% of zoning complaints, 5% of property standards complaints and 8% of noise complaints in 2009. The vast majority of complaints involved other types of properties including illegal shared rental housing units.

A zoning bylaw amendment dealing with shared-rental housing, which was passed by council in September 2010, was repealed by council in late January 2012. This decision came after the Ontario Human Rights Commission got involved in an appeal of the zoning amendment made by several local landlords to the Ontario Municipal Board. The interim control bylaw passed by council in June 2010, temporarily prohibited the development of any new shared-rental housing on residential property in Ward 5 and part of Ward 6. Council's decision to repeal the bylaw came after it received advice from city lawyers behind closed doors that it might adversely affect immigrants who lived in multigenerational arrangements in shared housing. It might not comply with the regulations or findings of the Ontario Human Rights Commission.

The city also received advice that it would be very expensive to contest the OMB appeal. That process, which was still in the pre-hearing stage, had already cost the city $50,000 and could have cost $200,000 if it had gone to a hearing. Despite these setbacks, Building Services staff continued to enforce the Property Standards and Yard Maintenance By-laws on a complaint basis. The 100 meter separation regulation also remained in force, but the licencing of lodging houses would have to be subjected to additional reviews and public consultation before being implemented.

By the middle of 2012, the city was back to "Square One" with its licencing proposal. It created a committee to examine the idea relative to the Ontario Human Rights Code and citizen input. It had to examine the classes of rental housing to licence, the proposed fees, the processes for appeals and possible penalties. It also was required to develop a phase-in strategy for licencing. The revised by-law and licensing scheme would attempt to prevent concentration of shared rental housing, reduce intensity of residential uses and decrease accompanying noise. The issue of absentee landlords would also be addressed. The city will examine licensing programs in cities such as Waterloo, London and Oshawa to determine what is possible in Guelph. So, after years of work and several by-laws, the problem of shared rental accommodation and rental housing in Guelph continued.

After much deliberation at council and many meetings with landlords, tenants, and neighbours, on Tuesday, August, 12, 2014 rental licensing was rejected by City Council in favour of stronger enforcement of existing regulations and zoning by-laws.

Condominiums and High Rise Apartments

Guelph has had a number of high rise apartments for many years including the venerable Park Mall on Quebec Street and the Twin Towers at the corner of Speedvale and Kathleen. More recently the Evergreen Residences were built on Woolwich St. next to the Evergreen Seniors' Centre. Downtown, the Cooperators Building remains the tallest office building. Recently a number of existing apartment buildings have been converted into condominiums while many new condominiums have sprouted in the suburbs. A number of historic buildings such as Len's Mill and Stewart's Lumber have also been converted into condominiums while several other former mills and factories have become retirement homes. Most of these generated some controversy and opposition among neighbours as NIMBY continued to raise its ugly head. More recently a number of proposals for high rise condominiums, student residences and affordable housing downtown have caused controversy and opposition from a wide spectrum of citizens.

Marianne's Park and Condominium Proposal

One of the most controversial planning applications in the past few years was the proposal to build condominiums next to Marianne's Park beside the Speed River at 180 Gordon Street. Opponents declared that any structure there would "dishonour" the memory of Marianne who was slain by her boyfriend, and ignore a number of planning restrictions related to the site and its proximity to the river. This protracted battle continued till early 2014. A few of the arguments on each side are presented below to illustrate the way in which concerned citizens participated.

In May 2010, contaminated soil was being removed from the planned location for the condos, alerting citizens that some development was to occur. Almost immediately representatives of the Old University Neighbourhood Residents' Association and community activists condemned the plan, saying that it privatized Marianne's Park, obstructed views of the river and would create traffic problems. One opponent argued that the plan violated a number of zoning bylaws, including the following:

> Its height was to be four stories instead of three;
> It was too high-density;
> It did not meet the infill criteria set out in Places to Grow legislation;
> It contravened regulations on development next to rivers.

Some supported the plans because they would supply luxury accommodation near the river and bring more residents downtown. They felt that the developer might compromise on his original design to meet some of the criticisms. Others asserted that the eleven unit project would be "downright disrespectful to ... a very sensitive piece of land." A sarcastic rebuttal to some of the opponents written by Greg Mercer appeared in the *Guelph Mercury* in October 2011:

> You see, it's not that they're opposed to a condo development in their neighbourhood - why, that's preposterous, they love condos!- it's that they feel condos beside a park honouring the memory of a woman killed by her partner is inappropriate.
>
> The problem is, the condos would be next door to Marianne's Park, named after Marianne Goulden, a women's shelter worker who was stabbed to death by her boyfriend in 1992. It was a horrific crime and renaming the park after Goulden was a poignant tribute.
>
> Reality, however, doesn't seem to matter much in these kind of fights. It's the same kind of mentality

that inspired someone to write "Go home yuppie scum" on a billboard promoting new townhouses recently built in a vacant lot across from Goldie Mill.

In January 2012, the application was taken to city council where staff recommended that it be approved with some conditions. Opponents were outraged and vowed to fight to the end. They asserted that neighbours were "universally negative". They referred to the four triangular hedges in Marianne (Johanna Goulden's) garden surrounding a boulder holding her dedication plaque. They described the riverbank and the park where seagulls and Canada geese often clustered. On a bench facing the river, the sound of the Speed River drowned out the sound of nearby traffic. Somehow the proposed town houses would spoil this tranquillity.

Representatives of Podium Developments asked for several amendments to the *Official Plan*, but argued that they did respect Marianne's Park. They offered to leave a right of way to the park and to the river. They would build a beautiful building to enhance and complement the park as a "gateway to the waterway." In March 2012, council considered Podium's revised plan to build a two storey, 11 unit building; a considerable reduction from its original proposal. After much discussion and impassioned presentations by opponents, council voted to permit a reduced setback from the river edge and to change the zoning of the property from a convenience commercial and floodway zone to permit cluster townhouses at 180 Gordon St. Opponents vowed to appeal this decision to the OMB.

In September, Podium Developments asked council to provide an additional grant of $138,000 in addition to the original $156,000 designated for cleaning the site which had once been the location of a coal ash dump and for many years accommodated a service station. The Ministry of the Environment had informed them that contamination was worse than expected and recommended additional remediation. City staff concurred and recommended that the grant be increased to insure that the land would become suitable for residences. Development was delayed because the appeal to the OMB was not to be heard until November 5, 2012. The OMB finally ruled in favour of the developer in a decision early in 2013.

A headline in the Guelph *Mercury* on 20 March 2014 stated: "*Marketing underway for controversial Guelph riverside condo project*". The developer is still seeking final site plan approval from the city, but work on the site has begun as has marketing. The building at 180 Gordon St. will be a 10-unit condominium structure, about 50 steps from the edge of the Speed River. Construction hoarding is being erected on the site to display marketing billboards for a lovely building that will feature spacious 1,483 and 1,509 square foot (138 and 140 square metres) condominiums. A website, www.180gordon.com has been developed to market the project.

The website shows a resident enjoying the view of downtown Guelph from a fourth floor outdoor patio, and other images depict the relaxing amenities of the river setting, including neighbouring Marianne's Park. The project is advertised as urban living in Guelph at its finest in a unique setting that is a combination of city and nature. Fine urban living within walking distance of grocery stores, dining, shopping, entertainment, and several kilometres of trails along the banks of the river are advertised. The four-storey complex will include units with high ceilings, granite counters, and soft-closing cabinetry. Construction will commence as soon as the city approves the site plan.

Controversy Over High Rise Condominiums

On March 6, 2012, The Tricar Group from London presented a condominium proposal to council that would drastically change the face of downtown Guelph. They requested zoning and *Official Plan* amendments to allow an 18-storey high rise building that would include 130 condominium suites on 16 floors at 148-152 Macdonell St. It would also have 3,550 square feet (329.8 sq. Metres) of ground-floor commercial space fronting onto Macdonell. At this meeting, public delegations were invited to address the issue before the planning department made any recommendations.

A number of delegations, many from downtown or representing local developers, spoke to this issue at the meeting. Although there was opposition, supporters outnumbered objectors about two to one. Tricar was praised by Guelph citizens as having a proven track record of building luxury condo highrises in southwestern Ontario. Those in favour of the proposal pointed out that there were very few locations in downtown Guelph suitable for a highrise building. They emphasized that such opportunities must be maximized if the city is to meet growth targets dictated by the province's *Places to Grow* legislation. The condo tower, with its ground-floor commercial space would become a key entrance to the downtown. The Guelph Chamber of Commerce suggested that the condo tower would help downtown businesses.

Early in May, City council overwhelmingly approved a new downtown plan that allowed highrises as tall as 18 storeys and was described by one councillor as "a real game changer." It was the result of the first comprehensive review of the central area since the 1970s. The Mayor suggested that it signalled a big change which would provide Guelph with the central business district (CBD) that it deserved. Some councillors commented that this new secondary plan was a real paradigm shift and a watershed moment for Guelph. Others said that people had been telling them that such a plan for the CBD was far overdue. For another councillor, the new plan was primarily about building beautifully in the centre of the city.

In the middle of May, council approved the application by Tricar with a decisive 10-3 vote, enabling building to commence. A dissenting councillor worried that in 30 to 40 years they would be judged by their children and grandchildren. Other dissenters suggested that the Tricar building did not reflect the "inspiring vision" portrayed by the new CBD plan and was neither unique nor innovative. It did not reflect the aim of "building beautifully." To some it appeared to be a "generic" highrise that did not reflect Guelph's creativity or beauty. Nevertheless, the project was approved and building is now well under way.

Market Commons Condominiums

In March 2009 the Market Commons Condominium was proposed for the empty lot opposite the Farmers' Market on Gordon Street. Its Development Consultant, John Farley of Creating Homes, a not-for-profit corporation based in Cambridge, suggested that it would be "market affordable," at 20 per cent less than market rates. This was in contrast to the "luxury" condominiums now being proposed and constructed in Guelph. The project by the Gordon Street Development Corporation had been designed for first-time buyers and half the units had already been sold.

In May 2012, Market Commons requested a $1.5 million grant from the city to assist with developing infrastructure for the building. They were also seeking a deferral of development charges to augment affordability for condo buyers, notably low-income first-time owners. This was done through an application to the city's *Separate Development Charges Late Payment Program*, which they had used in 2008 for an affordable housing initiative on Mountford Drive. The Market Commons development would add commercial space to the core and provide residents with an innovative financing structure. It is priced for first-time home buyers, investors, empty nesters and those of moderate income. According to a city official, its urban, mixed-use, live-work units were well-designed. Home Ownership Alternatives, a firm with 10 year's experience is assisting buyers through innovative financing and down payment options to help them into new home ownership, as it has with similar projects in Kitchener, Waterloo, Toronto and elsewhere in Guelph.

The one-half acre (0.6 ha.) condo complex comprises 57 residential units consisting of a mix of studio, one-bedroom, one-bedroom plus den, and two-bedroom units, as well as five live-work combination units. A ground-floor commercial space may accommodate a café or grocery store. The solid concrete structure will be a six-storey mid-rise building with the top two levels set back from the lower four. It will be oriented toward green space along Essex Street. The design generally conforms to the traditional buildings that were previously on the site, and which dominate the downtown. The affordability of the project will allow more people to live downtown and contribute to the city's CBD revitalization plans. Mid-rise buildings such as this are optimal because they allow the penetration of sunlight into the street; something that taller buildings don't permit.

There will be both underground and surface parking, as well as car-sharing, bicycle space and other "green" initiatives. Construction was to begin in Spring 2012 (Now 4 Nov. 2012) with occupancy in summer 2013. The condos, which vary in price depending on factors like size and features, will start at $164,900. The project conforms with the Provincial Government's *Places To Grow* efforts to promote infilling and limit urban sprawl in Ontario. It also reflects Guelph's similar objective to make better use of space through urban intensification. It would also increase the city's economic and tax base.

For buyers, it would provide accommodation and an excellent long term investment. The development makes it possible for someone with a lower or moderate annual income to move from renting to ownership, with "payment-free loans" of up to 10 per cent of the home's value. These would not have to be repaid until the homeowner resold the unit. The condos should be attractive to first time buyers, young families and people downsizing or going through life transitions such as a divorce. It could get people out of the rental cycle and into home ownership. The building was partially completed by the summer of 2013 and will become a major and positive addition to the housing stock of Guelph. It was completed in 2014.

Proposed Student High-Rise Development

On August 23, 2010 Abode Varsity Living, based in Mississauga proposed a highrise students' complex at the corner of Stone Road and Gordon Streets. The developer would like to turn the Best Western Hotel site into two high-rise towers for University of Guelph students. It asked for the following amendments to Guelph's zoning by-laws:

> *An Official Plan Amendment to redesignate the Site from 'General Residential' to 'High Density Residential' with site specific policies and a Zoning By-law Amendment to rezone the Site from 'Specialized Service Commercial 1-11 (SC1-11)' to 'High Density Apartment (R.4B) Zone' with site specific regulations.*

Local opposition began almost as soon as the proposal was made public and the Mayfield Park Community Association met City of Guelph planners and representatives of Abode Varsity Living several times. Abode's proposal was to house about 1,600 residents on the site of the Best Western Royal Brock Hotel. Abode provided several alternatives at the meetings, but those did little to address neighbourhood concerns. Residents pointed out that there was no transition between the huge buildings and their single-family homes. The developers also failed to address inadequate setbacks from the road, inadequate parking facilities and traffic issues that would result from a development of that size on that corner.

A second alternative reduced the size of the development to about 75 per cent of the original proposal. The two buildings would be 10 and 12 storeys, would accommodate about 1,200 bedrooms but would still require variances from city zoning bylaws. The community association retained urban planning experts who met with city staff to act on behalf of the group. In January 2011, Guelph city councillors heard from many residents urging them to reject the proposal. A representative of the university's student government who panned the development said that most first year students want to be incorporated into the community and live close to families rather than being in a residence-type situation. Of the 21 delegations to address council, only one had anything positive to say about the proposal. Some of the objections to the buildings were as follows:

The integrity, safety and stability of a neighbourhood with historic roots, cottage-like atmosphere and low density residential homes will be destroyed by the high density residential buildings right at our doorstep. The proposed high rises would be an insult to the privacy of the residents an established community.

The Official Plan and the Zoning By-law for this area allow low density residential homes
Half the historic trademark evergreens on the property would be destroyed.

The University of Guelph does not agree with the need for additional student residences in the city of Guelph.

There is no guarantee that this will be strictly student housing, especially given the fact it has nothing to do with the U of G..

Sunlight penetration will be affected by this development and become non existent on Evergreen Drive. Shadows from the buildings will cover all the houses, vegetable gardens and swimming pools on the adjacent street.

The outside developer would not understand and care for the city as do the residents. The well taxed value of their homes will drop drastically and the quality of their living will deteriorate.

Increased traffic density will be a concern as well. There will be a concentration of vehicles in a small enclosed corner of Gordon St. and Stone Road, which is also extremely populated with car and bicycle traffic.

Noise from the air-conditioning units, heating devices and the crowds of excited students will also affect the quiet neighbourhood of residents who have lived there for over 40 years with the expectation of safety and stability. Many homeowners have done extensive renovations and additions to their houses and large lots allow for swimming pools and backyard gardens. The high density residencies will undermine the excellent reputation of the area.

There are other sites in the city of Guelph within walking distance to the U of G which could be explored and which already have tall buildings.

We actively support Guelph's position on "maintaining the stability and character of the built forms in an existing established neighbourhood" and "minimizing potential conflicts between various housing forms". The student high rises will present an obvious conflict with the area and will not make Guelph a better place to live.

After numerous meetings, no compromises had been made, and when a year had passed the city had not yet responded to Abode Varsity Living's rezoning request. An informal public meeting had been held on 18 November 2010, the statuary public meeting occurred on 17 January 2011, and during the spring and summer of 2011 a series if facilitation sessions between the Mayfield Residents' association and Adobe Varsity Living occurred. On December 13, 2011 Abode confirmed that it had asked the Ontario Municipal Board to decide whether it should be granted the zoning bylaw and *Official Plan* amendments it requested. The *Planning Act* requires such decisions to be made within 180 days of an application being submitted and it had been more than twice that long since Abode made its original application. A pre-hearing conference was set for April 19, 2012 and a full OMB hearing for September 10, 2012. This hearing was continued in early October.

Adobe altered its original application to decrease the height of its buildings to 14 and 10 stories from 16 and 12. It reduced the total number of units from 341 to 264 and revised its building design to eliminate a raised parking deck and to provide parking on underground and surface parking lots. Revisions to the building design to comply to a 45 degree angular plane were also made. A representative of the developer hoped that a compromise could be reached before the issue was heard by Ontario Municipal Board in September. However, there were no compromises at a city council meeting on July 3. Without any debate, it voted 11-0 to support planning staff recommendations that the city fight Abode Varsity Living's proposal at the OMB.

A report from the planning department asserted that the two proposed highrises would actually be huge lodging houses at a scale with no precedent in Guelph, rather than apartment buildings. A consultant hired by the city agreed with many of the objections raised by the Mayfield Park Community Association;

> *The impacts on the adjacent residential properties on Evergreen Drive, in terms of shadows, loss of light and sky-views, and loss of privacy, are severe and unacceptable. The massing impacts on Gordon*

Street, Stone Road, the gateway intersection and long streetscape views toward the site are also severe and unacceptable.

The built form of the proposed development is entirely out of character with its surroundings and indeed with the overall character of Guelph.

During the OMB hearing, the city recommended that three buildings of five, six and seven storeys, would be more consistent with the zoning and *Official Plan* policies for the property. A University representative said that buildings intended to house 1,000 or 1,200 students were a concern. He suggested that the university was not opposed to an appropriately sized student housing development, but that the Adobe Varsity proposal represented over-development of the property and was incompatible with the nearby campus and with adjacent residential neighbourhoods. The OMB hearing ended on Wednesday October 3, 2012 with a promise that the ruling would be made as soon as possible.

A Final Resolution

On April 24, 2013, the OMB ruled that the proposed student highrises at the corner of Gordon St. and Stone Rd. were an appropriate use for the site. However, they imposed a number of conditions including a height limit of 11 stories at the intersection and 9 stories elsewhere on the site for an average of 10 stories. They also imposed a maximum tower area above the three and four storey podiums to 8,100 square feet (752.5 sq. metres) per floor and a 30 degree angular plane to the residences. While the decision supports Abode's plans to pursue amendments to the City's *Official Plan* and Zoning By-law, the Board imposed several restrictions to address concerns raised by the City and neighbourhood residents.

The OMB took residents' concerns seriously. It attempted to ensure that the development would be compatible with existing buildings, and would not overpower the intersection which is also the entrance to the university. It noted that neighbouring properties and the surrounding area are characterized by having trees at the front, and buildings at the back, and accepted the City's recommendation for larger landscaped setbacks along Gordon Street and Stone Road. The OMB also imposed restrictions to further limit the height of buildings on the east side of the property near the Mayfield Park neighbourhood. It agreed with the city that the facades of the proposed buildings were too big. However, the board had no problem with the proposed densities and felt that having the students concentrated in one area was better than having them dispersed around the neighbourhood.

BROWNFIELD REDEVELOPMENT

In February 2001 City Council authorized the establishment of a multi-departmental team to provide recommendations on the scope and characteristics of of a municipal brownfields strategy. The Province of Ontario had passed the *Brownfields Statute Law Amendment Act* which would guide Guelph's strategy. City Council identified 'brownfield' redevelopment/reuse as a priority as part of the City's Smart Growth initiative. The city developed a preliminary inventory of approximately 175 potential brownfield sites based upon historical land use documents. Its revised *Brownfield Redevelopment Community Improvement Plan*, approved in November 2012, defined Brownfields as follows:

> *Brownfields are abandoned, idled, or underused properties where expansion or redevelopment is complicated by real or perceived environmental contamination as a result of historical land use practices. Brownfields are often vacant and characterized by building deterioration and/or obsolescence, and/or inadequate infrastructure. Brownfields can include many uses such as old landfills and abandoned factories to dry cleaners and former gasoline stations.*

The report went on to list some of the reasons why developers hesitated to redevelop Brownfield sites:

> *Lack of funds to conduct required environmental studies;*
> *The cost of cleaning up contaminated sites;*
> *Difficulty obtaining project financing from traditional sources of development capital;*
> *Significant demolition and infrastructure upgrading costs;*
> *Fear of regulatory (government) and civil liability due*

*to environmental contamination
Uncertain, lengthy and complicated environmental
remediation and planning approval
processes;
Community and neighbourhood concerns and
opposition; and,
Poor returns on investment.
Numerous studies have shown that the costs to
develop brownfields are greater than greenfields.
However, positive experience and results in Canada
and the U.S. have shown that the challenges
to brownfield redevelopment can in fact be overcome
to produce a profit for the developer and
significant economic, environmental and social
benefits for the community.*

Despite these obstacles, Council accepted the revised policy, knowing that that every dollar spent in the Canadian economy on brownfield development generated approximately $3.80 in total economic output and increased local property values. Given such information, the city adopted a *Community Improvement Plan* (CIP) policy of subsidizing brownfield redevelopment. This policy would also help the City to achieve its target of accommodating 40 per cent of annual residential development within the built up area by 2015, as outlined in its *Local Growth Management Strategy.* The financial incentive programs in the 2012 policy are from the original *Brownfield Strategy* which was adopted by Council in May, 2002. Major provisions of the revised policy were adopted on April 6, 2010 and amended on December 5, 2011. Implementation Guidelines for the Community Improvement Plan were approved on April 23, 2012. The CIP contains the following incentive programs:

*i) Feasibility Study Grant Program – matching 50%
grant to a maximum grant of $5,000*

for a range of feasibility studies;
ii) Facade Improvement Grant Program – matching 50%
grant for building facade
improvements to a maximum grant of $10,000 per
property and a maximum grant of
$30,000 for properties with multiple addresses,
facades, owners and/or tenants;
iii) Minor Activation Grant Program – 30% grant to a
maximum of $120,000 for selected
capital costs of developing small of amounts of
commercial space or residential units;
and
iv) Major Activation Grant - a Tax-Increment Based
Grant for large projects that can
reimburse costs incurred in downtown development
that are not routinely encountered in
Greenfield development, using up to 100% of the 10-
year tax increment.

In addition to these provisions, supplements for additional studies and remediation are available in a number of circumstances. A few important applications of these policies and some important Brownfield sites will be discussed to illustrate their significance for downtown Guelph.

In 2001, J. Lammer Developments Ltd. bought a brownfield site at the corner of Waterloo and Beechwood avenues. The site, just over an acre (0.40 ha.), contained two stone barns built in the 1800s for storage and maintenance of rail cars for George Sleeman's electric railway, which the city later took over and operated from the 1920s to the 1960s. Thereafter the Sutton family operated an auto body repair shop on the site, which they sold to the Lammer firm in 2001. Building those units on brownfield sites relieves the pressure for greenfield development that paves over farmland and leads to urban sprawl. Lammer's firm had been involved with infill development projects, some in heritage buildings, for close to 25 years. The former street railway depot and auto body shop was eventually redeveloped as a luxury condominium, without the benefit of a brownfield grant.

In 2002, Reid Heritage Homes redeveloped the former Pirelli factory site at the corner of London and Edinburgh Roads. The environmental cleanup to remove copper from the soil was done by Pirelli at a cost of $250,000 before the sale, and Reids paid another $250,000 to remove underground debris such as concrete pipes. There were no government subsidies, but Reids sold the homes at competitive prices ranging from about $135,000 to $145,000, somewhat less than what they received for comparable units in another subdivision. The Pirelli development consisted of townhouses at relatively high densities. There were no government subsidies for this early infill development.

In 2003, a $711,500 grant, primarily in the form of property tax forgiveness over five years, was given to the developers of a condominium project in an existing 100-year-old structure which was usable but needed extensive mechanical, electrical and structural renovation. This was an excellent early trial of the city's new brownfields policy. The project produced some infilling within the city's downtown core and preserved a valuable landmark. The 78-unit condominium in the former Len's Mill Store on Cross Street was the first project to benefit from a brownfield grant. The Len's Mill project was ideally suited to the new policy. It was a sizable site with a large structure, and contamination was minimal. Its heritage features were worth preserving.

The developers had insisted that the beautiful modern loft condominiums with cathedral ceilings would not be built if council did not approve the tax incentives. Council approved the grant and it was completed successfully and the units were sold to tenants. More recently, the 18 storey condominium at the corner of Macdonell and Wellington Streets, as well as the Market Square project on Gordon Street were assisted by this policy. Several other applications are under review, but many other properties such as former service station lots, foundries, dry-cleaning operations, scrap yards, chemical plants and other industrial sites remain undeveloped and could become eligible for brownfield grants. A few are described below.

Some Polluted Brownfield Sites

The former gas works plant, at Fountain and Surrey Streets, now a large municipal parking lot across from the police station is among the most severely contaminated of the city's former industrial sites. The Guelph Gas Company was established in 1870 and in exchange for being allowed to lay gas pipes, agreed to provide free coal gas to light the streets, town hall and other public buildings in Guelph. The municipality took over of the gas works in 1903. By 1912 the coal-fired plants were decommissioned. The gas works included a 150,000 cubic foot (4247.5m³) underground iron gas container, and another that accommodated 30,000 cubic feet (849.51m³). There was also an underground tar tank. Coal tar was produced as a byproduct of gas production. Other buildings included an ammonia room, a coke shed, coal sheds, and a coal crusher.

Consultants recommended that additional studies were necessary to determine if any of the tanks were still in the ground and to measure the extent of the contamination. These studies were never conducted even though the site was at the top of a priority list and had alarmingly high contaminant readings. The Municipal parking lot remains the only use of a large plot that could accommodate an excellent CBD development if remediated and decontaminated.

The former International Malleable Iron Company on Beverley Street was abandoned in 1989 by owner Ian Carver, who returned to the United States. The Bank of Montreal also relinquished its equity in the property rather than assuming ownership and responsibility for the clean-up. After a series of eccentric owners and numerous toxic fires, the city seized the site when there were no buyers during a tax sale. The neighbourhood had indicated that it was interested in the 13 acre (5 hectare) site being redeveloped for mixed uses that would include residential and parkland as well as light industrial uses. It could cost more than $6 million to make the site suitable for building homes or parks. Cleaning it to a standard suitable for industrial use would cost much less. Many municipalities don't have the money to decontaminate brownfields, but leaving the chemicals in the ground also comes with a cost. Contamination slowly leaches into the groundwater table, and into the air and food chain, eventually causing long-term health problems.

In 2006, City council voted to invite companies that were interested in redeveloping the IMICO site to submit proposals. They specified that it could become an open space for community use, or a sports facility or a medium-density residential area, with possible office space. It might also become a railway facility or a location for government use such as a school or community centre. Developers expressed interest in building housing on the property. Family and Children's Services of Guelph and Wellington County said that it was a location that they might consider for a new building to consolidate three of their Guelph offices.

By 2010 the IMICO site had not yet been developed and was called an albatross by one local newspaper. Council decided to authorize a "risk assessment" of the location, costing up to $100,000. It then issued a Request For Proposals for developers to suggest an end use for the 13.1

acre (5 ha.) site. The city's environmental consultant proposed that the property be severed into two parts, resulting in a 10 acre (4 ha.) westerly portion that could be remediated relatively quickly, and an easterly portion that would take much longer to prepare for development. About $2.5 million has been spent by the city to remove PCBs, asbestos, waste oil, sludge and other contaminants from the property. The city has also demolished or removed eight acres of buildings, ovens and equipment and has removed some of the most hazardous soil from the footprint of the old galvanizing building. However, little is known about the condition of the remaining soil, especially below large concrete floors that have not been removed. In August 2014 a city hall report said that prospects are good for marketing the city-owned former IMICO site on Beverley Street for construction of medium-density rental housing.

The city regularly reports levels of zinc, lead, hydrocarbons and other contaminants to the Ministry of the Environment as part of the Ministry's clean-up order on the property. Groundwater flow under the site and the impact of contamination from surrounding former industrial sites continue to be studied. At the time of writing, no development has occurred on the site, and prospects for its future remain uncertain because of the costs of removing the contamination. The Ministry of the Environment's standards for soil and groundwater, along with provincial *Places to Grow* legislation have significantly changed the regulatory contexts for planning and brownfield development. The incentives to infill have encouraged developers to use brownfield sites, while tougher environmental regulations have made this more difficult to achieve. In 2014, several Councillors suggested again that appropriate uses should be found for the site and that city money be offered as an incentive to clean up the site.

Canadian General Electric was opened in 1954 on a 207

acre (83 ha.) site on Woodlawn Road to manufacture large power transformers. It became the city's biggest employer. By 1970 it had expanded to 322,000 square feet (29,915 square metres). The company used PCBs until they were banned in 1977, but large quantities were stored on the property and contamination was discovered in the bedrock under the plant. PCBs were also leaking off the site and into the Speed River. In 1985 General Electric reported that four of 120 employees had abnormally high levels of PCBs in their bloodstreams, but that levels were decreasing over time. Under the direction of the Ministry of the Environment, the company maintained a sophisticated on-site waste water treatment plant. Contaminated water was pumped from a dozen wells at the western boundary of the property and Polychlorinated Biphenyls (PCBs) were extracted to be shipped to Alberta for disposal. The plant and property were subsequently sold to ABB which continued the transformer business. After ABB closed, the plant remained vacant for several years until 2008 when Linamar entered into a long-term lease for the entire property. The large building accommodated the growth of Linamar's expanding Skyjack business and made space for Linamar's growing Energy & Heavy Machining business.

Eastview Road

The Eastview Landfill was created in 1962 on 200 acres (81 ha.) in the city's east end and was used by local industry in the 1960s and 1970s when little monitoring of dumping occurred. The leachate contained cancer-causing chemicals such as vinyl chloride, dichloroethane, benzene and dioxins. However, tests indicated that potential for exposure to carcinogenic compounds ranged from very low to zero. Only two areas were found to have toxic substances at levels above provincial regulations. Elevated sodium chloride was found from road salt runoff. Elevated levels of zinc and other heavy metals that are naturally occurring in the geology of the Guelph area were also discovered. A methane gas collection system was installed to address neighbourhood concerns about odours. The site closed in October 2010. After the closure, the gas collection system was converted into an electricity generating facility. The Guelph power project was approved as one of 10 to provide renewable energy to the province. Guelph Hydro saw the potential when methane collection pipes were built into the dump as required by the landfill closing plan. Guelph Hydro quickly began to generate electricity from the gas, instead of allowing it to be flared off continuously into the environment.

Following the closing of the site, a comprehensive plan for its redevelopment was proposed by the city in 2012. Forty five of the total 81 hectares (200 acres) had been land-filled. The plan included a pollination park to attract flying insects and especially bees, and trails on the land-filled portion of the park. On the non-land-filled areas, many uses such as sports fields, concessions, splash pads, an amphitheatre and play areas were proposed. Budget considerations will ultimately determine how much of this plan is implemented.

More Former Landfill Sites

Old landfill sites may be found throughout the city. It is estimated that there are about 420 in Guelph but most contain relatively inert materials, such as brick, sand, glass and lumber, but some contained industrial pollutants or domestic garbage that may still be producing toxic leachate. They include:

The north side of the Eramosa River between Victoria Road and the confluence with the Speed River which was used for landfill between 1935 and 1958. Leachate seepage from rotting domestic garbage has been detected there. Cinder and ash fill is also buried along this stretch.

Wellington Street at Edinburgh Road was used for dumping between 1950 and 1952.

There was considerable dumping on both sides of the

Speed River in the area of Riverside Park and the surrounding apartment buildings between 1958 and 1963. Some of the material was domestic garbage.

Land between Bristol Street and Wellington Street was used for landfill between 1959 and 1960.

In the early 1960s there was a large domestic landfill at the west end of Waterloo Avenue. A methane gas venting system was installed there adjacent to apartment buildings and methane has been detected in some apartment building basements.

Guthrie Park, on Edinburgh Road between Bellevue and Forest streets was once a gravel pit which was filled with about 10 metres of garbage in 1962 and 1963.

In the early 1960s fill was used to straighten the channel beside John McCrae school along the south side of the Speed River.

Areas near London Road between Bagot Street and Edinburgh Road, and near Edinburgh and Willow Road were filled.

Filling occurred from 1929 to 1930 in Royal City Park, north and south of the Speed River between Gordon Street and Gow's Bridge.

Garbage was buried from 1931-32 and during 1950-51 on the south side of the Eramosa River, upstream from the confluence with the Speed River near the east end of James Street, on property owned partially by the Cutten Club.

Landfilling was done on Alice Street in 1933 adjacent to Sacred Heart school.

The site of the former W. C. Wood plant on Arthur street which was demolished in 2010 is now being remediated. It was purchased by Kilmer Brownfield Management Limited in 2011 who applied for a grant to redevelop the property and build condominiums there. City council supported a staff report recommending a grant of up to $10,000, and forgiveness of property taxes for up to three years while the site is rehabilitated and redeveloped. Based on the site's 2009 tax bill, a three-year waiver could total slightly more than $700,000.

Now that Guelph's brownfield policy has been adopted and implemented for several development, all participants, including planners, developers and councillors have become familiar with its provisions which should be more easily implemented in the future.

Redevelopment of the the W.C. Wood Site

There have been a number of public meetings and consultations between representatives of Fusion Homes which ultimately purchased the land, and neighbours interested in the redevelopment of the W.C. Wood site. A set of designs will have residential units fronting onto an area along the Speed River called the "river walk." The original plan included indoor parking on the lower levels of buildings along the river. This parking had the effect of creating a high wall along the river walk. The new plan replaced the structured parking wall with three-storey townhouses overlooking the promenade. This concept provided more low-rise buildings. This change pleased the Ward Residents Association, which formed because it was worried about highrise development on the former Wood site.

Changing the river walk won't eliminate the taller buildings, some of which will be be as high as 14 storeys. Instead, the new design eliminated a north-south interior road, bringing buildings on the site closer together. The new designs also include a pedestrian bridge that was not obvious in other conceptual drawings of the site. The city included two pedestrian crossings from the site to the downtown as part of its *Downtown Secondary Plan*. One is north of the heritage building that is part of the site while the other is just south of that building. City hall is attempting to co-ordinate the timing of its bridge with the development of the site. Heritage Guelph would develop the heritage portion of the site as soon as possible, but Fusion has not yet determined the timing of its development. They are also maintaining a level of flexibility which will not limit possible land uses. Heritage Guelph supports mixed use for the heritage building, which might include community, commercial or residential functions. Ultimately, Fusion will proceed with plans that are "financially feasible". The Ward Residents Association has been involved in consultations about the property since before Fusion took over the project and height has always been a major issue.

By February 2014, an affiliate of Fusion Homes applied for a tax increment-based grant of $3.1 million through the city's *Brownfield Redevelopment Community Improvement Plan* and $8.6 million from a similar downtown intensification program. Guelph Council will have to provide almost $12 million in possible tax deferral incentives to help to transform the former W.C. Wood manufacturing property on Arthur Street into about 700 residential units and a mixture of commercial uses on the site in the city's core. The firm will get tax "forgiveness" of $11.7 million over 10 years, with the tax ultimately recouped by the higher assessment for the residences, retail stores and townhouses to be built on the vacant 3.25 hectares (8 acres). This will transform formerly vacant land into tax-generating properties. Downtown intensification and brownfield redevelopment is a positive policy and incremental financing is generally considered the best way to motivate private investment in areas where it will benefit a municipality.

The city estimates that the three phases would yield a total of about $140 million worth of property assessment. Together, the incentive grants awarded to Fusion are about 11% of this value, which is similar to that granted to previously approved projects. Fusion is obligated to proceed with its redevelopment work quickly and finish within a set number of years, so that it can't procrastinate. The sunset clause requires completion of the first phase by 2019, the second by 2021 and the final one by 2023. They can't wait five years and still receive their tax forgiveness. Fusion's project on the eight-acre former Wood site should yield 36 times more property taxes than the site had been generating as an industrial location. Fusion desires incentive grants from the city primarily to offset an extra cost of more than $18 million for underground parking which will be required on this site. The incentive grants that city hall proposes to give to Fusion Homes will exhaust all the funds in its two year old program for major downtown redevelopment projects. If council approves the proposed grants, it won't accept any more applications for Downtown Major Activation Grants because the program's funding limit will have been reached.

40 Wellington Street Plaza

Belmont Equity Partners and First Plazas are redeveloping the dormant brownfield site on Wellington Street near its intersection with Gordon, where Rockwell International once made tools and electronics. In the summer of 2012 City Council approved rezoning to allow a cluster of retail and office space in four buildings of various sizes. This site has been vacant for over 20 years and has been remediated for commercial development, but not for residences, which a city planner said in 2011 would be prohibitively expensive. It promises a balanced mix of stores on this former industrial site. Plans are to offer a natural food store, restaurant, liquor store, coffee shop and other retailers.

The proposed plaza which is adjacent to Royal City Park, residential neighbourhoods, commercial operations and fast food restaurants, and is receiving a generally positive response from local residents. They believe that it will serve them well, but as with all such developments, there are concerns about traffic congestion at such a busy corner. Guelph politicians and planners hope that the developers design the plaza to be compatible with the adjacent Royal City Park and Speed River, and with Gordon's streetscape. The developer stated that it has balanced urban design, municipal and Conservation Authority requirements, servicing constraints, site contamination and the stringent design and functional requirements of prospective tenants to create an excellent new plaza.

THE DOLIME QUARRY: CONTINUING CONFLICT

The Dolime quarry was developed on part of Lots 1, 2, 3, 4, and 5, Concessions 4 and 5, Division G, Township of Guelph-Eramosa, just beyond the city limits on the western edge of Guelph. The quarry exposes 16 metres of the Middle Silurian Guelph Formation underlain by 3 metres of the Amabel Formation. The Amabel Formation (Eramosa Member) consists thin-bedded, coarse crystalline dark brown bituminous dolostone. Overlying this is 5.5 metres of Eramosa-Guelph Formation dolostone which consists of grey-green, medium-crystalline, massive, fossiliferous dolostones. Overlying this is 2.5 metres of pure white to buff coloured fine to medium crystalline, massive dolostone of the Guelph Formation. The overburden is composed of 8-12 metres of coarse sand.

Over 100 years old, the quarry began operations in the 1860s and Canadian Gypsum worked the site until 1978 when Guelph Dolime followed as Licensee until the 1990's. Lafarge Construction also operated there during the Guelph Dolime period. The licence was transferred to River Valley Developments Inc. in March 2004. James Dick Construction has been operating quarry since Fall of 2005. The original focus was on Guelph Formation Limestone for lime products, which supplied lime kilns and produced dust problems. The current operations are concentrated on the Lower Amabel Formation Stone which is valued for concrete and construction purposes, so the kilns have been eliminated and dust is no longer a major concern. For a few years, flat plains, steep cliffs and a lake filled the 150 acre (60.7 ha.) site until it reopened in 2006 as an aggregate quarry. Increasingly, the city has grown outwards with sprawl surrounding the quarry site. Ever since, there have been disputes between the quarry and the City of Guelph. These focus primarily on concerns about how proposed future quarry operations may affect regional groundwater resources. It is now a below water table quarry, having an "A" Class Licence, # 5672.

In 2009, workers at the Quarry excavated four or five metres into a confining bedrock layer, exposing the city's water supply aquifer and creating concerns about potential contamination. These were reported in findings of the Ontario Geological Society. Then the Ministry of Northern Development and Mines conducted complex geological mapping for an ongoing project examining the bedrock along the Niagara Escarpment. It concluded that blasts along a 100 metre area of the quarry were probably accidental and it was not known whether they would affect the aquifer. Given the irregular surface of the strata, only a geologist would have been able to recognize the aquifer. In 2007 it was still not exposed, but by 2008, the aquifer had been uncovered and additional concerns were expressed by the city.

The resource manager at James Dick Construction said that operators had excavated only to the depth allowed in its Ministry of Natural Resources-approved licence. He claimed that the lowest level in the quarry was reached 20 years ago and that there was no danger to Guelph's groundwater from present operations. The quarry's licence had been disputed by the city ever since it applied to excavate at twice the approved annual rate. Despite this, the city appealed the quarry's request for an amendment. The Quarry management asserted that the city was misinterpreting geological mapping and that it should not be appealing the licence of a business that has been operating for years. The Ministry of Natural Resources requested advice on possible groundwater contamination from the Ministry of the Environment.

Before new geological mapping discovered the Gasport Formation which is the primary confined bedrock aquifer, the Ministry of the Environment was not concerned about possible contamination. In light of the new mapping, it recommended that no further excavation of the Amabel

Formation take place pending further investigation. The city recommended that the Ministry limit excavation to prevent additional damage to the protective layer. It contended that contamination could occur when the quarry stops operations and shuts down its sump pumps. Without the pumping,the quarry would flood and allow water to seep into the aquifer.

The City of Guelph continued to be concerned that operations of the quarry so close to city wells would adversely affect the quality of Guelph's drinking water. On 26 July, 2011, Mayor Karen Farbridge wrote to the Ministry of the Environment objecting to the Management Plan for the quarry approved by the Ministry of the Environment. She pointed out that a peer review of the plan done for the city by Golder Associates discovered that:

> The "Fines Layer" would not provide adequate protection for the city's water supply because its composition, thickness, layering, density, particle size and filtration potential would be inadequate to protect the city's otherwise well confined aquifer from water and contamination in the quarry. The report concluded that operation of the quarry under the management plan proposed would pose a threat to the health and safety of the citizens of the city of Guelph. The city also opposed a proposal to increase the extraction rate at the quarry.

In 2007, River Valley Developments Inc., the owner of the the Dolime quarry made a request to the Ministry of Environment to double its extraction rate from 500,000 tonnes a year to one million tonnes a year. This application is still being processed, but if accepted, the company will have depleted the quarry in 15 years. The current plan is to extract rock for the next 30 years and then turn the site into a lake. The company has also applied to amend its permit to take water. This application was made in 2010 and is still being reviewed by the ministry. Meanwhile, the city of Guelph has continued its objections to River Valley

Development's plans for the quarry into 2013.

The quarry operators contend that within the same lake, they want to move the pumps from one side to the other side of the lake. They contend that the city has made this into a bigger deal than it actually is. The company has a two-stage pumping system with three pumps and is hoping to replace that system with one pump, on the other side of the lake, closer to Speed River. It was not planning to change the rate or the depth at which the water is going to pumped.

In response to the company's permit to take water application, Janet Laird, the executive director of Planning, Building, Engineering and Environment Services in Guelph, wrote a letter to the Ministry of Environment citing three main reasons why the application should not be approved. It demands a long-term management plan to protect the quality and quantity of the water in municipal wells. It also asserts that the current monitoring program is inadequate to determine whether future well interference will be caused by quarry operations. It suggests that a financial assurances plan be implemented to protect taxpayers financially if operations at the quarry lead to unforeseen environmental costs in the future.

The company contended that the three requests made in the letter were unnecessary. A management plan had been provided to the city, and the monitoring program was one of the most sophisticated plans for any quarry in the province. They suggested that the city was just trying to make money to reduce the cost of adding additional water treatment to the wells when the quarry became a lake. Because the city's municipal wells were so close to the quarry, it was inevitable that the well water would eventually need additional processing and treatment before entering into the drinking water system. They suggested that the city had not foreseen the requirement for additional drinking water treatment when the quarry became a lake.

On January 18, 2013 Robert Baxter, general manager of River Valley Developments Inc., owner of the Dolime quarry, sent a letter making the following points to the City of Guelph. He stated that there had been no contamination at the quarry and that no deepening or expansion of the limits of extraction had been requested. He said that an application was submitted to double the rate of extraction within the approved limits of the quarry, which would significantly reduce the quarrying life of the site based on the current licence.

He reiterated that the quarry had existed since the late 1800s and that the the City of Guelph has expanded toward the quarry since then. The current quarry's plans were approved in 1992 but the Membro production well, the closest city water supply well, was commissioned only in 1994. He suggested that the City should plan and design its water supply system based on the details of the legal licences, knowing that the quarry will eventually become a lake. The city's problems with water quality at Membro occur because of its proximity to the river which manages water quality by altering its flow. The city should be proactive and add treatment components to Membro to mitigate these potential issues, rather than suggesting that the quarry would affect the municipal water supply.

Baxter also stated that the upper part of the Gasport formation provides protection to the much deeper and more porous part of the gasport formation from which the city extracts its groundwater. Management continues to work with the Ministry of Environment and the Ministry of Natural Resources to improve the protective qualities of the quarry base as described in the Quarry Management Plan.

The August 10, 2010 application to the Environment Ministry was to amend and renew the permit to take water. This requested the relocation of pumps in the quarry pond, updating of the pumping system and improving the monitoring system. It would remove an unnecessary set of pumps, improve overall efficiency and reduce electrical consumption. The renewal of the permit was not a revision to its management plan and would not affect the city's water supply.

Baxter reiterated that in 2004, the new owners of the quarry had met with city staff and presented a vision for early closure of the quarry and the creation of a residential development around the lake. The city declined to embrace this proposal. Nevertheless, management might consider revising its quarry business plan by reducing the 30 year life of the site to approximately 10. This would decrease its licensed volume of extraction, abandon any future option of expanding the footprint of the quarry, and change the land use from quarry to residential development, which is integral to the city's water system. Quarry management would welcome a meeting with citizens and city staff to review these suggestions, but such a meeting did not occur.

Permit Approved

On January 25, 2013, the Ministry approved an amended permit that allowed the daily total maximum water-taking requested by Dolime. The average water-taking at the quarry had historically been around 6,000 cubic metres per day which is approximately one half the maximum permit rate of 13,750 cubic metres, allowing them to actually take much more water than normal. At their highest permitted rate, this would make Dolime the largest water taker in the Guelph area.

The current management plan for the quarry allows extraction in areas of the quarry that may further expose Guelph's aquifer and increase inflow to the quarry. According to city reports, this may increase the average pumping rates out of the quarry, adversely affecting the quantity and quality of water available to city wells. The city therefore insisted that the management plan be linked to the water-taking permit. The movement of the pump sumps to a new location is part of the original management plan and the amendment for the approved water-taking permit is to reflect the new sump location. The city and Wellington Water Watchers therefore concluded that the current management plan would not protect our water. The timing of the approval of the water-taking permit was unfortunate, given that the new management plan was to be submitted to Ministry of the Environment in February 2013. The city had only 15 days to seek leave to appeal which it did, since the plan was not satisfactory to the city.

Continuing Controversy

In May 2013, the Quarry became the target of Mike Schreiner, Leader of the Green Party and a candidate in Guelph. He planted the first of about 200 signs on the lawn at 360 Woolwich St. It stated: *"Protect Our Water: Say No to Dolime Quarry."* Quarry management labelled the campaign an exercise in political opportunism. Schreiner contended that there is a broad concern in Guelph that the longstanding and ongoing quarry operation is a threat to the city's water supply. He said that he supports the City's efforts to limit activity at the quarry because it could impede or contaminate the city's drinking water supply.

Quarry management responded that it operated within the terms of its permits and that an increase in the rate of rock removal would reduce the operating life of the quarry and be a benefit to the community. Earlier this year the Ministry of the Environment had stated that the operation's water-taking permit would not result in more water being taken or increase the risk to water quality. Schreiner insisted that the ministry failed to protect Guelph's drinking water adequately. His sign campaign was intended to apply political pressure to the Liberal government.

He said that the current Liberal government tends to respond to public pressure, as it did when there was an outcry over the proposed "mega quarry" in Melancthon. The sign campaign is intended to apply similar pressure. Quarry management claimed that the Green party is bullying the company and engaging in a witch hunt for crass political purposes. They suggested that in the current environment in which no one is willing to defend quarry operators, Schreiner is taking advantage and turning a simple approval certificate into a major issue to defame the quarry operation unjustly. The permit has been granted and the controversy will continue into the next provincial election.

May 09, 2014: The Environmental Review Tribunal gave the City of Guelph the chance to appeal the provincial decision on River Valley Developments Inc.'s permit to take water at the Dolime quarry. On May 2, the provincial adjudicator approved the city's application for appeal, which was submitted at the beginning of 2013, beginning a process that could end at a future tribunal hearing. The city is appealing the conditions in the permit allowing the company to take water till the end of 2017. Guelph now has the right to a full hearing on this issue. If the issue is heard before the parties reach a settlement, the tribunal will make a decision as to whether the permit should be altered. The city will file a formal Notice of Appeal which will trigger a hearing process, bringing together the ministry, the city and the quarry owners to discuss the conditions of the permit.

The City will request that the permit include a revised management plan for the quarry. It must include strategies to mitigate the impact on the city's drinking water when the quarry ceases operation, an improved monitoring program and financial assurances that taxpayers won't have to pay for long-term mitigation costs caused by quarry operations. The hearing could be very expensive for the city and the quarry owners. The city will meet with River Valley Developments and the Ministry of Environment to discuss conditions of the permit to take water in an effort to avoid a Tribunal hearing. In September 2014, the city, the Ministry of the Environment and Dolime quarry owner River Valley Development Inc. agreed to mediation in a bid to resolve the dispute without the necessity of a lengthy hearing. The results have not yet been announced.

OTHER IMPORTANT ISSUES

Conflict with Wellington County

Guelph's Land Ambulance Performance Agreement with the service provider, Royal City Ambulance Service Ltd. expired on December 31st, 2008. Council directed that emergency medical services be delivered as a municipal operation serving the City of Guelph, the County of Wellington and other areas as required by the Ontario Ambulance Act. This transition to a municipally operated Guelph–Wellington Emergency Medical Service was completed January 1, 2009.

In February 2008, city council unanimously passed a resolution giving Wellington County one year's notice that the city planned to terminate the existing cost-sharing agreements on social services and social housing, and that the city wanted arbitration of the matter. In March 2009, the county notified the city that it desired arbitration of the costs of land ambulance services, which had been shared on the basis of population. This resulted in 57% of the ambulance costs that weren't paid by the province being borne by the city and 43% by the county. Under a cost-sharing agreement dating back to the 1990s when social services, including social housing, were downloaded by the province to municipalities, Guelph and Wellington County had split the costs based on where the recipients live. The city considered this to be unfair because recipients of social services disproportionately reside in Guelph, where social service offices are located. Guelph also provides public transit, which is needed by people on welfare.

In January 2010, the County of Wellington filed a $4 million breach of contract lawsuit against the city over the funding of the Wellington Terrace long-term care home near Fergus. Then Guelph councillors severed committee relationships with Wellington County, ending the city's participation in a joint social services committee and scrapping the land ambulance committee. When a Toronto arbitrator supported Wellington County in a hearing about the funding of shared services, the ruling shifted about $2 million in annual costs from the county to the city.

In March 2012 the city and county settled their lawsuit about the cost of maintaining the county owned Wellington Terrace Long Term Care home near Elora. The settlement required the city to pay almost $4.2 million to cover maintenance obligations between 2006 and 2012. This and the arbitrator's decision ended years of bickering about costs between the city and Wellington County.

City Reorganization Plans

Beginning in 2011, Council spent considerable time and effort discussing the merits of having an Integrity Commissioner. In that year, lawyer Robert Swayze was retained to investigate complaints about the behaviour of several councillors, to investigate breaches in the Council's Code of Conduct and to provide councillors with guidance on the application of the code. In October of 2011 he was appointed as the City's Integrity Commissioner. His first report dealt with a dispute between four councillors and staff about the release of an air quality report. They objected to his findings and voted to reject his report which was ultimately "received" by council. Thereafter, he investigated several other complaints. Considerable discussion and controversy surrounded his function and his fees. This continued until the end of 2015 when council discussed not renewing Swayze's contract and sharing an Ombudsman with other councils.

In July 2013, the city of Guelph decided to change fundamentally the way it conducts city hall business, especially as it affects economic and residential development. The goal of the Integrated Operational Review has evolved in three phases since 2011. It is to make Guelph more "businesslike" in the way it does business. It would promote a "whole systems" approach to "improving the city's business investment and development processes." Through an organizational rethinking process involving over 60 staff members in four principal service areas, the review identified ways to streamline development processes, to improve interdepartmental communications, and to identify new economic development investment opportunities. Phase 1, completed by an Oakville-based consultant Glenn Pothier in late 2011, identified a "constellation" of issues creating barriers to development in the city. Some of the issues were a "culture of fear" among municipal employees, low staff morale, contradictory communications between city staff and developers, undue interference in development projects by city staff, and an overly long application process. The term "Guelph factor" was used by developers to describe the impediments associated with doing business in the city, and the costs of dealing with unexpected delays and problems with municipal procedures.

Based on numerous recommendations, the review process has initiated major changes to addresses those issues. While the Integrated Operational Review's implementation will take three and a half years, ten "immediate improvements" have been identified and are being implemented. They included standardized mapping templates for corporate reports, a new standardized site plan agreement, and a site plan inspection protocol. There was also a review of all open development application files to identify the most promising economic development investment opportunities, and to enhance communications between city departments and stakeholders. Some counsellors criticized the fact that the review had begun in 2010 and would not be complete until 2016.

Implementation of the plan would require expenditures of $270,000 for operating and $720,000 in capital costs which include positions for two new planners. In 2014, an estimated $240,000 will be spent on consultants to implement elements of the plan, including establishing a "triage protocol" for new development proposals. They would also conduct a technology gap analysis and develop an Integrated Operational Review technology implementation plan, as well as a new communications and customer service strategy.

City hall has plans for an open-government action program that may have national and international influence. The city awarded a contract to Delvinia, a digital strategy firm in Toronto, to help with development of the plan. Delvinia in association with with the University of Toronto's Innovation Policy Lab at the Munk School of Global Affairs will work with the city and community participants in Guelph to prepare a five-year project and action plan for the Guelph's open government initiatives. City council endorsed an open government framework and approved $100,000 for the project as part of the city's 2013 budget.

This open government action plan, the first of its kind in Canada, will involve the local community and depend on community interest, insight and active participation. The exercise will offer community members new ways to get involved and participate in a major initiative for Guelph's municipal government. According to Mayor Farbridge, more "open, accountable, transparent and engaging municipal government will empower the Guelph community to work together on innovative solutions and, ultimately, all civic decisions." She said that "open government is defined as creating a fully transparent and accountable city, one that leverages technology and empowers the community to generate added value as well as participate in the development of innovative and meaningful solutions."

An audit of Guelph's operating expenses in November 2013 reported that poor tracking tools, and 'a culture that views overtime as obligatory,' in some city departments contributed to excessive overtime costs that could exceed $5 million in 2013. It demonstrated that if Guelph were to reduce its overtime costs to a "maximum target" comparable to overtime rates in cities like Kitchener or Waterloo, Guelph could save over $3 million a year. It suggested that estimates of overtime Guelph's costs were based on "historical data rather than on actual business needs." Guelph's City Administrator promised to review and remedy this situation.

Residential Development Charges

In January 2014, City councillors passed an updated development charges bylaw that increased residential rates by 12.5 per cent. This could add $3,000 to the price of a newly built single-detached home. The bylaw will increase development charges levied on a single detached home or town home built after March 2, 2014 from $24,208 to $27,232. The levy for a two-bedroom apartment will rise to $16,389 from $14,568 and for a condominium, the rate will increase to $20,508 from $18,232. Many developers opposed these increases, but a number of Councillors wondered whether they were high enough. They maintained that growth should pay for itself, but staff desired to keep increases reasonable. Planned infrastructure such as new roads, parks, transit vehicles and city buildings qualified for development charges were projected to cost $547 million, part of which would come from the increased levies.

Council also voted to reduce development charges on new commercial and industrial developments to $9.09 per square foot, down from $12.27 for commercial projects and $9.97 for industrial projects. New buildings constructed by the University of Guelph continued to be exempt, but a new charge of $64 on each new townhouse or single-detached home was added to help pay for Wellington-Dufferin-Guelph Public Health's new headquarters. The cost of cleaning up after the December 22 ice storm and January blizzards is somewhere between $500,000 and $750,000 which didn't include the cost of restoring the city's tree canopy, which was badly damaged by the ice storm. Council also passed a bylaw that will allow residents to pay their property taxes with a credit card.

Isobel Warren Death from Wall Collapsing

On June 16, 2009, after she boosted herself onto a change table attached to the privacy wall in a city washroom, Isobel Warren was crushed and killed by the collapsing wall. She was on a break from a physical education class at neighbouring Bishop Macdonell Catholic High School. In a ruling on 12 February 2013, Justice Michael Epstein said that there was abundant evidence that the privacy wall at the South End Community Park washroom was improperly tied and anchored, and since its construction in 2004 had been a hazard and a danger to the public. However, he ruled that the City of Guelph was not guilty of a breach of the province's Occupational Health and Safety Act. He stated that the city took reasonable precautions and followed standard practices when it relied upon the professional standards of the engineers, architects and masons who built the washroom and its privacy wall.

The city, the architect and engineer were originally charged by the Ministry of Labour. In pretrial proceedings Epstein dismissed the charges of providing negligent or incompetent advice against architect Alan Grinham and engineer Larry Argue, the experts hired by the city to oversee the design and construction of the washroom. Epstein dismissed the charges because the one year time limit to lay such charges had expired. The ministry appealed that ruling but was unsuccessful.

Isobel's parents launched a $2.8-million civic lawsuit against the city in 2010 which was settled out of court. Court records revealed that a payment of $40,000 to Warren's younger brother, James Theodore Warren, was part of the resolution.

Epstein stressed that evidence proved that the washroom's privacy wall was improperly constructed. It was neither properly anchored to the floor nor tied to the structure's main wall, as required. Had it been properly anchored it would have withstood a heavier load. The washroom building at Southend Community Park never reopened and was demolished by the city in August 2013. A new one is being constructed.

Guelph Police Headquarters

The original estimate of $13.6-million for Guelph Police Service's proposed headquarters renovation had escalated to $34-million by November 2013. The city treasurer is working with the Chief of Police to review and possibly reduce these costs. Some councillors are worried that the large cost for the police headquarters might defer planned expenditures for other projects such as a south end community centre. In December 2013, despite the controversy about its high cost, municipal staff recommended approval of the new police headquarters. However, the Police Board must elaborate the benefits of new construction versus renovation and assess its impact on police operations. It must also determine its impact on the city's tax assessment and its effect on police satellite facilities like that on Clair Road. Questions of how a new headquarters will affect working relations with other emergency services in the city were also raised. The Police Board asserted that it would cease operations from the Clair Road facility.

Guelph Farmers' Market

The Guelph Farmers' Market has been a focal point in Guelph for over 180 years. It is a friendly location where fresh fruit and vegetables can be purchased directly from local farmers. It is also a community meeting place where families come to shop for quality meats, cheese, produce, baked goods, preserves, and delicious foods prepared by the vendors. Customers enjoy a one-on-one relationship with producers. The snack bar and picnic tables provide a congenial space where friends can meet and visit. Many "regulars" look forward to this every Saturday morning. During the winter most market activity is inside while the summer market extends outside and includes the Market parking lot.

In December 2010, market vendors were moved to the City Hall to accommodate necessary repairs to the market building roof. Based on a structural assessment of the building, engineers who inspected the roof declared it unsafe and in danger of collapsing from the weight of snow. The city closed the building in the interest of public safety and invited arts and crafts vendors to relocate to the lobby of City Hall. Produce vendors used the entrance and foyer. Unfortunately, vendors requiring hot and cold water for the operation of their booths could not be accommodated at either location.

The market operated from City Hall every Saturday while the roof was being repaired. The temporary location at City Hall served about 3,000 shoppers each Saturday while it was there. The Guelph Farmers' Market was reopened in its original building at 7 a.m. on Saturday, March 5. Not all vendors and shoppers were happy about the move, but most agreed that it was better than cancelling the market while repairs were being made.

Temporary Move to Exhibition Park Arena

From June 15 until Saturday, September 14, 2013 the Guelph Market operated at Exhibition Park arena while many necessary repairs were being made to the old market building. The floor required recoating, an accessible washroom was added, walls were painted, new vendor partitions and millwork were installed, plumbing was modified, offices were renovated, fire suppression and exhaust hoods were added, the entrance vestibule and doors were upgraded, cracked concrete was repainted or filled and the foundation wall was coated.

To accommodate customers' parking and transportation requirements during the renovations, the city offered free parking at the Fountain Street lot and shuttle service between it and the Exhibition arena. There was also free on site parking at the arena. When the move was announced there were the usual "Guelph Reactions". Some neighbours of the Exhibition Park arena worried that traffic and parked cars would disrupt the area on Saturdays while others didn't like the idea of all those people coming to "their" arena.

Guelph's 2013 capital budget included $170,000 for upgrades to the hundred year old market building at Gordon and Wilson streets. When detailed inspections had been made, it became apparent that the cost would be far more than this. However, the Downtown Secondary Plan, approved in 2012, envisioned the market moving and its current home demolished. This plan even included a suggestion to extend Freshfield Street to connect to Wilson Street once the building had been demolished. Critics suggested that if this were to occur, money spent on market building improvements would be wasted.

In June 2013 the city retendered the renovations at the Guelph Farmers' Market building to keep the project on budget. Bids were received from three of six pre-qualified general contractors but none were within the City's project budget of $500,000. The City then reduced the scope of work and retendered to the original six pre-qualified contractors but only one bid was received and it was significantly over the allocated project budget. The City then further reduced the scope of work, re-designed some of the systems, and re-specified some of the materials in an effort to bring the work in on budget.

The new tender was released to a broader group of general contractors. Planned work focused on health and safety such as flooring and plumbing. A significant amount of work was also to be done on the individual vendor booths. All the doorways in the market were to become more accessible. Some cosmetic issues that were included in the original tender were postponed because of budget constraints. They included an office renovation, some cosmetic work around doorways and some work on kitchen exhaust hoods. Stahle Construction and Beitz Construction Innovations completed the required work on budget and the market returned to its original location on September 14, 2013.

Police Chief Resigns

On August 30, 2014 Bryan Larkin, Guelph's popular and excellent Chief of Police resigned to become the Chief of Waterloo Regional Police Service. He will be greatly missed by the citizens and police of Guelph. A search found a replacement, Jeff DeRuyter.

2014 Petrie Building Considered Endangered

The Petrie Building at 15 Wyndham St. N. features one of the most unique facades in Canada, a stamped galvanized iron decorative element that dates back to the 1880s. It is one of just three pre-1890 buildings in Canada with a full sheet metal façade. Some fear that this historically significant part of Guelph's downtown could eventually be lost if nothing is done to restore it. Heritage Canada and The National Trust agree. Petrie's stamped galvanized iron front displays extraordinary craftsmanship and obvious historical significance but is a state of advanced deterioration. The Apollo Eleven diner has occupied the ground floor of the building since the mid-1970s, but the upper floors have been unoccupied and unheated for decades. The building is owned by Agelakos family of Guelph which feels that the cost to restore the metal façade alone is prohibitive.

The state of the Petrie Building is unfortunate, especially given that it has been designated by the City of Guelph under the Ontario Heritage Act for nearly 25 years. The building was nominated for the Top Ten Endangered Places and has been added to the infamous list. It has since been purchased and is being renovated.

The Transit Strike

During July 2014,Guelph's transit workers voted to reject the city's final contract settlement proposal. The city then threatened to lock them out. When city made another offer which both the union executive and Council accepted, it was rejected the the membership. The city then locked out the workers despite their offer to continue without a contract until a settlement was reached. After a two week lockout, the city's new offer was accepted by the union members and transit service returned. Members were pleased that some of their concerns about washroom and lunch facilities had been addressed. Free rides were offered to lure passengers back to Guelph's buses.

Contamination along the Speed River

In September 2014, six or seven barrels were found at a construction site on the north side of Wellington Street behind the Phoenix Mill apartment building on Waterloo Avenue. Subsequently, several more barrels, some leaking, were discovered in the area. Nearby residents were told to stay indoors and close their windows as the noxious smell from the spilled material became overwhelming. The contents were sent to be tested for toxicity. Geophysical surveying tools were being used to discover if any more barrels were buried in the way of the future watermain construction.

More than 100 chemicals were analyzed from samples taken from the test pits and 15 were discovered to exceed the concentration standard set out by the Ministry of Environment and Climate Change. Of the 15 chemicals, 12 were identified as those typically found in industrial fill where coal burning operations were located. The other three included petroleum hydrocarbons, ethylbenzene and xylene mixture. They were found to exceed ministry standards in only one test pit and only by a small amount. While all 15 chemicals are of concern, the 12 associated with typical industrial contamination don't tend to move once buried. The other three are associated with a liquid and are more likely to spread underground. Because these liquid chemicals exceeded ministry standards by so little there's little possibility that they will spread. However, efforts should be made to remove the drums and the contaminated soil around them as hazardous waste before watermain construction resumes.

The Tree Canopy and the Emerald Ash Borer

Guelph's updated tree by-law provided increased protection for trees on private property. Effective August 3, 2010, damage or destruction of any tree measuring at least 10 centimetres in diameter at 1.4 metres above the ground on lots larger than 0.2 hectares (0.5 acres) was prohibited without permission from the City. Trees on lots equal to or smaller than 0.2 ha. will be cared for by residents and property owners. Some trees are exempt from the by-law and can be removed without a permit. These include dead or dying trees, trees posing danger to life or property, or trees affected by unforeseen causes or natural events. The bylaw listed other exemptions.

In April 2014 the City planned to spend $15 to $16 million over the next ten years to fight the threat of the Emerald Ash Borer (EAB).Since it arrived in North America around 2000, the ash borer, an invasive insect from Asia, has been spreading slowly throughout Ontario. It targets and kills virtually all ash trees, but leaves other species alone. An estimated 10,000 city-owned street and park trees are at risk. As a result of EAB infestation, all untreated ash trees are expected to die over the coming decade, or sooner. Guelph's plan is to reduce the risk of injury and property damage, by reducing damage to city trees and assisting in recovery. Three hundred thousand dollars has been allocated to assist EAB work in 2014. This will include monitoring the extent of the damage and creating an inventory of the city's ash trees. It will pay for removing and replacing some 750 trees, treating 500 trees, planting 50 trees, and acquiring a "tub grinder" to grind up large amounts of wood. Traps spread around the city indicated that the borer has spread quickly across Guelph.

All public trees showing signs and symptoms of the ash borer will be cut down and removed. Trees not showing visible signs of infestation will be assessed for possible treatment with TreeAzin, a pest control product approved by the Canadian government. Guelph's plan suggests that only larger trees be treated with this product. Treatment involves injecting a tree with TreeAzin every two years for about $250 per treatment. It is hoped that after 5 treatments (10 years) the effects of the Emerald Ash Borer will decrease because of lack of food and increased predation. Protecting large trees over this period can be less expensive than the cost of removing and replacing them. The cost is also comparable to the services provided by the trees, such as air and water filtration, moderating storm water flows, carbon sequestration and micro-climate improvement.

As the infested ash trees are removed they will be replaced, primarily with a native, site-appropriate species of tree. A small percentage will be replaced with non-native, non invasive species. When all untreated trees have been killed, the EAB should suffer a massive population decline. Because the infestation is already well advanced, and because funds are limited, the city will probably treat less than 30 per cent of the ash trees in Guelph. To gain the longest service life possible, trees that are untreated will be left standing as long as they are safe. Guelph is expected to reach its peak of ash tree mortality in 2016, and a plan with how to deal with the dead trees will evolve in the future. Some cities such as Detroit and Windsor have been overwhelmed with dead trees.

During the winters of 2013 and 2014, severe ice storms damaged many trees, a number of which had to be removed. The city asked the Ontario Ministry of Municipal Affairs and Housing for $917,300 to help clean up the damage from the December 2013 ice storm. Despite the number of trees planted by Trees for Guelph volunteers (over 10,000 between 2012 and 2013), the city's tree canopy experienced mass devastation from ice and wind storms. More than 4000 volunteers from this group planted 5326 trees in 2013. Nevertheless, the city's tree canopy includes far fewer mature trees than before the storms and will take years to replenish.

Tricar Condominiums on Wellington street

In February 2014, City council approved an 18-storey condominium tower on the former Marsh Tire site in Guelph's downtown. Subsequently it approved a grant of $4.6 million to assist with site remediation. Funds from both the brownfield tax increment based grant reserve fund and heritage redevelopment reserve grant program would be be used; $2.8 million from brownfield and $1.8 million from heritage. These grants are incentives to encourage redevelopment of lands based on the estimated increase in municipal taxes generated by the completed project. The funds are recouped through future taxes based on a 10 year tax increment. The grants are to help offset the costs of off site infrastructure upgrades and the construction of underground parking spaces.

A tax increment based grant was previously approved for a planned residential development at 5 Arthur St., the former W.C. Wood manufacturing site. Some councillors and citizens were critical of these grants and felt that money should have instead been granted to the IMCO site on Elizabeth Street.

Controversy about St. George's Square

A proposal for the rebuilding of St. George's Square after renewing underground infrastructure has caused considerable controversy. It suggested a square with a single lane roadway running around the outside. Most of the open space would be in the centre in an area with trees lining the roadway. There would also be some small grassy areas with stylized benches and a shade structure to one side. That structure could house washrooms and a maintenance building, where temporary seating could be stored for special events. There might also be a concession stand. A cross delineated by paving stones on the ground would represent the former location of St. George's church.

During the public meeting, the consultant suggested that a Christmas tree might stand in the centre of the circle and that it could accommodate a public market. Questions of traffic management and snow removal were posed by the audience. Costs were estimated to be $18.5 million for reconstruction of Wyndham Street plus another $6 million to $6.5 million for St. George's Square. The new city council will have to wrestle with this contentious issue which may be postponed for several years.

Wyndham Street Railway Underpass

Soon after it was constructed, it was discovered that the new underpass on Wyndham Street was too low for long transport trucks. Since the bridge opened in October 2013, five transport trucks hit a beam under the bridge, causing minor damage to the trucks. There were no reported injuries. Apparently someone misjudged the slope under the bridge and did not allow for the fact that long trucks could hit the beam. Truck cabs could clear at 4 metres, but because of the slope, trailers hit the beam. Temporary signs were installed, but it was almost a year before permanent signs were posted in both metric and imperial units. The final solution was to install flashing amber warning beacons on the beam underneath the bridge and permanent signs on the sides of the road in both directions. The new sign attached to the crash beam will continue to indicate a clearance of 3.8 metres, but also includes the imperial height of 12 feet, 5 inches.

Guelph's Innovative District Energy System

A project called the Galt District Energy System is being implemented by Envida Community Energy, a company managed by Guelph Hydro Inc. and owned by the City of Guelph. It began operating in late December 2013 at the Sleeman Centre and is an important first step in developing North America's first city-wide district energy network. The city plans to use more local energy sources to supply at least 50 per cent of the community's heating needs in the next 30 years. The system will become an interconnected thermal grid to serve industrial, commercial and residential buildings across Guelph. It will operate initially in the area around the city's downtown Sleeman Centre arena.

The network will be supplied by the central heating and cooling plant at the Sleeman Centre which uses natural gas to heat water in boilers for space heating. It also has a central chilling unit to chill water for cooling during the summer. Later the system will be expanded to heat and cool the nearby River Run Centre and other commercial and residential developments in central Guelph.

Insulated pipes running from the Sleeman Centre and to other buildings in the area are being buried and will transport hot water, steam or cold water through an underground network to heat or cool additional buildings. In cold weather, the system at the Sleeman Centre will use natural gas to heat the water before it runs through the closed loop system. In warmer months, water will be chilled and piped to provide cool water for air conditioners. There is very little heat loss with such a system. If there is community support for the project, the network of pipes will eventually spread throughout the downtown and beyond. The work under way is part of a long term strategy to have the entire city connected to district energy by 2041.

New heating and cooling systems, or nodes, will eventually be established throughout the city wherever there is concentrated demand for heat and a group of businesses wanting to be part of the grid. The nodes will eventually be connected and form a network. When nodes are established and have a strong economic base, the incremental cost to add customers to the nodes will decrease considerably. Neither the taxpayers of Guelph nor Guelph Hydro's ratepayers will be required to pay for this system which is common in many European cities.

In August 2014 the Tricar Group, an environmentally responsible builder, announced that its 18-storey condo development, River Mill Condominiums will be the first residential building in Guelph to be heated and cooled by district energy. Its residents will benefit from the reliability, convenience and lower fuel costs associated with this system. Heating and air conditioning equipment in the 139 condominium suites will look the same as conventional equipment. Individual programmable thermostats will enable residents to monitor and control the temperature in their units.

Guelph Municipal Holdings Inc.

In June 2014, City Council approved the amalgamation of Guelph Hydro Inc. with the city's municipal holding company, Guelph Municipal Holdings Inc. (GMHI).The City of Guelph is GMHI's sole shareholder, and GMHI is the sole shareholder of Guelph Hydro Inc. which holds Guelph Hydro Electric Systems Inc. It provides electricity to customers in Guelph and Rockwood, and holds the unregulated company

Envida Community Energy Inc.

GMHI was established by the city in 2011 to manage city owned assets and maximize the value of those assets. It could include a new real estate based development corporation to direct City assets and operations such as downtown land parcels and parking; a thermal utility to implement the District Energy Strategic Plan and Guelph Junction Railway. All officers of the holding company are city of Guelph employees.

The Guelph Municipal Holdings Inc. portfolio, with assets of $66.8 million, has focused on energy related corporations supporting Guelph's Community Energy Initiative. Barry Chuddy became its Chief Executive Officer on July 23, 2014, replacing Ann Pappert, the City of Guelph's Chief Administrative Officer who had served as CEO of GMHI since its inception.

Baker Street Development Plan

In June 2014, City Council endorsed the *Baker District and Parking Master Plan* on city-owned land that is currently the Baker Street parking lot. It suggested a Conestogo College Campus, 1,075 parking spaces, 350 residential units and 183,000 square feet (17,001 square metres) of institutional uses including a new main library, YMCA, Innovation Guelph, plus retail and office space. The cost of the city's portion of the Baker District project, including its contribution to the proposed new college campus and library, could be $43 million, but it will increase the value of the property to $222 million and generate an additional $1.2 million annually in property taxes. It includes the 750 new parking spaces recommended for downtown related to the project's development. Some of the proposed cost would be the city's responsibility and some could be covered by private partners or other levels of government. The scheme would also attract some 3,777 visitors downtown each day, which would generate $43.7 million annually in retail sales.

A new 350 space parking structure is also needed to meet current demand and provide infrastructure support for increased GO Train service. The parking structure would cost $13.4 million, $9.6 million of which would be covered by development charges. The city has been planning for a new 90,000 sq .ft. (8,361 square metres) library to replace the Guelph Public Library headquarters on Norfolk Street. There might be a low rise library facing upper Wyndham Street, with a residential tower at the back. Innovation Guelph, which is part of a network of regional innovation centres across Ontario is also interested in having some space in a Baker Street redevelopment.

Innovation Guelph, which was established in 2010 by the Guelph Chamber of Commerce has expanded its roster of mentors to eight. Its new "Fast Lane" program for small and medium size enterprises will support innovation and growth in the manufacturing sector. Since 2010 it has assisted 450 companies with business advisory services, and maintains about 100 active clients monthly. Its team of business mentors has facilitated the creation of more than 200 new jobs and has helped its clients to retain an additional 300 jobs. Innovation Guelph is now a key player in the development of the Guelph region's local innovation economy.

The Central Student Association at the University of Guelph would like a study space that could be used by U. of G. students to be part of the redevelopment. They would also like to be able to use a new main public library and to connect with Conestoga College students. All organizations that became the city's partners in a Baker Street redevelopment would contribute financially to the redevelopment. Some had already signed draft Memorandums of Understanding about the redevelopment with the city. The fate of this innovative scheme will be decided by the new council elected in November 2014.

Guelph Heritage District

The Brooklyn and College Hill Heritage Conservation District Plan was passed on September 9, 2014 after many meetings with residents and discussions at City Council. The plan provides for the management, care and protection of the heritage character of the District. This includes the Speed and Eramosa riverscapes and associated open space, the Gordon Street corridor and buildings fronting onto the street, and the residential areas of Brooklyn and College Hill. It differentiates between structures that are designated for heritage preservation and those not affected. The provisions of the Ontario Heritage Act apply to the designated structures and areas. Designating a district enables council to preserve the important heritage character of this large historic neighbourhood. This may be the first of many applications to designate heritage districts in Guelph.

Mitchell Farmhouse

In 2005, city council approved a demolition permit for the 1912 farmhouse on top of the Paisley Road hill, despite public opposition. The granite fieldstone house had been on land owned by the Mitchell family since 1834. Years of controversy about the home's heritage value and impassioned debates at city hall preceded this decision. It meant that there will no longer be a physical reminder of a pioneering farming family in the community. Armel Corporation which owns the land located a Costco Store on the property.

Wilson Farmhouse

On May 21, 2014 city council passed a resolution to allow for the demolition of the Wilson Farmhouse which had been designated as an Historic Site. It was an important symbol of Guelph's agricultural heritage. The Wilson family was one of the first to acquire a farm in 1836, less than 10 years after John Galt founded the City of Guelph. The farmhouse was built in the 1880s.

In early August the building was demolished, while documenting and salvaging significant architectural and heritage features. During demolition, the City protected two existing mature black walnut trees on the site by creating a fenced Tree Protection Zone.

The land surrounding the farmhouse was retained as parkland and staff integrated the parcel into the Wilson Farm Park Master Plan. Council's decision was subject to many hours of discussion and debate before the demolition decision was taken. Much of the debate revolved around the issue of whether neglect had left it in a condition too poor for restoration.

New University Entrances

A Gryphon sculpture was erected at a newly redesigned campus entrance at Stone Road and Gordon Street as part of Guelph's 50th anniversary celebrations and Alumni Weekend. The Gryphon (namesake of U. of G. sports teams) is a mythical creature with the head, talons and wings of an eagle and the body of a lion. It was funded by donations.

The sculpture is a key piece of the U of G master plan, which included construction of stone walls bearing the university's name at Gordon Street entrances at both Stone Road and College Avenue.

THE 2014 MUNICIPAL ELECTION AND SOCIAL MEDIA

Guelph's 2014 Municipal election was one of the hardest fought and most divisive since the epic battle between Karen Farbridge and Kate Quarrie in 2006. During that election,which also featured "progressive liberal" versus "conservative" candidates, accusations of dirty tricks and mud slinging permeated the campaign. In 2006, the Guelph Civic League worked diligently to successfully oust Quarrie and in 2014, GrassRoots Guelph/Gerry Barker worked just as assiduously to oust Farbridge.

In 2014, things became even nastier when social media in the form of blogs and tweets were used to promote and denigrate many candidates. The large number of articles written about Karen Farbridge by Gerry Barker in *GrassRoots Guelph* appear to have influenced many voters. Although seven candidates stood for mayor (Karen Farbridge, Cam Guthrie, Jason Blokhuis, John Legere, Andrew Donovan, Nicolas A. Ross, Joseph St. Denis) only Farbridge, Guthrie and Blokhuis were in contention. Guthrie won with 19,672 votes, Farbridge received 14,174 and Blokhuis trailed with 3987. None of the other candidates received over 300 votes.

GrassRoots Guelph supported Guthrie for mayor, and suggested the following candidates for seats on council:

Ward 1: incumbent Bob Bell and Dan Gibson
Ward 2: incumbent Andy Van Hellemond and former councillor Ray Ferraro
Ward 3: Craig Chamberlain and Jason Dodge
Ward 4: former councillor Christine Billings and former PC provincial candidate Greg Schirk
Ward 5: former PC provincial candidate Bob Senechal and Jim Galatianos
Ward 6: Glen Tolhurst and Mark MacKinnon.

Of these, Gibson, Bell, Van Hellemond, Billings and MacKinnon were elected.

In essence, the election was between supporters of Farbridge and those who favoured smaller government, tax cuts, possible privatization of services and zero-based budgeting. Cam Guthrie campaigned on such a platform while Farbridge ran on her record. Although Guthrie was not officially aligned with GrassRoots Guelph, its blogs and activities contributed considerably to his ultimate victory. It is difficult to say how much it helped the council candidates that it had endorsed. Quotations from the Farbridge campaign and GrassRoots Guelph (Gerry Barker's) postings capture the flavour of the mayoral race.

MAYORAL PLATFORMS

Guthrie's Five Promises:

Limit property tax increases to the rate of inflation or lower by controlling excessive spending and borrowing. Mandated services must be provided. Everything else is discretionary.

Deliver cost-effective and efficient core city services. Waste management, park maintenance and snow removal could be provided for significantly less than the city currently budgets without any disruption to service levels.

Create an actual transparent government that avoids costly mistakes. Have the city post all expenditures by council members and city staff online.

Eliminate the so-called "Guelph Factor" by changing the culture at city hall, rebuilding trust and valuing business. Extensive use of regulations, restrictions, delays and unrealistic guidelines drive away potential employers, residents and opportunities

Support downtown without the use of a punitive tax levy, while promoting development that ensures all corners of Guelph are equally respected.

Some Guthrie Questions

Will more commercial opportunities create a better Guelph?

Will more jobs right here in our community create a better Guelph?

Will an improved environment for more private sector jobs create a better Guelph?

Will lower taxes create a better Guelph?

Will moulding transit to us, rather than us to it create a better Guelph?

Will the improved delivery of core city services create a better Guelph?

My answer to these questions is a resounding yes!

Yes to increased commercial opportunities.

Yes to initiating job creation.

Yes to lower taxes.

Yes to ensuring efficient, cost-effective transit.

Yes to improved core service delivery.

Because a better Guelph makes our lives better. It makes yours better!

Farbridge Platform

Bring more jobs to Guelph

Guelph is successfully competing regionally and globally for talent, investment and jobs. As your mayor, together we will:

Protect the talent, investment and jobs we're bringing to Guelph
Keep attracting new jobs and businesses to Guelph
Continue growing local businesses and opportunities for youth

Make Guelph Canada's greenest city

Rising energy costs and extreme weather events place our community at risk. As your mayor, together we will:

Create even more green jobs
Protect our city and citizens from unpredictable energy costs
Increase energy security through local production that's by Guelph and for Guelph

Ensure everyone has the opportunity to thrive

Guelph is a safe, affordable and sustainable place to live and raise a family for many people but not all. Not yet. As your mayor, together we will:

Continue to improve services for all
Partner with the people, organizations and businesses of Guelph to make a difference in our community
Continue to reduce the cost to government and taxpayers while making a difference for low income children and families

I commit myself fully to the idea that Guelph can be more. Guelph can have more jobs, be more green, and provide more opportunities for people to thrive. I'm the only candidate in this election with a real plan to continue to build and protect our City.

My record is clear:

Guelph has seen more than 8,000 new jobs since 2006
Guelph continues to close the gap between tax increases and inflation with a 2015 target of 2%.
We deliver a balanced budget every year to ensure we live within our means
We have lowered our debt to build a brighter and stronger future
We have increased our financial reserves to protect us from the unknown and unexpected
We have received a AA+ credit rating with Standard & Poor's, one of the most respected financial institutions in the world
We have finished Value for Dollar audits, identifying $3.5 million in potential savings

We have one of the lowest crime rates in all of Canada

We have doubled our bike lanes, built new parks, added new trails, and started new community gardens

We have a world class composting facility that is helping to divert more than two thirds of our residential waste from landfill We're doing all of this – and more – while building a liveable, sustainable city that's ready for the 21st century and we're doing it as a caring, thriving community.

THE REAL (DIRTY) BATTLE

Both candidates resorted to questionable tactics near the end of the campaign. GrassRoots Guelph (Gerry Barker) in his blogs continued the criticism of the Farbridge administration that he had expressed for years in his *Guelph Mercury* columns, which ceased before the election. Surprisingly, despite the fact that they were harsh and relentless, no one threatened a libel suit over their contents. This is probably because the data quoted therein were accurate but most problems and errors were attributed directly to Farbridge. In the opinion of many, Barker's blogs played a major part in the defeat of Farbridge and several of her supporters. Nevertheless, Guthrie claimed that he was not associated with GrassRoots Guelph or with Barker who is a major Conservative supporter.

In response to numerous harsh attacks by Grassroots Guelph and the Guthrie campaign, the Farbridge campaign responded by running a photograph of Guthrie beside Michael Sona. He was the Conservative operative who was convicted of using robocalls to mislead Liberal voters about the location of polling stations in the last Federal election. Its caption was "A person is known by the company they keep". This was done to counter what Farbridge called "a nasty and bitter and toxic campaign." The photo ran beside a Farbridge advertisement in the Guelph Tribune listing her accomplishments during the last four years. Unfortunately, permission had not been obtained to use this *Guelph Mercury* photograph of Sona and Guthrie. Guthrie claimed that he had never collaborated with Sona and that they just happened to be together in 2011 when the photo was taken. Many commentators concluded that this photograph had damaged the credibility of Farbridge and her campaign.

In many of Guthrie's speeches he claimed that City Hall did not listen to citizens, that the "Guelph Factor" (difficult bureaucracy and regulations) was deterring new investment. He implied that Farbridge was responsible for the Urbacon lawsuit which cost the city $8 million. In retaliation, Farbridge pointed out that Guthrie had been a member of council during the last four years. She complained about bullying of women candidates, hateful messages and displays. She also blamed conservatives for the toxic campaign which continued to become even nastier. However, only by perusing the Internet can one appreciate the full extent of "toxic campaigning" during this election.

Numerous Tweets and Blogs contributed to the 2014 election campaign, but GrassRoots Guelph was by far the most detailed and persistent. Almost every day it attacked Mayor Farbridge's policies, administration and character. There was considerable controversy about Grassroots Guelph's possible financial contributions to candidates who opposed Farbridge.

Susan Watson claimed that a $400 donation to Glen Tolhurst's campaign by Grassroots Guelph was illegal. She also argued that Tolhurst benefited from a series of paid advertisements run by that organization which he did not claim in his campaign filings. The advertisements were published in the *Guelph Tribune*. Watson filed a request for a compliance audit of the financial statements of Glen Tolhurst which was rejected after a hearing in 2015. Nevertheless, she raised the issue of who is eligible to finance candidates for City Council.

The only way to illustrate the impact of Grassroots Guelph is to reproduce direct quotes from a few of its (eventually very repetitive) offerings:

Excerpts from Grassroots Guelph

Posted October 1, 2014:

Who are these extreme conservatives, pictured with horns and cloven feet? Those who dare to question the Farbridge record of unfettered waste of the city treasure? Money misspent on projects that voters didn't approve such as the $35 million organic waste processing facility. That's the project that was built to process organic feedstock that was triple the tonnage required by the City of Guelph for the next 20 years.

The solution? Sell the excess capacity to others. Was this the intent of the Farbridge administration to overbuild a facility at the taxpayer's expense? Build it for others to use and not explain the associated costs?

The newsletter states: "Financial stability and prosperity need not come at the expense of our friends and neighbours, or our future."

Okay, let's subsidize the Regional of Waterloo, organic plant contractor Maple Reinders, the farmer who bought some 3,000 tonnes of compost, or hiring a second shift at the recycling plant to process tonnes of Detroit trash.

Is this what the voters wanted in the 2006 election?

The Farbridge folks get their shorts in a knot every time someone complains about the taxes the city charges. Guelph's property taxes are among the highest of the 444 Ontario municipalities. In eight years, Guelph property taxes have increased by 38 per cent. Compare that to the Consumer Price Index growth in the same period of just 17 per cent.

Why? Because the Farbridge administration's record of spending money on projects that dilute its ability to create facilities that serve all the people all the time.

Examples include the millions spent on the downtown at the expense of other areas of the city. More interesting, is the money not spent in eight years on a new downtown library or a south-end recreation centre.

Both these capital projects were promised in the first Farbridge term in 2000/2003.

Guess a funny thing happened on the way to 2014. Promises made but never kept.

But hey! We spent more than $15 million over the $42 million city hall contract because the Farbridge-led administration thought they could kick the general contractor off the job and finish the project themselves.

The actual costs of that management debacle may never be known because the administration doesn't want to reveal them as it will affect the re-election of the Farbridge team, the same ones who caused the problem in the first place.

Posted October 19, 2014

If anyone wonders where the Guelph Mercury stands in this election just look at its pick-up reprint of the phony one-sided story carried in the Toronto Star written by a futurist consultant carrying academic credentials.

A reporter he isn't. In his glowing non-description of our city that does not exist, Don Tapscott never introduced any counterpoints in his essay. It is apparent that he never visited Guelph or spoke with the citizens. He never questioned any of the material provided by the Farbridge team. The mayor initiated this piece as Tapscott has acknowledged.

This distortion of the facts does a monumental disservice to the people of Guelph who have just experienced a mayor who is out of control, petulant and in danger of losing her job.

There was a total absence of fact checking, especially in the middle of an intense election campaign.

More important is that the Mercury ran this pie-in-the-sky drivel without as much as changing a comma. How can readers trust a newspaper that is so blatant about its support for an administration that is in disarray over its loss of the people's trust?

Posted October 23, 2014

Mayor Karen Farbridge and the Mercury use the word "toxic" when referring to this election campaign. It's a word carrying a negative connotation, like it shouldn't be like this. This isn't the Guelph way, or so the Mayor and Mercury would like you to believe.

The truth is that there has been constant and accurate exposure of the Mayor's record. Cumulatively, the details have been highly critical of the city operations led by the Mayor, including the Urbacon financial fiasco that has cost citizens, year to date, $15 million.

What has now come to light is the professional relationship between the city's $213,000 Chief Administrative Officer, Ann Pappert, and Mayor Farbridge. According to information recently received, the city staff is demoralized because every report, recommendation and even planning proposals sent to the CAO are immediately referred to the Mayor for approval.

This would indicate that the mayor personally decides the outcome of all city business. The members of council are not always consulted. An example was the firing of Urbacon that all members of council say they were not consulted nor asked to ratify the decision.

The committees of elected councillors and council itself eventually are presented with the Farbridge approved version. The mayor has complete control of the council in which her supporters are the majority and are dominating the committees.

It is now apparent that one person made the decision to fire Urbacon. It was not former CAO Hans Loewig as CAO Ann Pappert now claims. He was only following orders when he fired Urbacon off the job in September 2008. It was Mayor Karen Farbridge. For the mayor to now say that "we fixed the problem" is simply an indictment of her leadership.

Posted October 24, 2014

Okay, here we have a mayor whose fingerprints are all over every decision the city makes including, presumably, the width of the toilet paper rolls. Nothing happens at City Hall without the mayor's express approval.

Having said that, the mayor takes credit for winning awards and achieving recognition of her vision of the city. But when the feathers hit the fan, the mayor's name is never associated with the problem, big or small.

A prime example is who ordered the firing of Urbacon Buildings Systems Corp in September 19, 2008? According to Chief Administrative Officer, Ann Pappert, consigliore of the mayor's inner circle, former CAO Hans Loewig carried out the order with the assistance of the Guelph police.

Yes, but who told him to do it? With the exception of the Mayor, members of council at the time said they were not consulted on the decision or asked to ratify it.

The mayor ducks.

The story goes underground as the Farbridge administration frantically hires two outside construction firms to complete the new City Hall that was 95 per cent finished. Also required was renovation of the old city hall into a provincial offenses court. The details of this arrangement including the costs have never been revealed.

What we do know is both projects were part of the original $42,000,000 contract.

Two months after the firing, acting CAO Hans Loewig was

rewarded with a permanent, four-year contract with a starting salary of $198,000 plus the unusual provision allowing him to take up to 12 weeks a year in unpaid vacation. Great, for almost $200,000 a year we get a part-time CAO.

The Mayor ducks again. This time it was to protect her reputation in the upcoming 2010 civic election.

In 2009, there was an attempt to mediate in the differences with Urbacon to reach a settlement that failed because the city offer was not acceptable to Urbacon. The company had launched a $19.2 million lawsuit for wrongful dismissal. The city counter-sued for $5 million.

Comingled in all these inner workings of the administration was the hiring and subsequent firing three years later of Margaret Neubauer as Chief Financial Officer. There was never any explanation other than the theory she was demanding that capital projects must all have business plans.

The mayor ducks again. Her reputation as the Teflon mayor grows as nothing sticks to her.

Mayor Farbridge is re-elected in 2010 and the citizens were still in the dark as to the looming impact of her decision to fire Urbacon in 2008.

Of 86,574 eligible voters, 45 per cent participated in the election. This was an 11 per cent increase over 2010. It is difficult to tell how much Internet posts hurt Farbridge, but it is interesting to note that more of the 12,768 people who voted online supported Guthrie.

The other interesting race was between incumbent June Hofland and Craig Chamberlain in Ward 3. Hofland initially had three more votes than Chamberlain, but the official count showed that she had 2050 to his 2045. This was reconfirmed by an official recount on November 18.

ELECTION RESULTS - CITY COUNCIL:

Candidates for Mayor (1 to be elected)

Votes: Cam Guthrie 19672, Karen Farbridge 14174, Jason Blokhuis 3987, Andrew Donovan 296, John Legere 269, Joseph St. Denis 250, Nicholas A. Ross 112

Ward 1 Candidates (2 to be elected)

Votes: Dan Gibson 3419, Bob Bell 2984, Karolyne Pickett 2705, Terry O'Connor 1705, Maria Pezzano 1386

Ward 2 Candidates (2 to be elected)

Votes: Andy Van Hellemond 3266, James Gordon 2990, Ray Ferraro 2615, Martin Collier 1314, Sian Matwey 1109, Chris Keleher Sr. 583

Ward 3 Candidates (2 to be elected)

Votes: Phil Allt 2299, June Hoffland 2050, Craig Chamberlain 2045, Maggie Laidlaw 1861, Bob Moore 1131, Jason Dodge 878

Ward 4 Candidates (2 to be elected)

Christine Billings 2300, Mike Salisbury 2179, Laurie Garbutt 1061, Scott Tracey 992, Gary Walton 760, Greg Roffey 620, Greg Schirk 608, Robb Dunn-Dufault 559, Mark Briestensky 224

Ward 5 Candidates (2 to be elected)

Leanne Piper 3386, Cathy Downer 2795, Scott R. Butler 2316, Bob Senechal 1599, Dimitrios Galatianos 1049, Alex Green 759

Ward 6 Candidates (2 to be elected)

Mark MacKinnon 3806, Karl Wettstein 2886, Todd J. Dennis 2044, Glen Tolhurst 1968, Keith Poore 671

PERFORMANCE OF GUELPH CITIZENS AND CITY COUNCIL, 2000 TO 2015

After a many years of studying and writing about Guelph planning and politics I have reached some (probably unscientific) conclusions. I have also drawn upon my earlier experience during eleven years as a member and Chair of Guelph's Planning Advisory Committee.

The first and most striking conclusion is that successive Guelph Councils have dithered and/or changed their positions on numerous occasions and on many issues. Such (in)activity has often lasted for months or even years. The second conclusion is that Councils have often been prompted to behave this way because of powerful citizen participation by groups supporting or opposing their actions, or because of lengthy OMB hearings. A third conclusion is that the "default position" of many citizen groups is to oppose all developments, regardless of their merits, if they are perceived to adversely affect their lives or property values.

On other occasions, citizen groups have performed well and encouraged sensible, prudent developments. For some reason, not always made clear by Council, there have been a surprising number of senior staff dismissals, "retirements", "leaving for other opportunities" and "resignations" since 2000. In some instances, generous "golden handshakes" were given to those departing, but because of "personnel confidentiality" the amounts were not made public. The examples below will exemplify Council and citizen performance between 2000 and 2015.

Considerable controversy and citizen input accompanied the city's attempts to close its Eastview landfill site and move to recycling between 2000 and 2013. Citizen participation encouraged the city to close Eastview and try several solutions to recycling. This positive input culminated in a new Wet-Dry facility that was built in 2013. This occurred only after the lawsuit with Subbor was settled, and after many complaints about foul odours emanating from the plant and its predecessor! However, citizen reaction to the introduction of the three cart waste collection system was initially very negative. After considerable controversy, it began in 2012 and has been generally successful despite the opposition. *Nevertheless, it took thirteen years to achieve a successful and environmentally friendly system of waste disposal in Guelph.*

From 2001 to 2009, several Guelph councils debated the possibility of a pesticide By-Law and finally passed it in 2009. Many long and heated public meetings, with the usual Guelph opposition, accompanied this process. One particularly vehement opponent said that she and her family would flagrantly and repeatedly break the By-Law and that she would willingly fight this to the Supreme Court of Canada by becoming the first test subject in Ontario. "If my neighbour wants to tell me what I can or cannot do on my property, he better buy it," she said. *Ironically, on April 22, 2009 the Province proclaimed legislation that was weaker than that passed by Guelph which superseded Guelph's hard-fought pesticide By-Law.*

In 2008, for reasons that remain obscure, the City decided to end its cost sharing with the County of Wellington and request arbitration. In 2010 the City ended participation in a joint City-County social services committee and scrapped the joint Land Ambulance Committee. A Toronto arbitrator supported Wellington County and the ruling shifted about $2 million in annual costs from the county to the city. In March 2012 the city and county settled their lawsuit about the cost of maintaining Wellington Terrace Long Term Care facility This required the city to pay almost $4.2 million to cover maintenance obligations between 2006 and 2012. *These* *curious legal actions initiated by the city, cost taxpayers at least $6.2 million plus legal fees!*

In 1995 Council negotiated a public-private agreement with a company called Nustadia to operate the Guelph Sports and Entertainment (now Sleeman) Centre. In 2005 the city assumed ownership. As had been negotiated, Nustadia terminated the deal with no financial consequences. This left the City of Guelph with nearly $3.5 million in payments, plus a $9 million loan and a $10 million loan that it had guaranteed. *This time the cost to taxpayers was at least $22.5 million.*

In 2000, then city administrator David Creech recommended that the city spend $50,000 to hire a consultant to recommend a site for the new central library. In 2005, the Quarrie Council voted not to purchase the former Canada Post building which had been chosen by the Farbridge administration as the library site. Wellington County Council then purchased the building and assessed the City of Guelph $2.7 million for its share of renovation costs to cover joint services administered from the building. *Some estimated that this decision cost the city $2 million more than if Guelph had purchased the Post Office building.*

In anticipation of a library where the Post Office had been, Council decided to purchase and demolish four buildings on Wyndham Street and convert the space into a parking lot. City staff estimated that it would cost $360,000 to demolish the Mitchell building which the city had purchased for $1.25 million. Since then the date for constructing a new library has continued to recede into the future. *Despite demonstrated need, no action has been taken on a new library, but Guelph did acquire additional downtown surface parking while losing several downtown businesses and apartments.*

In 2005 the city hired Adamson Associates for $1.4 million to design a new city hall. In 2006 the city accepted Urbacon

Buildings Corporation's bid for the new Civic Administration Centre at $32.5 million. Architect fees, underground parking and various other costs increased the total to $37.7 million. On October 30, 2008 the City fired Urbacon and hired a new contractor, Alberici Constructors Ltd. to finish the job begun by Urbacon. Urbacon then initiated a $19 million suit against the city. Guelph responded a month later with a $5 million counterclaim against Urbacon and a similar suit against Aviva Insurance Company, which the city alleged was obliged to indemnify the city from damages. Eventually Alberici finished the contract for $52.3 million and Urbacon won its suit. *After the trial, Guelph paid $6.635 million to Urbacon to settle the company's wrongful dismissal case out of court. Guelph's legal costs were $2.23 million.*

The city began studying downtown rowdyism in 2003. Various schemes were attempted to control drinking and public urination. Despite many meetings and expert recommendations, no permanent public toilets (pissoirs) have yet been established. *Recent attempts to control rowdyism have been more successful than those in the past, but after 12 years of study, council has done nothing to provide permanent secure toilets downtown.*

In a report to City council in 2000, Assistant Planning Director Jim Forbes warned that the rapid development of single family homes would make it difficult for low income families to find affordable accommodation. Despite many meetings and reports on this issue, little has been done to provide more affordable housing in the city. Unfortunately, neither the Provincial nor Federal government has provided much financial assistance.

Beginning in 2000, City Council, with encouragement from many citizen groups has studied the problems presented by group homes and student accommodation. Since then there have been many controversies about group homes, with several being prevented by NIMBY reactions. Others were approved after much debate. Early in 2001, council contemplated revising the lodging house by-law. Between 2002 and 2012, when attempting to create a definition of lodging houses that would be fair and withstand legal challenges, city council discussed and debated this issue many times. After much deliberation at council and many meetings with landlords, tenants, and neighbours, it appeared that a solution on lodging houses had been achieved. However, on Tuesday, August, 12, 2014 a motion on rental licensing was rejected by City Council. Instead it decided to implement stronger enforcement of existing regulations and zoning by-laws. *After fifteen years of study, OMB hearings and several legal opinions, neither the proposed by-law nor licensing have been implemented!*

Considerable controversy has accompanied almost every application for a high rise or condominium development in Guelph. In several instances, OMB hearings were required to settle differences among applicants, the city and interested citizens. Occasionally NIMBY has delayed such development as have OMB hearings. The condominium proposed for Marianne's Park has not yet been built, but several downtown high rise apartments have now been constructed and plans for others were approved after OMB hearings.

Guelph has developed excellent policies on Brownfield redevelopment and many have been restored and reused. The former International Malleable Iron Company on Beverley Street which was abandoned in 1989 and eventually taken over by the city has not yet been redeveloped, despite major efforts to clean up and market the property.

In 2005 the Ontario Realty Corporation decided to dispose of a large parcel of land owned by the province that once housed the Guelph Correctional Centre (Ontario Reformatory). The York Road Secondary Plan was developed for this area with considerable citizen and Planning Department input. Despite approval of the plan on May 12, 2014, nothing has materialized there, despite the major potential for population and employment growth.

Guelph Council has wrestled with traffic calming beginning in 1998 when speed humps were installed on Dufferin Street. Great controversy accompanied the impassioned debates on traffic calming, but *after almost 15 years of dithering and public debates, Guelph Council finally adopted and retained a Policy on Traffic Calming in 2012.*

Guelph's new Inter Modal Transit Terminal (Guelph Central Station) was approved in April 2010 and is functioning without the Via Rail Station which was expected to be renovated in 2013. Unfortunately, this has not yet occurred and Greyhound continues to use its temporary facility at 17 Wyndham St. South. Because of "insufficient finances", renovation documents for the former Via Station will be resubmitted for tender in late February or early March of 2016. The city plans to begin the renovations *in April 2016 and hopes that the work will be completed by April 2017. Why was too little allocated for this important transportation hub in earlier city budgets?*

On June 9, 1997 city council voted to reject power centres (big box stores) on land zoned industrial at the corner of Woolwich St. and Woodlawn Rd., and on land zoned institutional on Stone Road. After a change in Municipal Government, a lengthy OMB hearing and court cases, Walmart opened on November 8, 2006. *The city had spent almost $1 million on lawyers' fees during the Walmart hearings. The cost of staff time and effort during the nine year saga has never been calculated.*

CONCLUSION

Why did it take Council so long to adopt by-laws to calm traffic, ban pesticides, implement the York Road Secondary Plan and renovate the former Via Station? Why did the City fire Urbacon which had almost completed the new City Hall? Why did it not purchase the old post office? Why has it (after fifteen years of deliberation) never passed a rental licensing by-law? Why has a new library never been built? Why have public toilets never been installed in the CBD? Why did the number of "Senior Staff" increase from five in 2000 to twenty-two in 2015? How much has the city spent on lawsuits and Buy-Outs since 2000? How many employees have "left the city" since 2000? Why? Unfortunately "Personnel Confidentiality" has prevented me from answering these questions.

The following are the best estimates that I could obtain to calculate the cost of some of Councils' decisions since 2000. They are far from a complete accounting, but they have been described in detail in the text. Confidential "Golden Handshakes" protected by "personnel confidentiality" of terminated staff would add millions to the total!

(a) Settlement with Wellington County	$ 6,200,000
(b) Settlement with Nustadia	$ 22,500,000
(c) Payment for Post Office Renovations	$ 2,700,000
(d) Purchase of Mitchell Building	$ 1,250,000
(e) Architect Fees for City Hall	$ 1,400,000
(f) City Hall Lawsuit	$ 6,630,000
(g) Legal Costs of City Hall Lawsuit	$ 2,230,000
(h) Legal Costs of Walmart Hearings	$ 1,000,000
(i) Lenna Bradburn Severance	$ 300,000
(j) City Hall Severances	$ 1,000,000

TOTAL   **$45,210,000**

Between 2000 and 2015, Guelph has elected City Councils led by Joe Young, Karen Farbridge, Kate Quarrie, Karen Farbridge (twice) and Cam Guthrie (since November 2014). The Council led by Kate Quarrie was by far the most controversial and was defeated by Karen Farbridge in a bitter election in 2006. Thereafter, Farbridge was elected easily until her defeat by Cam Guthrie in another acrimonious election in 2014.

There were many controversial and expensive decisions during Quarrie's term, some of which continue to affect the city. A number of the decisions made by Farbridge Councils were bitterly disputed during the election against Guthrie in 2014. "Grassroots Guelph" published numerous damaging accusations against the Farbridge administration during the campaign.

At times, all councils made only glacial "progress" on passing by-laws and taking decisions. The apparent "purges" of senior staff resulting in large "settlements" and buy-outs for staff who disappeared were nothing short of scandalous. In most instances, Guelph citizens have never discovered why senior staff, who seemed to have performed well, were summarily dismissed. And we will never know the total cost to taxpayers! Has the city grown enough to require twenty-two senior staff in 2015 when five seemed to suffice in 2000?

Decisions by all Guelph councils have cost the city enormous amounts of money for lawyers' fees and for settlements imposed by the courts. Unfortunately the reasons for such expensive actions have not always been clear. Dithering, procrastination and reversals of policies have been common to all Guelph City Councils since 2000.

Unfortunately, bickering, differing political ideologies and personal animosities have influenced crucial council votes far too frequently. Councillors have appeared to be voting to please their personal constituencies, rather than to benefit all Guelph's citizens. At times they seemed to vote primarily to spite a previous council and to reverse earlier decisions with which they disagreed. On many occasions they missed opportunities because they were afraid of offending a pressure group or were intimidated by innovative motions. It hasn't helped that a significant segment of Guelph's population is inclined to oppose almost any proposal or suggestion that might alter the character of their neighbourhood or that of the city.

Since 2000 (and long before then) Guelph councils have consistently neglected to fund major essential (often unseen) infrastructure problems. Given their obsession with keeping taxes low, many councillors seem content to continually defer the cost of replacing old, disintegrating water and sewage pipes. Over 30 years ago Planning Advisory Committee received a report detailing the pathetic state of Guelph's underground infrastructure. So far, repairs seem to have been made only on an emergency basis, often when sewage pipes collapse during the winter. Add to this the sad state of roads and sidewalks and the cost to our children and heirs will be enormous.

In their frantic pursuit of "growth" some councillors have forgotten the cost of necessary upgrades to our water and sewage treatment plants. Drilling new wells will not solve Guelph's water shortage problems, because they all draw from the same aquifer. If these problems are not addressed in every budget, future citizens will inherit enormous debts and astronomical tax assessments.

On the positive side, Guelph councils have enjoyed some major successes. Unemployment in the city is very low, but it is difficult to ascertain the effect that council decisions have had on local employment. Guelph's innovative District

Energy Initiative is North America's first city-wide district energy network, and is thus far a success. Market Square in front of the new city hall is a lovely and functional public space. The city has almost eliminated what was once a major termite problem. Guelph has been a leader in solid waste reduction and recycling. Its Brownfield rehabilitation policy has been successful. The new Civic Museum is an outstanding example of heritage preservation and conversion of an important public building. Our record on being "Green" and environmentally friendly is outstanding.

Contrary to some opinions, Guelph's tax rate is comparable to Ontario communities of a similar size. In 2015, Guelph homeowners paid an average of 4.9 percent ($1,590) of their income for residential taxes. This was slightly higher than the 4.7 percent average for the 104 Ontario Municipalities in the study (BMA Management Consulting Incorporated, *Municipal Study,* Hamilton, 2016).

Being a city councillor is an important and stressful occupation. After writing this book, I have become sceptical about the ability or desire of some councillors to govern our city in the best interests of all its citizens. Many positions in debates have reflected personal party politics, which is unfortunate. Voting "Blocks" are usually "left/liberal" versus "right/conservative."Even after strenuous debate, councillors seldom deviate from their rigid political perspectives. There are far too many decisions on important issues that are carried by votes of seven to six. It would be gratifying indeed if all councillors would put aside their personal agendas and attempt to govern for everyone in Guelph.

APPENDIX 1

SENIOR STAFF RESIGNATIONS AND BUY-OUTS

Many observers of city hall have been concerned about the number of senior staff resignations, terminations and buy-outs since 2000. City administration has been reorganized on a number of occasions, with large severance payments being made. Unfortunately, because these are "Personnel Matters" I could not tabulate all the amounts being paid for buy-outs. The personnel changes that I found are listed below as are the names of senior staff in 2000, 2005, 2010 and 2015. My repeated requests for lists of senior staff were ignored until I contacted C.A.O Ann Pappert who directed Human Resources to supply them.

1999

Lenna Bradburn resigned as Chief of Police in October and received a $300,000 buy-out

2000

Tom Slomke, Director of planning resigned in February to return to university

SENIOR STAFF 2000

NAME	POSITION
Giles Lois	Director, Information Services/City Clerk
Payne Lois	City Solicitor
Stalhman Gus	Director Community Services
Funnell Raymond	Director Works
Creech David	City Administrator

2004

David Creech, Chief administrative Officer, resigned at the end of December.

SENIOR STAFF 2005

NAME	POSITION
Kotseff Larry	Chief Administrative Officer
Laird Janet	Commissioner, Environment/Transportation
Stahlmann Gustav	Commissioner, Community Services
Mackay Robert	Director Culture
Cartwright Peter	Director Economic Development
Tolkunow Rick	Director Engineering

Etienne James	Director Environmental Services
Kennedy David	Director Finance/Treasurer
Blais Pauline	Director Human Resources
Giles Lois	Director Information Services/City Clerk
Kivell Jay	Director Parks
Riddell James	Director Planning & Building Services
McCaughan Derek	Director Public Works
Goldie Andrew	Director Recreation
French Randall	Director Transportation
Armstrong Shawn	Fire Chief
Payne Lois	City Solicitor

2006

It cost the City of Guelph slightly less than the projected $575,000 in settlements to eliminate nine senior management positions this year. The costs were offset by $955,000 in annual savings as a result of the cuts. The positions were eliminated as part of a restructuring plan.

2007

Larry Kotseff, Chief Administrative Officer retired
David Kennedy, Director of Finance and Treasurer retired
Lois Giles, City Clerk retired

2010

Lois Payne, City Solicitor and Director of Corporate Services retired
David Corks, Manager of Downtown Development left
Murray McCrae, Manager of Corporate Property left
Rob Mackay,Manager of Facilities and Programs left
Marion Plaunt, Manager of Policy Planning and Urban Design left

SENIOR STAFF 2010

NAME	POSITION
Loewig Hans	Chief Administrative Officer
Laird Janet	Director Environmental Services
Riddell James	Director Community Design and Development
Pappert Ann	Director Community Services
Armstrong Shawn	Director Emergency Services
Neubauer Margaret	Director Finance/ Treasurer
Payne Lois	Director Corporate Services/ City Soliciter
Giles Lois	Director Information Services
Amorosi Mark	Director Human Resources
McCaughan Derek	Director Operations

2011

Margaret Neubauer, City Treasurer since 2008, "left the employ of the city"

Dan Chapman who worked his first day in Guelph on November 1 offered his resignation on November 5

Rob Mackay, Manager of Recreation and Culture left

Bob Burchett, who replaced Mackay is also no longer with the city

Robert Walters, resigned as Guelph's Manager of Development Planning He made public a consultant's report that severely criticized the "Guelph Factor". It said that Council "lacks a clear, coherent and cohesive vision" for development in Guelph. Guelph's Chief Administrative Officer Ann Pappert said she could not take issue with the report.

Jim Riddell left after seven years to become Director of Planning and Development in St. Catharines.

It was estimated that severance packages could cost the city $1 million

2014

Dr. Janet Laird received a buyout from her position as Director of Environmental Services

Derek McCaughan received a buyout from his position as Director of Operations

2015

The General Manager of Finance and Deputy Treasurer, the Corporate Manager of Strategic Planning and Corporate Initiatives, the Manager of Parks and Open Space, the Manager of Business Services, and Supervisor of Aquatics all became redundant. The five were given severance packages and 25 more staff members will have different jobs.

Al Horsman, Guelph's Deputy Chief Administrative Officer of Infrastructure, Development and Enterprise Services, left the city.

The city is advertising for a Deputy Chief Administrative Officer, to oversee Infrastructure, Development and Enterprise at a salary from $163,993 to $204,992

Bruce Poole was released from his job on Aug. 26. Poole would be offered a severance package under the terms of the city's non-union employee agreement. He is now suing the city.

Ramesh Ummat was hired as the General Manager of Environmental Services

SENIOR STAFF 2015

NAME	POSITION
Pappert Ann	Chief Administrative Officer
Amorosi Mark	Deputy CAO Corporate Services
Stewart Scott	Deputy CAO Infrastructure Development & Enterprise
Thomson Derrick	Deputy CAO Public Services
O'Brien Stephen	City Clerk
Swartzentruber Barbara	Intergovernmental Relations, Policy and Open Government
Cartwright Peter	General Manager, Business Development & Enterprise
Sprigg Tara	General Manager Corporate Communications & Customer Service
Coutts Bradley	General Manager Court Services
Clack Colleen	General Manager Culture, Tourism, Community Investments
Dedman Kealy	General Manager Engineering and Capital Infrastructure Services/City Engineer
Ummat Ramesh	General Manager Environmental Services
Petricevic Mario	General Manager Facilities Management
Sheehy Janice	Manager Finance/Treasurer
Petroczi Laszlo	General Manager Guelph Junction Railway
Meagher Phil	General Manager Guelph Transit
Godwaldt David	General Manager Human Resources
Jaques Donna	General Manager Legal Services/City Solicitor
Keller Rodney	General Manager Operations
Scott Kristene	General Manager Parks & Recreation
Salter Todd	General Manager Planning, Urban Design, Building Services
Labelle Blair	General Manager Technology & Innovation

SOURCES

All sources for this book were on-line; many discovered through Google. A number of important links are included in the text and all are listed below.

INTERNET ADDRESSES

www.guelphmercury.com/ News

www.guelphtribune.ca/ News

www.therecord.com/ News

www.mah.gov.on.ca/ *Citizen's Guide to Land Use Planning Ontario*

www.guelph.ca/plans-and-strategies/official-plan/ *Guelph Official Plan*

https://guelph.ca/wp-content/.../policy_TrafficManagement.pdf/ Guelph Traffic Calming Policy

https://www.omb.gov.on.ca/ Ontario Municipal Board

https://www.placestogrow.ca/index.php *Ontario Places to Grow Act*

www.180gordon.com Market Commons Website

PDF DOCUMENTS FOUND ON GOOGLE

ONTARIO

A Practical Guide to Brownfields in Ontario, 2007

Greenbelt Plan, 2005.

Infrastructure Ontario, *Expression of Interest, Guelph, Ontario Canada,* nd. (Guelph Innovation District)

Ministry of Municipal Affairs and Housing, *Citizen's Guide to the Planning Act,* 2010.

Ministry of Public Infrastructure Renewal, *Places to Grow:Growth Plan for the Golden Horseshoe,* 2006.

Provincial Policy Statement, 2005.

CITY OF GUELPH

Brownfields Strategy, 2002.

Brownfields Redevelopment Community Improvement Plan, 2012.

Community Development and Environmental Services Committee, Phase IV - Implications Analysis of the City of Guelph's Local Growth.

Envision Guelph, City of Guelph Draft Official Plan, 2012.

Facilities Management, City of Guelph, 2016.

Guelph's Local Growth management Strategy, 2009.

Guelph Innovation District Recommendation Booklet, 2011.

Guelph Innovation District Secondary Plan, 2012.

Guelph-Wellington Transportation Study Final Report, 2005.

Human Resources,Corporate Services,City of Guelph, 2016.

Lafarge Site Urban Design Guidelines and Concept Plan for Commercial and Mixed use Brownfields Development, 2007.

River Systems Management Study, Final Report, 1993.

River Systems Advisory Committee Terms of Reference, 2007.

Smart Guelph: Building Tomorrow Today, 2002.

OTHER

Bennett, Ben, *Secrets and Lies and No Replies: An Inside Report on the Wal-Mart Issue,* 2006.

Bennett, Ben, *The Story Since the Book was Written,* 2006.

BMA Management Consulting Incorporated, *Municipal Study, Hamilton,* 2016.

Silvercreek Guelph Developments Ltd., *Lafarge Property City of Guelph Planning study in Support of an OP Amendment and Zone Change for a Mixed Use Commercial Development,* 2005.

Fred Dahms